Abel Polese

LIMITS OF A POST-SOVIET STATE

How Informality Replaces, Renegotiates, and Reshapes Governance in Contemporary Ukraine

With a foreword by Colin C. Williams

ibidem-Verlag
Stuttgart

Bibliografische Information der Deutschen Nationalbibliothek
Die Deutsche Nationalbibliothek verzeichnet diese Publikation in der Deutschen Nationalbibliografie; detaillierte bibliografische Daten sind im Internet über http://dnb.d-nb.de abrufbar.

Bibliographic information published by the Deutsche Nationalbibliothek
Die Deutsche Nationalbibliothek lists this publication in the Deutsche Nationalbibliografie; detailed bibliographic data are available in the Internet at http://dnb.d-nb.de.

Cover picture: Stary Krym bazaar. © Abel Polese, 2005

∞

Gedruckt auf alterungsbeständigem, säurefreien Papier
Printed on acid-free paper

ISSN: 1614-3515

ISBN-13: 978-3-8382-0845-9

© *ibidem*-Verlag
Stuttgart 2016

Alle Rechte vorbehalten

Das Werk einschließlich aller seiner Teile ist urheberrechtlich geschützt. Jede Verwertung außerhalb der engen Grenzen des Urheberrechtsgesetzes ist ohne Zustimmung des Verlages unzulässig und strafbar. Dies gilt insbesondere für Vervielfältigungen, Übersetzungen, Mikroverfilmungen und elektronische Speicherformen sowie die Einspeicherung und Verarbeitung in elektronischen Systemen.

All rights reserved. No part of this publication may be reproduced, stored in or introduced into a retrieval system, or transmitted, in any form, or by any means (electronic, mechanical, photocopying, recording or otherwise) without the prior written permission of the publisher. Any person who does any unauthorized act in relation to this publication may be liable to criminal prosecution and civil claims for damages.

Printed in the EU

146 Lenka Krátká
A History of the Czechoslovak Ocean
Shipping Company 1948-1989
How a Small, Landlocked Country Ran
Maritime Business During the Cold War
ISBN 978-3-8382-0666-0

147 Alexander Sergunin
Explaining Russian Foreign Policy
Behavior
Theory and Practice
ISBN 978-3-8382-0752-0

148 Darya Malyutina
Migrant Friendships in
a Super-Diverse City
Russian-Speakers and their Social
Relationships in London in the 21st Century
With a foreword by Claire Dwyer
ISBN 978-3-8382-0652-3

149 Alexander Sergunin, Valery Konyshev
Russia in the Arctic
Hard or Soft Power?
ISBN 978-3-8382-0753-7

150 John J. Maresca
Helsinki Revisited
A Key U.S. Negotiator's Memoirs
on the Development of the CSCE into the
OSCE
With a foreword by Hafiz Pashayev
ISBN 978-3-8382-0852-7

151 Jardar Østbø
The New Third Rome
Readings of a Russian Nationalist Myth
With a foreword by Pål Kolstø
ISBN 978-3-8382-0870-1

152 Simon Kordonsky
Socio-Economic Foundations of the
Russian Post-Soviet Regime
The Resource-Based Economy and Estate-
Based Social Structure of Contemporary
Russia
With a foreword by Svetlana Barsukova
ISBN 978-3-8382-0775-9

153 Duncan Leitch
Assisting Reform in Post-Communist
Ukraine 2000–2012
The Illusions of Donors and the Disillusion of
Beneficiaries
With a foreword by Kataryna Wolczuk
ISBN 978-3-8382-0844-2

154 Abel Polese
Limits of a Post-Soviet State
How Informality Replaces, Renegotiates, and
Reshapes Governance in Contemporary
Ukraine
With a foreword by Colin C. Williams
ISBN 978-3-8382-0845-9

155 Mikhail Suslov (ed.)
Digital Orthodoxy in the Post-Soviet
World
The Russian Orthodox Church and Web 2.0
ISBN 978-3-8382-0871-8

156 Leonid Luks
"Zwei Sonderwege"? Russisch-
deutsche Parallelen und Kontraste
(1917-2014)
Vergleichende Essays
ISBN 978-3-8382-0823-7

157 Vladimir V. Karacharovskiy, Ovsey I.
Shkaratan, Gordey A. Yastrebov
Towards a New Russian Work Culture
Can Western Companies and Expatriates
Change Russian Society?
With a foreword by Elena N. Danilova
Translated by Julia Kazantseva
ISBN 978-3-8382-0902-9

ibidem-Verlag
Melchiorstr. 15
D-70439 Stuttgart
info@ibidem-verlag.de

www.ibidem-verlag.de
www.ibidem.eu
www.edition-noema.de
www.autorenbetreuung.de

Soviet and Post-Soviet Politics and Society (SPPS) Vol. 154
ISSN 1614-3515

General Editor: Andreas Umland,
Institute for Euro-Atlantic Cooperation, Kyiv, umland@stanfordalumni.org

Commissioning Editor: Max Jakob Horstmann,
London, mjh@ibidem.eu

EDITORIAL COMMITTEE*

DOMESTIC & COMPARATIVE POLITICS
Prof. **Ellen Bos**, *Andrássy University of Budapest*
Dr. **Ingmar Bredies**, *FH Bund, Brühl*
Dr. **Andrey Kazantsev**, *MGIMO (U) MID RF, Moscow*
Prof. **Heiko Pleines**, *University of Bremen*
Prof. **Richard Sakwa**, *University of Kent at Canterbury*
Dr. **Sarah Whitmore**, *Oxford Brookes University*
Dr. **Harald Wydra**, *University of Cambridge*

SOCIETY, CLASS & ETHNICITY
Col. **David Glantz**, *"Journal of Slavic Military Studies"*
Dr. **Marlène Laruelle**, *George Washington University*
Dr. **Stephen Shulman**, *Southern Illinois University*
Prof. **Stefan Troebst**, *University of Leipzig*

POLITICAL ECONOMY & PUBLIC POLICY
Prof. em. **Marshall Goldman**, *Wellesley College, Mass.*
Dr. **Andreas Goldthau**, *Central European University*
Dr. **Robert Kravchuk**, *University of North Carolina*
Dr. **David Lane**, *University of Cambridge*
Dr. **Carol Leonard**, *Higher School of Economics, Moscow*
Dr. **Maria Popova**, *McGill University, Montreal*

FOREIGN POLICY & INTERNATIONAL AFFAIRS
Dr. **Peter Duncan**, *University College London*
Prof. **Andreas Heinemann-Grüder**, *University of Bonn*
Dr. **Taras Kuzio**, *Johns Hopkins University*
Prof. **Gerhard Mangott**, *University of Innsbruck*
Dr. **Diana Schmidt-Pfister**, *University of Konstanz*
Dr. **Lisbeth Tarlow**, *Harvard University, Cambridge*
Dr. **Christian Wipperfürth**, *N-Ost Network, Berlin*
Dr. **William Zimmerman**, *University of Michigan*

HISTORY, CULTURE & THOUGHT
Dr. **Catherine Andreyev**, *University of Oxford*
Prof. **Mark Bassin**, *Södertörn University*
Prof. **Karsten Brüggemann**, *Tallinn University*
Dr. **Alexander Etkind**, *University of Cambridge*
Dr. **Gasan Gusejnov**, *Moscow State University*
Prof. em. **Walter Laqueur**, *Georgetown University*
Prof. **Leonid Luks**, *Catholic University of Eichstaett*
Dr. **Olga Malinova**, *Russian Academy of Sciences*
Prof. **Andrei Rogatchevski**, *University of Tromsø*
Dr. **Mark Tauger**, *West Virginia University*

ADVISORY BOARD*

Prof. **Dominique Arel**, *University of Ottawa*
Prof. **Jörg Baberowski**, *Humboldt University of Berlin*
Prof. **Margarita Balmaceda**, *Seton Hall University*
Dr. **John Barber**, *University of Cambridge*
Prof. **Timm Beichelt**, *European University Viadrina*
Dr. **Katrin Boeckh**, *University of Munich*
Prof. em. **Archie Brown**, *University of Oxford*
Dr. **Vyacheslav Bryukhovetsky**, *Kyiv-Mohyla Academy*
Prof. **Timothy Colton**, *Harvard University, Cambridge*
Prof. **Paul D'Anieri**, *University of Florida*
Dr. **Heike Dörrenbächer**, *Friedrich Naumann Foundation*
Dr. **John Dunlop**, *Hoover Institution, Stanford, California*
Dr. **Sabine Fischer**, *SWP, Berlin*
Dr. **Geir Flikke**, *NUPI, Oslo*
Prof. **David Galbreath**, *University of Aberdeen*
Prof. **Alexander Galkin**, *Russian Academy of Sciences*
Prof. **Frank Golczewski**, *University of Hamburg*
Dr. **Nikolas Gvosdev**, *Naval War College, Newport, RI*
Prof. **Mark von Hagen**, *Arizona State University*
Dr. **Guido Hausmann**, *University of Munich*
Prof. **Dale Herspring**, *Kansas State University*
Dr. **Stefani Hoffman**, *Hebrew University of Jerusalem*
Prof. **Mikhail Ilyin**, *MGIMO (U) MID RF, Moscow*
Prof. **Vladimir Kantor**, *Higher School of Economics*
Dr. **Ivan Katchanovski**, *University of Ottawa*
Prof. em. **Andrzej Korbonski**, *University of California*
Dr. **Iris Kempe**, *"Caucasus Analytical Digest"*
Prof. **Herbert Küpper**, *Institut für Ostrecht Regensburg*
Dr. **Rainer Lindner**, *CEEER, Berlin*
Dr. **Vladimir Malakhov**, *Russian Academy of Sciences*

Dr. **Luke March**, *University of Edinburgh*
Prof. **Michael McFaul**, *Stanford University, Palo Alto*
Prof. **Birgit Menzel**, *University of Mainz-Germersheim*
Prof. **Valery Mikhailenko**, *The Urals State University*
Prof. **Emil Pain**, *Higher School of Economics, Moscow*
Dr. **Oleg Podvintsev**, *Russian Academy of Sciences*
Prof. **Olga Popova**, *St. Petersburg State University*
Dr. **Alex Pravda**, *University of Oxford*
Prof. **Erik van Ree**, *University of Amsterdam*
Dr. **Joachim Rogall**, *Robert Bosch Foundation Stuttgart*
Prof. **Peter Rutland**, *Wesleyan University, Middletown*
Prof. **Marat Salikov**, *The Urals State Law Academy*
Dr. **Gwendolyn Sasse**, *University of Oxford*
Dr. **Jutta Scherrer**, *EHESS, Paris*
Prof. **Robert Service**, *University of Oxford*
Mr. **James Sherr**, *RIIA Chatham House London*
Dr. **Oxana Shevel**, *Tufts University, Medford*
Prof. **Eberhard Schneider**, *University of Siegen*
Prof. **Olexander Shnyrkov**, *Shevchenko University, Kyiv*
Prof. **Hans-Henning Schröder**, *SWP, Berlin*
Prof. **Yuri Shapoval**, *Ukrainian Academy of Sciences*
Prof. **Viktor Shnirelman**, *Russian Academy of Sciences*
Dr. **Lisa Sundstrom**, *University of British Columbia*
Dr. **Philip Walters**, *"Religion, State and Society", Oxford*
Prof. **Zenon Wasyliw**, *Ithaca College, New York State*
Dr. **Lucan Way**, *University of Toronto*
Dr. **Markus Wehner**, *"Frankfurter Allgemeine Zeitung"*
Dr. **Andrew Wilson**, *University College London*
Prof. **Jan Zielonka**, *University of Oxford*
Prof. **Andrei Zorin**, *University of Oxford*

* While the Editorial Committee and Advisory Board support the General Editor in the choice and improvement of manuscripts for publication, responsibility for remaining errors and misinterpretations in the series' volumes lies with the books' authors.

Soviet and Post-Soviet Politics and Society (SPPS)
ISSN 1614-3515

Founded in 2004 and refereed since 2007, SPPS makes available affordable English-, German-, and Russian-language studies on the history of the countries of the former Soviet bloc from the late Tsarist period to today. It publishes between 5 and 20 volumes per year and focuses on issues in transitions to and from democracy such as economic crisis, identity formation, civil society development, and constitutional reform in CEE and the NIS. SPPS also aims to highlight so far understudied themes in East European studies such as right-wing radicalism, religious life, higher education, or human rights protection. The authors and titles of all previously published volumes are listed at the end of this book. For a full description of the series and reviews of its books, see www.ibidem-verlag.de/red/spps.

Editorial correspondence & manuscripts should be sent to: Dr. Andreas Umland, c/o DAAD, German Embassy, vul. Bohdana Khmelnitskoho 25, UA-01901 Kyiv, Ukraine. e-mail: umland@stanfordalumni.org

Business correspondence & review copy requests should be sent to: *ibidem* Press, Leuschnerstr. 40, 30457 Hannover, Germany; tel.: +49 511 2622200; fax: +49 511 2622201; spps@ibidem.eu.

Authors, reviewers, referees, and editors for (as well as all other persons sympathetic to) SPPS are invited to join its networks at
www.facebook.com/group.php?gid=52638198614
www.linkedin.com/groups?about=&gid=103012
www.xing.com/net/spps-ibidem-verlag/

Recent Volumes

149 Alexander Sergunin, Valery Konyshev
Russia in the Arctic
Hard or Soft Power?
ISBN 978-3-8382-0753-7

150 John J. Maresca
Helsinki Revisited
A Key U.S. Negotiator's Memoirs
on the Development of the CSCE into the OSCE
With a foreword by Hafiz Pashayev
ISBN 978-3-8382-0852-7

151 Jardar Østbø
The New Third Rome
Readings of a Russian Nationalist Myth
With a foreword by Pål Kolstø
ISBN 978-3-8382-0870-1

152 Simon Kordonsky
Socio-Economic Foundations of the Russian Post-Soviet Regime
The Resource-Based Economy and Estate-Based Social Structure of Contemporary Russia
With a foreword by Svetlana Barsukova
ISBN 978-3-8382-0775-9

153 Duncan Leitch
Assisting Reform in Post-Communist Ukraine 2000–2012
The Illusions of Donors and the Disillusion of Beneficiaries
With a foreword by Kataryna Wolczuk
ISBN 978-3-8382-0844-2

154 Abel Polese
Limits of a Post-Soviet State
How Informality Replaces, Renegotiates, and Reshapes Governance in Contemporary Ukraine
With a foreword by Colin C. Williams
ISBN 978-3-8382-0845-9

155 Mikhail Suslov (ed.)
Digital Orthodoxy in the Post-Soviet World
The Russian Orthodox Church and Web 2.0
ISBN 978-3-8382-0871-8

156 Leonid Luks
"Zwei Sonderwege"? Russisch-deutsche Parallelen und Kontraste (1917-2014)
Vergleichende Essays
ISBN 978-3-8382-0823-7

Table of Contents

Acknowledgements 9
Foreword by Colin C. Williams 13
Introduction: where is informality? 17
    How much of this book is about Ukraine? 21
    What is informality? 23
    Main themes of this book: (Over) Regulation and informality 27
    'In spite of the state' and 'beyond the state' 31
    Morality, compliance Informality
    and the cubic watermelon paradigm 34
    Cited works 38

Informality and the (welfare) state 47
    1   Introduction 47
    2   Welfare and the role of the state in post-socialism 49
    3   Individual agency and bottom-up welfare provision 52
    4   Reforms to the pension system from the bottom: Uzbekistan 55
    5   Access (or lack thereof) to healthcare: Lithuania 57
    6   Welfare as childcare: Romania 59
    7   Conclusion 63
    Cited works 64

Informality, borders and boundaries 71
    1   Redefining borders and their morality 74
    2   Scenes from a border 78
    3   A false bottom train 79
    4   Alternative ways of crossing 83
    5   Concluding remarks 86
    Cited works 87

Border crossing, petty trade and the role of informality in breaking artificial monopolies 91
   1 Introduction: a running bazaar 91
   2 Hum, I am Sorry. . . Where is the Border? 93
   3 Smugglers or Traders? 96
   4 Do you have a Tomato? Scenes of "Legal" Corruption 102
   5 Conclusion 105
   Cited works 107

Informality and grey areas: introducing the "brift" 111
   1 If I receive it, it is a gift. If I demand it, then it is a bribe. 111
   2 Informal payments and the role of the state 113
   3 Switching moralities 120
   4 The academic 'moral code' 121
   5 'Survival techniques' of hospitals 126
   6 Concluding remarks 129
   Cited works 131

Informality between private and state initiative 137
   1 Introduction 137
   2 Informality and (lack of) Welfare 138
   3 Structure and agency in debates on informality 143
   4 Chernobyl 145
   5 Chernobyl Welfare 147
   6 Food and welfare 148
   7 Rejecting welfare and embracing place 153
   8 Conclusion 156
   Cited works 157

**The guest at the dining table:
economic transitions and informal renegotiations of hospitality** 165
    1   What's So Special about Eating? What All that Food Means...168
    2   What is Hospitality? 171
    3   Who is a Guest? Who is a Stranger? 174
    4   Step I: Entertaining the Host's Belly 178
    5   Food without Borders: The Dinner 180
    6   Discovering your Limits: Drinking 181
    7   Final Reflections on Hospitality, Food and Guests 183
    Cited works 184

**Why bazaars are not wiped out by supermarkets:
reflections on a possible bazaar economy** 187
    1   Introduction: the role of bazaars in Odessa 187
    2   On the persistence of informal economic practices
        in the (post-Soviet) world 189
    3   The origins of bazaars in Odessa 192
    4   The morphology and function of bazaars of Odessa 194
    5   Post-1991 bazaars and their challenges 201
    6   The transformation of bazaars 205
    7   The future of bazaars in Odessa 211
    Cited works 212

**New directions in informality studies?
policy making and implementation** 219
    1   Methodological considerations 223
    2   The context: evolution of language statuses in Ukraine 226
    3   Domesticating Ukrainian identities 230
    4   Concluding remarks 235
    Cited works 236

**By way of conclusion:
on current and further directions in informality research** 241

Acknowledgements

In our frenetic rush to satisfy our national ranking systems, mostly based on quantitative criteria, social scientists have been hearing with increased frequency that many journal articles can be regarded as evidence of academic quality. Keen to emulate a model that has been widely accepted in science and in countries where a book is considered slightly better than an article and thus not worth the effort, we have been indoctrinated that we need to publish "more" with little or no incentive to publish "better". I have to admit that I have not been immune to this pressure and, whilst this being my seventh book in six years it is my first, and sole, monograph.

In my attempts to publish a plethora of articles every year, I had little or no time for a book. However, I was faced with a double necessity, from which the idea for this book arose. On the one hand, I had to adjust to the formal criteria when competing for positions in some countries, including my own, where a lack of a monograph could be used as a reason to exclude you from a job panel. On a more positive none, there was the necessity to make the point of showing what over ten years of my research on informality has found. My initial attempts to challenge a too normative framework on corruption have gradually expanded into attempts to find the place for informality in a number of aspects related to theory and practice of governance, understanding social and cultural change.

The result was a hybrid work, containing some reprinted articles for which I thank the original publishers for their permission to reprint and some parts that were written ex novo for this book. This was partly due to the limitations in reusing my own material, which I was not aware of when I started thinking of a collection of articles. However, given the speed at which I was able to produce the new parts, or update the old ones, I am no longer afraid to write a monograph.

This book was also my first attempt to go beyond the geographical area that has "adopted me" since 2002. I was born (academically speaking) as an area study specialist and I initially saw myself as such. I think it is now time to go past this classification. Most of my empirical work has been focussing on post-USSR spaces from a number of perspectives. The most interesting result has been, so far, that political scientists see me as an anthropologist and anthropologists see me as a political scientist with an interest in ethnographic methods. I am neither, and this inspired me to search for employment in a geography department at the University of Edinburgh. My colleagues studied stones, fossils, soil but also development, medical geography and were interested in the accounts of the first geographical expeditions. I am grateful to each and every one of them for intriguing me with many different pieces of something that we all like, knowledge. It is in the same period that I was accepted to join the Scottish Crucible, which brings together the 30 most promising researchers of Scotland (well, we were 31 that year) from any discipline. I befriended colleagues from engineering, ICT, history, psychology, medical and nutritional sciences and I was even invited to give a talk in the School of Medicine at the University of Glasgow (thanks to Emilie Combet for believing in my idea on "food democracies" and to Ruth Neiland for her support many years after the Crucible).

While most of the material contained in this book draws from examples from post-USSR spaces it has to be said that if my academic work has been focusing on the region, my practical work on development, capacity building of NGOs, and empowerment of marginalised and vulnerable groups has happened mostly elsewhere. Since 2007 I regularly work in Vietnam; I have also had the chance to work extensively in Cambodia, China, Laos, Myanmar and, more recently, India and Nepal, visits that have helped me put things in perspective.

I have to thank Chris Schoen and Andreas Umland for believing in this project and giving me all the freedom I needed. My gratitude also goes to all the people and institutions that have offered their support by hosting me, giving me the chance to discuss my ideas or simply informally and formally discussed and criticised my ideas. First and foremost, the institutions I am currently affiliated with. At the School of Law and Governance of Dublin City University I am grateful to my old friend and colleague Donnacha Ó Beacháin but also to John Doyle, Eileen Connelly and Karolina Stefanczak. At Tallinn University I wish to thank all my colleagues from the School of Governance, Law and Society and especially Emilia Pawlusz and Raivo Vetik, the latter being the main reason why I ended up working in Estonia. I also thank Peeter Muursepp at Tallinn University of Technology for his constant support since my early Estonian days. I wish to thank Firouzeh Nahvandi who has adopted me at the Centre for International Development at the Free University of Brussels, to which I became affiliated with recently, and Sarah Murru who was the main initiator of the collaboration.

My initial idea was that this book would be written, at least partly, at the Jawaharlal Nehru University in Delhi. Unexpected, but welcomed, opportunities made this impossible but I have still benefited of the hospitality and support of my colleagues in the School of International Studies and in particular my friend Rajan Kumar, for whom I have no words to express my gratitude. Most of my understanding of Vietnamese informal practices, Vietnamese society and Vietnam in general is due to the hospitality and friendship of Don Tuan Phuong, his wife Que and his staff at the Centre for Sustainable Development Studies, where I have always been welcomed as part of the family. The list of people to thank is long and includes Thazin and Chan Aung at Charity Oriented Myanmar; Borith, Kalyan and Sitha at the Khmer Youth for Sustainable Development; Cui Shoujun at Renmin University of China. A special thank goes to Colin Williams at the University of Sheffield, who has always been supportive of my ideas and has kindly accepted to write the foreword to this book; to Sally Cummings for all her encouragements and help, to my friend and partner in crime Jeremy Morris at the University of Birmingham who has had a role in virtually anything that I have written on informality since 2011 to Oleksandra Seliverstova, who had a role in anything I have written on informality before that and on many other things after that, and to Sergey Seliverstov, to whom I owe some of the best insights on informality I have had.

In the course of the last few years I have also been lucky enough to find more and more amazingly nice people with whom I share the informality approach and that I wish to thank. Bori Kovacs and Lela Rekhviashvili, Nicolas Hayoz, Tanya Stepurko (whom I also with to thank for her help with the figures in this book), Christian Giordano, Gul Berna Ozcan, Ioana Ursachi, Rodica Ianole, Ida Harboe, David Jancsics, Alena Ledeneva, Huseyn Aliyev, Bettina Bruns, Olga Sasunkevich, Lale Yalçın-Heckmann, Kristine Müller, Judith

Miggelbrink, Ida Harboe, David Karjanen, Ioana Ursachi, Anna Cieślewska, Aet Annist, Karla Koutkova, Anna Danielsson, Thom Davies, Jingqing Yang and Aleksandr Prigarin. May I be forgiven by the ones I have forgotten here.

Finally, I am thankful to a number of people who do not necessarily study informality but make me realise, every time I meet them, how lucky I am to have the chance, thanks to my work, to meet such amazing people: Raquel Freira and Licinia Simao at Coimbra, Heiko Pleines at Bremen, Bruno De Cordier at Ghent, Simon Tordjman at Toulouse, Ilona Baumane at Riga, Markku Lonkila who is now in Jyvaskula, Jan Kohler in Berlin, Filippo Menga at Manchester, Rick Fawn at St Andrews; Pal Kolsto at Oslo, Rico Isaacs at Oxford Brookes University. Finally, I wish to thank Gina Mzourek for proofreading most of the manuscript and the editorial team at Ibidem and in particular Florian Boiter and Valerie Lange who have been extremely helpful with editing and support. The encouragements and moral support are to be credited to them. Else, for anything you might not like in the book I am the one to blame.

Morelia, April 2016

Foreword

All societies develop a way of producing, distributing and allocating the goods and services required by its citizens. In consequence, all societies have an economy of some type. Economies, however, can take different forms. To understand how an economy can be structured, it is common to differentiate between three modes of producing, distributing and allocating goods and services, namely the 'market' (private sector), the 'state' (public sector) and the 'informal' sector, even if different labels are sometimes attached to these realms. In recent decades, the widespread view has been not only that there has been a transition to the use of the 'market' in post-Soviet societies, but that globally the market is increasingly becoming hegemonic. In other words, there is firstly a view that in all economies goods and services are being increasingly produced and delivered through the formal (market and state) sphere rather than through the informal sphere (known as the 'formalization' thesis) and secondly, that this formal production and delivery of goods and services is increasingly occurring through the market sector, rather than by the public sector, (the 'marketization' thesis).

Given the dominance of this discourse regarding the trajectory of economies, it might be assumed that a voluminous evidence-base exists supporting this view of the direction of economies. However, the worrying and disturbing finding once one starts searching for evidence is that hardly any is ever provided. Put simply, it is such a widely accepted canon of wisdom that evidence is all true frequently deemed unnecessary. Indeed, perhaps the growing hegemony of the formal market economy is so obvious and uncontroversial to all that evidence is not required. Perhaps, however, it is not. No other idea in the social sciences is accepted without an evidence-base and there are no grounds exist for exempting this meta-narrative regarding the totalising shift towards a formal market economy.

The importance of this book by Abel Polese is that it begins to contest the belief that there is an irreversible, inevitable and inescapable shift towards a formal market economy in post-Soviet societies by re-evaluating the role of informal economies in this region of the world and the limits of the state and market. In doing so, it provides a seminal contribution to the much wider scholarship on post-Soviet spaces that addresses the recurring question of 'transition' in order to dispute not only the past hegemony of the command economy system but importantly also the notion that there is a universal linear trajectory of development in post-Soviet spaces towards a hegemonic ideal-type formal market economy system as some end point. What this book reveals through its in-depth analysis of informality is the need for a more nuanced argument to be adopted that allows recognition of how there has been a transformation of post-Soviet economies in varying ways from different starting points and along different economic development trajectories.

On the issue of the past hegemony of the command economy system, this book through its rich and nuanced understanding uncovers that this was never the case and that the 'second economy' was a pervasive force in such systems. More importantly however, and on the inevitability of a formal market economy, this book makes it very clear that a future where the formal market economy becomes hegemonic is far from being cast in stone. Instead, it reveals that to assert that the formal market economy is inescapable and inevitable would be to fly in the face of the empirical evidence presented here on not only the trajectories of post-Soviet economies but also the lived practices in post-Soviet societies.

By revealing how the advent of a formal market economy is not a natural process, but has to be facilitated with massive intervention and encouragement, and how informality sometimes replaces the formal market economy and renegotiates and reshapes the role of the state and state intervention, this book begins to make readers question quite how expansive the formal market realm would have been if left to its own devices. The outcome is a rethinking of the 'economic' and a move beyond a closed view of economic development as a transition towards market hegemony. Instead, it reveals that economic development is an open-ended, heterogeneous and transformative process. This book in other words deconstructs the all too familiar and comfortable notion of economic development as a transition to a formal market economy by revealing that formal market economic practices are just one of a plurality of economic practices in post-Soviet spaces. In doing so, it thereby decentres the formal market economy from its pivotal position and recovers alternative futures for economic development so as to disrupt those dominant economic discourses about the future of post-Soviet economies as being one in which the formal market economy is hegemonic, totalising and universal.

However, the intention in doing so is not simply to replace one universal conceptualisation of the trajectory of economic development with another alternative universal. Instead, the contribution of the chapters in this book is to reveal that the informal economy may be persistent and even growing in many post-Soviet spaces (negating the formalization and marketization theses) but also that the role it plays in contemporary post-Soviet spaces is not always the same and that it varies according to both the type of informal work being considered and the population groups and places being evaluated. In doing so, this book brings out of the shadows the important and varying role that informal economies play in not only people's livelihood practices but also renegotiating and shaping governance and the role of state in post-Soviet spaces. In doing this, readers are being asked to re-think not only the discourse of 'transition' in the post-Soviet world but also the meanings of the 'economic' and 'economy'.

At the heart of this book is therefore a critique of the notion that economic transition is at an end in post-Soviet societies and that the move from the command system to the market economy is complete. Through examining the lived experiences of people and the everyday, this book reveals that post-Soviet societies are composed of a diverse repertoire of practices and that if the 'economic' and 'economy' are to be understood, it is necessary to move beyond such simplified accounts where one mode of production or another assumes a hegemonic status and all other systems of exchange disappear. Rather, it reveals that the processes of transformation are about a shift in the balance afforded to different systems of exchange and that these transformations are in different directions in different populations, places and sectors.

This book thus unpacks the diverse relationships that can exist between the market, state and informal economy across the post-Soviet world and unravels how these relationships vary in different contexts. The outcome is a very rich and nuanced understanding of the multifarious nature of the relationships that can and do exist between informality, the state and the market in contemporary post-Soviet societies. I hope that you enjoy reading it.

Colin C. Williams, June 2015
Sheffield

Introduction: where is informality?

July 2015, Cambodian-Vietnamese border. People are waiting in a line to get their passports stamped. From time to time some people enter the room, skip the line and go directly to the passport window. They handed their passport to the border guard and get it back stamped almost immediately. When bypassed the first two or three times I felt outraged by the lack of formal rules and this apparent favouritism. However, after a few more of them passed I thought I understood the typology of the person and the secret pattern behind it. The border control was equipped with two indistinctly separate lines: tourist and business track. Many airports and other busy hubs have it. You pay for the privilege to be passed through customs, passport or security control thanks to an annual subscription fee. It is an exclusive club only for a few fortunate and busy people. At that border this was not an option. Instead, customers were subscribed to a pay-as-you-go service. They would pay only when they needed the service.

Corruption is often defined as the use or abuse of a public function for a private benefit. The border guards were using their position to earn some extra cash. However, I would ascribe this, and other situations presented in this book, to a broader category where individual and state morality diverge, or simply do not overlap (Polese 2008, 2014). In a market-like fashion this gap between supply and demand could be seen as the beginning of a new business. There is a demand by a significant number of customers that is not matched from the supply side. There are a number of people who need to regularly get through border control quickly but there is no mechanism or practice allowing this. I would expect that one day someone approaches the head of the post with a proposition to train and pay extra staff, which would allow for a designated passport control for business customers and thus formalise this informal practice.

In a standard situation, the state would welcome a private initiative as long as it does not invade its competencies or challenges the symbolic order, which it is based upon. At other times the state decides to outsource a service to cut down on fees but, until this happens, any intrusion into state-regulated areas can be seen as an infraction.

Therefore, state rules and state morality are not static and immutable things. They evolve along with the state, its people and institutions so that new generations, products, systems of productions and dynamics generate new moral standards, or stretch current ones. In general, innovation generates new challenges, new demands and new needs. Initial views on informality would, at least in some cases, tolerate these informal practices. Transitionalists would see them as the starting point, slowly evolving into formal institutions (Geertz 1963, Lewis 1959) while ultra-liberals would see it as a way to make things work better in transitional countries (Leff 1964). This book certainly shares the vision that informality may be seen as a starting situation, a mechanism that may then be formalised and be used to propose new formal rules; it argues, however, that formalisation of an informal practice is not the end of a story but a phase in a cycle that might bring informality back in or might not.

If we take an area that is unregulated or under-regulated (that is, where the state has only started adopting formal rules to manage a particular aspect of a community life or of society) most habits and rules will be informal. If we take a country where migration is only a recent phenomenon, most of the services delivered will be managed by non-state actors (sometimes NGOs, sometimes informal groups or personal connections with no regularity and on a case-by-case basis) since institutions are busy regulating what they see as more urgent needs. How migrants gain access to education, healthcare and a number of other services and opportunities is outsourced to the people themselves, and can remain like this for a long time, even if the migrant population grows exponentially. At some point the state will feel the need to regulate certain aspects, create new services, obligations, prohibitions and opportunities. If they address all the urgent needs then informal rules will be gradually sided by formal rules, regulating most aspects, and might be swallowed by them. However, any inelastic and dysfunctional aspects of the new system, sets of rules and institutions will rely, for a solution, on informal renegotiations, person-to-person interaction and the use of a human agency. Assuming that the new set of rules and institutions perfectly fit the current situation and lead to a total formalisation of all aspects of management of migrants and their integration, the ideal situation will be limited to "here and now" that is fitting to the number of migrants present in a given moment within a given territory (they will have a certain educated/non-educated ratio, a given ethnic and gender distribution). Whilst small changes in the migrant population (in terms of gender, age, occupation, ethnic and religious background) are likely to be absorbed by the system, more significant changes will generate new needs, new issues and new challenges.

In a democratic state, newly introduced rules have to be proposed, evaluated, voted, adopted and then implemented. This means that, even in the most effective state, there will be a fair delay between the moment a new phenomenon or tendency manifests itself, the moment it is perceived and the moment new measures are adopted. Institutions will have to identify a new problem, propose solutions, debate them, adopt and test them, before something starts changing. Even assuming that the first proposed solution turns out to be "the perfect one", the decision chain is likely to bring institutions to address, today, yesterday's problems.

From this point of view, informality originates in existing formal rules and structures to complement them. As such, the definition used in this book is that informality is the space between two formal rules. We can visualise this as a surface covered with dots that represent formal rules. The more the state is regulated the more there will be dots and the smaller the distance will be between them. But dots cannot cover the entirety of the surface. There will always be some unregulated space and informality is here to fill it.

This view suggests that there are two ways to limit informality in a system, either quantitatively or qualitatively. The first one rests on a drastic reduction of the amount of informal transactions. By filling our surface with dots one leaves an agency so little space that it becomes virtually impossible not to play by its formal rules. Theoretically possible, this is a bit utopian and impossible to achieve without any damage. Most repressive systems, striving to regulate and limit individuality and initiative, have high amounts of informality and overregulated countries are often seen as suffocating people's initiative so to make economic or social development almost impossible (interestingly enough, evidence shows that informality, in both situations, blossoms). The second one is to limit informality qualitatively.

Informal transactions, in other words, are tolerated or even encouraged as long as they do not affect the way a system works. This means not to fill the surface with dots but to place the dots in the right place so to leave a clear message: play informally with anything, but with this particular aspect. This more liberal approach is likely to give better results as people still feel that they have their freedom, can express their creativity, initiative and entrepreneurship while working together with the state towards common goals. It is, at least in my view, the way more effective states give the impression to have gotten rid of informality. They have not. But they have substantially reduced the role of informal practices in some aspects of life that are crucial to good governance. After all, it makes little sense to measure state, institution, or even individual performances by scoring them against an ideal theoretical model. It is perhaps more beneficial, and realistic, to measure how much better a state performs against other similar states, measuring this empirically. Which country may claim to collect taxes on a hundred percent of taxable incomes? There are countries whose collection is very low and those whose is higher but, the more we near the ideal figure of a hundred percent, the more costly it becomes to locate undeclared income and force people to pay taxes. Control has a price and extensive control a higher one. In the end, each government shall find the balance between how much to spend in tax collection (including positive and negative incentives) and how much tax is brought back into the state budget.

It is important to highlight that there is no lack of informality in the Western world but there seems to be a double standard when referring to informality. Informality may be seen as negative, neutral or even positive depending on where informal practices are noticed. In some areas informality is tacitly acceptable, and accepted, whereas in some other aspects of a society this is stigmatised. This is possibly based on the assumption that regulation, and formalisation, in the Western world has happened to a sufficient extent confined it to practices that are unharmful to the state or not sufficiently relevant to be tackled (Dixit 2007; Helmke and Levitski 2004). As such, informality on the job market, in neighbour relations or in some spheres where trust and personal connections are crucial, are treated as either exceptions or, borrowing from maths, a discrete case that has nothing to see and does not affect the standard functioning of a system. Informality is seen, in many respects, as the cartilage that keeps solid bones together and allows them to function together. Only when informality invades areas that are perceived as being state competencies, or when its presence and influence cannot be denied, then it is treated as something evil to eradicate.

How much of this book is about Ukraine?

I started reflecting about informality during my PhD fieldwork in Ukraine, where I was studying something apparently unrelated: the reaction of a Russian speaking city (Odessa) in attempt to construct a homogeneous Ukrainian identity over the whole territory of the country. Having lived in Ukraine between 2002 and 2006, I became increasingly allergic to corruption reports and analyses claiming that it was endemic to the country and present in all spheres of life. My starting point was that it is normal to have deviant behaviours that need to be corrected. If there are some rules, and a few people do not play by them, then coercion might be used to bring people back onto the right behaviours to use. However, when there is a rule and more than half of a community, or of a country, ignores it then there must be something wrong with the rule, rather than with the country. By force of this, if offering a doctor a little amount of money (1–2 EUR equivalent in local currency) was a widespread practice, would tough control and anti-corruption campaigns hit the weak spots and convince people not to engage in the supply/demand mechanism that alimented these transactions? I doubted it and I doubt it today.

Starting from this assumption, I started exploring some alternative interpretations of informality, the most provoking of which was that hospitals in Ukraine are de facto private (Polese 2006). I suggested that if a public worker's salary is not sufficient to pay for basic living expenses the person should not be considered a full-time public worker (Polese 2009) and that the meaning of a transaction cannot be given in absolute terms but depends on the relationship between the individual and the state. A state should not only be there but, to be respected as a state, should act as a state (Polese 2007) and engage in a balanced give and take relationship with its citizens, rather than just taking.

As in many other cases, my research on informality emerged as a hobby, or a lateral project, beside my main project, that I believed being identity. It soon took most of my time and energy so that I first applied it to my identity research, suggesting that identity formation mechanisms created and alimented by a central government can be renegotiated locally and most of these negotiations are informal. I then turned full time to informal mechanisms and practices thanks to a Marie Curie fellowship that allowed me to collect more material and systematise my findings from 2008 through 2011. In total, I can claim almost a decade of systematic data collection on Ukraine, to which one could add the surveys that I commissioned and the further engagement with the country up to today (2016). The natural consequence of this commitment is that, as one could imagine, most of the material I collected is coming from that part of the world.

This is not to say, however, that Ukraine was the only place where I had the chance to observe informality. Since 2005 I have spent a good amount of time in other countries such as Georgia, Poland, Russia and Turkey (where I also conducted a survey on informality) and, since 2007, I have increased my engagement with development projects in South East Asia. In addition to regularly visiting Vietnam for several weeks a year, I have also worked intensively with Cambodia, China, Myanmar and, to a lesser extent, Indonesia and Laos.

I gradually started seeing some of the patterns I had observed in Ukraine elsewhere. My post-Soviet field experience helped me to better understand other situations, but also showed me that a lot of what I had seen was in no way unique to one single geographical area. There are, of course, practices that belong to a particular place because of historical, geographical or cultural specificities but I increasingly believe to have identified a common denominator to all these transactions.

So, is this a book about Ukraine? I would not claim so. In spite of my devotion to the country I believe there are people who can take much more credit than I can for being Ukrainian experts. I am certainly aware of its evolutions and peculiarities but claiming to be an expert on Ukraine would not be an honest statement, if one compares me to people who have spent their life only in that country. Am I am expert in any other country? I would not claim so either. My Vietnamese language skills are limited and so my knowledge of all underlying facts and events of the countries I work with. I recently found myself, however, at an Irish Aid funded event in central Vietnam where I realized that few people had lived in the country for as long as I had. A fair statement would be that I know these places better than the average person but (much) worse than anyone with a monogamous long-term relationship with the country. What makes this book special and what might make my contribution worth reading, at least in my view, is my capacity to connect events, tendencies and phenomena beyond one single region and the attempts to find a common pattern that could be then theorised for a better understanding of how governance works. I have observed a growing interest in issues of real, informal, participative, local governance and my wish is that this book may help by identifying and understanding some underlying mechanisms so to help improve governance at the local, international and global level.

What is informality?

The word informality has been used to refer, since its identification, to several different, although related, phenomena. Keith Hart was possibly the first scholar to identify, and study, a number of informal economic practices (1973). However, ILO's increased interest in informal labour from 1972 on ignited a variety of debates concentrating on the same issue but from different viewpoints. Initially, informality was seen as a transitional phenomenon that would be wiped out by modernity (Lewis 1959; Geertz 1963). Some seminal works, however, led to reconsider a number of paradigms and discussed them from a different angle. Scott was one of the major frontrunners, initiating both the debate on moral economy (1976) and then looking at how informal economic practices had a major impact on power relationships between peasants and their landlords (1985), which has then been continued in major economic anthropology works (Hann and Harth 2009; Hann 2010). It is in the same period that other social facts started being challenged and scholars discovered the dynamic nature of objects (Thomas 1991) and even money (Parry and Bloch 1989) that changes according to the situation and context. Informal economies became an object of interest also for policy makers and political scientists and the subsequent debates found common issues with the debates on effective governance of post-colonial states (Leff 1964; Palmier 1983; Rose-Ackman 1978).

The nineties, with the opening up of post-socialist spaces, saw a revitalisation of the debates on development, governance and corruption (Harboe 2014, 2015; Humphrey 2002; Millington et al.2005; Jancsics and Javor 2012; Temple and Petrov 2004; Smith and Stenning 2006; Urinbojev and Svensson 2013, 2014, 2014b; Wamsiedel 2013). Critical works, however, challenged what had been the mainstream approach, which is the use of a transitional paradigm using Western experiences to align the non-West with the industrialised world in terms of practices, mechanisms and institutions.

Indeed, most of the critics of this approach have highlighted the questionable approach of installing prefabricated structures and institutions that are allegedly working properly in the West into new countries. By importing know-how and practices, they are confident that the new country will, in the end, work in the same way the model country was. Only after Stieglitz (2002) have economists started questioning the "out of the box" macro approach used indistinctly for diverse realities and only after Gibson-Graham (1996) have critics of the capitalist model seriously engaged in thought-provoking debates suggesting that there are alternatives to the neoliberal capitalist model, which is taken for granted almost everywhere. These voices have been echoed by social scientists showing that diverging ethos (Gill 1998), social acceptability (Van Schendel and Abrahams 2005) or simply limited or different intellectual skills (Morrison 2007) prevent policies and reform to be accepted, understood or implemented into as a whole package, sometimes suggesting the use of institutions, procedures and practices that do not exist, or do not function properly, in the West itself (Carothers 2002).

This critical view has also inspired ed new terminology in development studies, as the term "developing countries" is now sometimes skeptically looked at. The very word "transition" seems to imply that a country or a sector is inevitably moving from point A (pre-transition) to point B, where point B means being like a certain model (or country). In other words, it sounds that it is all clear and pre-determined that we know, from the very beginning, where a country should head and we exclude all possible variations and different paths of development that are not the one we can imagine. This also challenges the expression "international standards", being unclear what standards one should refer to. Germany is not France or Japan but the three are often seen as models for development. They have little in common but the fact to be considered is their success stories along with a relatively high degree of satisfaction of their citizens.

The influence of informality has been found to be wider than generally acknowledged. Inspired by Granovetter's works (1984), informality is seen now as embedded in social phenomena (Gudman 2001; Yelcin-Hackman 2014) but also in other spheres of action of a state (Helmke and Levitsky 2004, Isaacs 2011, 2013, Ledeneva 1998, 2013; Misztal 2001, Morris 2011, 2012, 2013). They have also grown partially away from the original understanding of a mostly monetary logic (Williams 2005) and they permeate both societies in the Global South and North. In addition, whilst class and social status may influence the way informal practices are conceived and perpetuated, the studies have in common that they exist among all segments of a society, with many similarities between both winners and losers of transitions (Morris 2012, Morris and Polese 2014b).

Informality here is not considered as something merely economic or monetary but affecting potentially all aspects of a society, of a state and its governance. This brings into question the difference between informal and criminal activities. It becomes more complex since the boundary between what is criminal and what is not may be very subjective so two reflections are called upon. The first is the matrix legal/illegal licit/illicit by Van Schendel and Abrahams (2005) where licit can be considered as socially acceptable and is a sub-portion of illegal. There are things that are illegal by local criminal codes but people do not perceive them as "bad" (Fogarty 2005; Rasagayam 2011), they are socially acceptable and, thus licit. There are even things that are perfectly legal but a population, or part of it, does not accept them, at least in the short term, as licit.

Table 1: The relationship between legality and licitness (adapted from Van Schendel and Abrahams 2005)

	Legal	Illegal
Licit	State and society norms overlap	The society allows something that is forbidden by state institutions or codes
Illicit	The state does not punish actions that are stigmatised socially (by one or more communities)	State and society norms overlap

There is a second notion that I have based on direct and indirect harmfulness (Polese 2009). Murder harms a society, since it deprives it of its labour force, but also harms directly a fellow human being. Trafficking, kidnapping and theft, follow the same logic. However, fiscal noncompliance harms first the state and then, only indirectly, fellow citizens. A lower fiscal income either puts more pressure on honest tax payers or lowers the amount available for the population of a state. Non-transparent hiring practices rarely harm a single person directly (unless this person was given a job and then a last minute change took it from him), but indirectly harms the society by placing incompetent people in key positions.

Table 2: Direct (affecting fellow citizens), indirect (affecting a society) harmfulness and legality

	Direct harm (mostly illicit)	Indirect harm (might be licit)
Illegal	Murder, trafficking, heavy drug dealing, ethnic violence (might be licit in some cases)	Fiscal fraud, nepotism, ethnic or religious discrimination
Legal	Use legal action against unaware people to extort money or property; clauses written in a smaller font at the end of a contract	Laws that favour one (ethnic, religious) group over others (are licit for the favoured ones)

The above matrix can be used to circumscribe the scope of this book and suggest what kind of informality we will be looking at, that is the area of activities that are not regulated by the state (Routh 2011) but are either socially acceptable or do not harm directly a fellow human being. This definition excludes, to a certain extent, activities by organised criminal organisations and activities punished by both criminal codes and people's moral standards in most of the world.

Main themes of this book:
(Over) Regulation and informality

The study of informality, at least as it is intended here, is meant to engage with the attitude of two main actors: the first is called an overarching entity (this is generally a state but can be a company or any other entity claiming to regulate the relationship between two or more of its subordinates); the second is a community of people whose life, or some aspects of it, is regulated by this entity. The formal overarching entity is the one delivering instructions and creating the formal role that regulates a system. Since informality is the way not to pass through that entity, and the formal rules that it has established to regulate a system, absence of a formal overarching entity means that everything is regulated informally. In such case, it makes little sense speaking of informality since, de facto, everything is informal.

Lack of formal rules does not mean that there are no rules. In a primordial, or pre-state, society there are rather clear rules and norms that regulate the behaviour or a population in a given territory. Rules are not necessarily accepted by everyone but, in a small society, social control may be sufficient to ensure compliance, coercion and punishment of deviant actors. When the community enlarges some members might not agree with all the rules and act by sub-mechanisms and rules that are either tolerated or repressed by the community. The conflict or, better, friction between them becomes more evident when formal institutions step in. An overarching entity is then established, institutions are created and mechanisms initiated to regulate the society and this goes in parallel with the de-personification of a community. Informal mechanisms and unwritten rules may result effective only as long as the community to which they are applied is "personal". I refer to the fact that the community is small enough to know who does what and individually-tailored pressure can be applied to ensure compliance (this includes the use of community solidarity that is the pressure to behave correctly to the rest of your kin). In both cases individual desire and the good of the community might not overlap and some mediation is needed. Individuals are prone to think short-term and for their personal gain. The role of community chiefs, or its ground rules, is to ensure that individual desires and needs are mediated to come up with rules that benefit the whole community (or society). This is relatively a straightforward thing in a small community, where feedback mechanisms are direct, relationships are personal and communication between decision makers and decision takers happens with little distortion (Ledeneva 2006, 2013; North 1990).

In larger systems, decision makers are selected (directly or indirectly) and they (claim to) represent the society. However, even in the best cases, the feedback mechanisms are usually slow and not always direct. In addition, critics of representative democracies have pointed out the possibility to have a minority deciding for the majority or lack of overlap between the ruling class and the desires of the population (De Mesquita 2005). If the first party in a country gathers 30 or 40% of the votes, that is does not represent even half of the country and a new law adopted by 51% of the parliament is potentially leaving out 49% of the electorate's needs, which may mean several tens of million. Finally, the effects of the adopted policy will not necessarily benefit the majority of a population (think, among others, of a case where a policy was informed by wrong assessments or assumptions). If we consider that these people might belong to the same geographical area, or segment of the population, one can imagine that the gap between the state and the people may be quite significant for several reasons. One is that there is a gap between what the people expect to get and what they get in reality. This is endemic to all societies since individual desires, needs and expectations are different from what the state provides. In addition, there may also be a gap between what the state promises and delivers, a thing that can be linked to the gap between what the state symbolically represents and provides and what gives in reality. Informality grows and establishes itself in areas where the state cannot or does not want to rule (Polese et al. 2014; Davies and Polese 2015).

In the course of history, a constant, if not growing, amount of people have been trying to take advantage, collectively or at the level of in-group status, of a given position so to bring material or symbolic advantages to themselves, their family or their kin. In a pre-state world, this could be limited only by a similar force opposing and limiting the power of this or this group or family. Once the state stepped in trying to regulate, competition between the state and its citizens became tougher. The state would impose a set of rules that everyone living on its territory should abide to. Entrepreneurs would look for unregulated territories or ways of playing with the rules to maximise their gain. This search will continue, until a new rule is created to regulate, and possibly limit, the influence of this or that actor in one or another sphere of life of the state. Informality may be seen as originating with one or more people or groups of people, and stems from a natural human desire to maximize one's advantages. If there's no overarching entity regulating the relations between people, groups of people and groups of interests then most of the rules are informal.

However, as soon as an overarching entity starts regulating a geographical territory or a certain sphere of life (think of entities not as powerful as the state but that have a say in human interaction, such as trade organisations acting over a given territory, tax collection organisations in the Ottoman empire, privately operating but endorsed by the ruler, see Cizakca 2011) formal and informal rule enter competition. As Hart (2009) suggested for economic phenomena, informality becomes relevant politically only once there is a state, or at least an overarching entity, trying to regulate relationships and interactions between people.

The incapacity of a system of institutions to get rid of informality *in toto* is thus due to at least two parallel phenomenon. One is the impossibility to regulate, once and for all, every single aspect and sphere of life of a state. Informality is the space between two formal rules and actually the ligament bringing together two or more parts of a state's formal rules, making possible to conciliate or to solve issues due to the rigidity of a system. States that are less capable to assert their control might have formal rules more distant and allow for more informality while states with good decision-making mechanisms might have enough rules to leave a little room for subjective choices.

However, even the most repressive, or controlling, state can't possibly regulate people's life from dawn to dusk, or forecast all possible reactions and attitudes of their people to every single instruction. This is partly why black markets may be regarded as safety valves, unlawful habits are sometimes tolerated or ignored and their repression concentrates on some aspects while neglecting others.

In a previous statement "informality is here to stay" (Morris and Polese 2014:1) we were not claiming that informality is always stronger than the state. In principle, once a state has identified an informal practice to get rid of, they have the power to do it. The question is the price of liquidation in operational (how much the reform costs), social (how many people will be negatively affected and how much an alternative solution will cost) and broader (what will be the consequences of squeezing a practice) terms. It is always possible to get rid of an informal practice but the question is at what price and if it is worth doing, or it is more suitable to concentrate state resources on more urgent issues.

The relationship between informality and regulation is the first main theme of this book that permeates all its chapters. In particular, chapter one will deal with the rising of informality in a situation where the state claims to control welfare but only partly does that. This is partly connected to chapter two, where we will appreciate the tensions between state-laden public morality and anti-corruption rules and the way citizens come to understand these rules. Lack, or deviated, regulation informs chapters three to five, dealing with cross-border petty trade (technically smuggling) and the partial absence of rules in an area (Chernobyl) where the state does not necessarily want to regulate. Chapters six and seven will deal with the social and economic factors influencing people's attitudes and preferences at the everyday level (hospitality rituals and shopping patterns). Finally, chapter eight will propose new ways of looking at policy making with formal rules not regulating economic phenomena (linguistic policies, in our case) still being challenged informally.

'In spite of the state' and 'beyond the state'

In a post-Weberian vision of a state regulation goes well beyond the monopoly on the use of force, at least in theory. This brings about a conflict between what the state does, and should be doing, or between what the state claims to do and does in reality. A series of projects on imagined development I designed over the past years were intended to identify a gap between the way social and development policies are imagined in the head of policy makers and how they are actually carried out. The bias between theory and practice can go as far as to completely denature a policy. Once my father told me "once, when I was a child, I got a bad grade in maths despite having guessed the result. There were so many mistakes in my maths exercise that I actually came up with the right results". This recalls the main issue of chapter eight, which takes over a previous study on the way nation-building has been put through in a way that, allowing various regional and local actors to exert their agency and thus distort the political messages, seemed to produce the results they were intended for. The study looked at the way a Ukrainian identity, and in particular, Ukraine language policies, was applied into a Russian speaking city in the south. The perverse mechanism unchained during the process of policy implementation involved the use of an official narrative claiming one single state language (Ukraine) always and everywhere, mixed with a loose control on the real use of the language. As a result, a facade of Ukrainians is created in public schools and institutions in Odessa and Ukrainian is used at some particular moments and when communicating with the capital, giving the impression of total compliance with language directions.

The way informal practices are introduced has been divided into two main ways: in spite of a state or beyond a state. 'In spite of' a state refers to customs, habits, structures or even rules that overlap with, or do not correspond to, state instructions, codes and formally adopted laws and rules. 'Beyond the state' refers to attempts to regulate what the state is not yet regulating or where an insufficient number of instructions are in place. Not only may the categories above be blurred, but also the spectrum of situations between them is unclear (Polese and Morris 2015).

In spite of the state refers to the capacity of informal rules to overrule state ones. The most evident example is international organised crime and mafia-like structures that have their own rules, codes and mechanisms in a way that replicates and overlaps the one of the state. They are, of course, not legitimate from a state perspective but they might be seen as more legitimate than the state in some areas. Think of a case where a criminal organisation lands money, provides support for families and even helps people look for a job. It comes as no surprise that when the police come to arrest one of the members, the neighbourhood locals may get very aggressive. In their eyes the state that is doing little or nothing for their welfare is coming to stop the only person (or people) who is helping them. In other words, criminal actors may become socially legitimate and licit actors in the views of some local people. In his book *The Other Path: The Economic Answer to Terrorism*, de Soto (2002) showed that depriving a criminal organization of its popular support meant its sudden death. At a recent workshop on organised crime (Naples, December 2015) there was a lot of talk on beheading criminal organisations and harshening punishment while ignoring Gene Sharp's theory of power (1973) that, although conceived to deal with dictators and tyrants, seems to point at the fact that delegitimisation of criminal organisations and thus loss of support by the local population is a major step in liquidating it.

'Beyond the state' refers to an aspect of a state life that is not regulated by the state. This is not to say that the state is not there, one could say that the state is getting there but it remains unclear when the process will be completed. There are at least two reasons for the state to be absent or "delayed" in a particular area. One is that a certain need has not been yet identified and policies have not been adopted. Notwithstanding this, people live in that area (or belong to that particular category) and cannot wait for the state to start acting as it might take years. They can organise themselves without invading the sphere of influence of the state. The state might also be there but "not enough" that is, for people to be aware that the state is taking care of an issue but it looks like this is not sufficient to take care of the citizens' needs.

The issue of positioning of informal actors, and practices, with regards to the state, permeates all the following chapters. Chapter one describes situations of people de facto replacing the state for some services that the state claims to provide but in fact does not. Chapter two and three illustrate practices, common throughout most border regions of the world that is used to supplement the state. Chapter four demonstrates that an economic transaction may be regarded from different angles, and thus have different meanings, depending on whether the state is present or not. Chapter five explores the way to integrate, or again supplement, state structures and mechanisms once they turn out not to effectively function in a given region. The amount of people living in the Chernobyl area is not enough to justify the deal of policy making efforts that re-regulation of a vast territory would need. The state has other priorities but the people living there cannot possibly agree with this prioritisation and create their own rules beyond the state.

The developments described above are intended to demonstrate that informality is not a micro but a macro phenomenon. A single informal practice can start micro but become embraced by a growing number of individuals that, de facto, make it socially and politically significant. It is then up to the state, or its government, to decide whether to try and challenge the practice and change people's attitudes and habits (with no guarantee that it will succeed, revolutions can be seen as a response to a too hazardous or clumsy attitude of the ruling elite to repress or contain a certain phenomenon) or buy them to institutionalise them. In either case informality may have a longer life than it is often predicted and the outcome of a given measure not predictable, as shown in the figure below.

Figure 1: The evolution of an informal practice

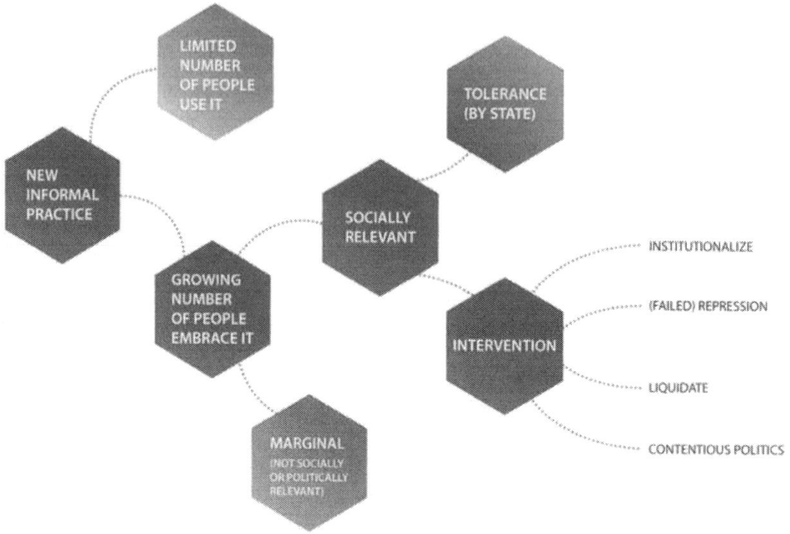

- NEW INFORMAL PRACTICE
- LIMITED NUMBER OF PEOPLE USE IT
- GROWING NUMBER OF PEOPLE EMBRACE IT
- SOCIALLY RELEVANT
- TOLERANCE (BY STATE)
- INTERVENTION
  - INSTITUTIONALIZE
  - (FAILED) REPRESSION
  - LIQUIDATE
  - CONTENTIOUS POLITICS
- MARGINAL (NOT SOCIALLY OR POLITICALLY RELEVANT)

Morality, compliance Informality and the cubic watermelon paradigm

Recent developments in informality debates have engaged with the discussions on the gap between individual and state morality and what happens if they do not overlap (STSS 2014; Wanner 2005) Previous works have dealt with variations in the level tax morality (Williams and Martinez 2014) or the role of major institutional reforms (Aliyev 2014, 2015; Özcan, 2010) or the relationship between economic and ethnoreligious ties (Mollica 2014). How likely is that, in a system, individual and state morality overlap? In a constructivist perspective, this is possible only after several efforts that "educate" the citizens.

Moral norms may be both exogenous, be suggested by a state, and endogenous, be embedded in some religious and social aspects of morality as defined by the citizens themselves. In spite of these norms states are often affected by the divergence between individual and state morality. The best scenario for an individual is not necessarily the best scenario for a state and vice versa, at least not in a short-term perspective. Lack of confidence in a state makes individuals wary of the role of the state and the benefits of paying taxes. People who expect a return for their payment are more likely to pay for a service even if they see a way not to pay, whereas people used to see payments for a service only as an additional cost will be more reluctant to comply with a given rule. In a previous work (Polese 2007) I suggest that the desire to pay for a bus fare is largely informed by one's attitude towards the state, or overarching entity. As a result, it is possible that, in an environment where you expect nothing from the state, you decide that, unless forced, you will tend not to pay for a service even if you have the money to do so. Although initially informed by an economic logic, the cause is more complex and rests in a mutually exploitative relationship through which you do not expect a good service but become unable to pay for it once this happens to be the reality. Empirically, Bovi (2003) has found that compliance with economic demands by the state comes from a mix of positive (advantages) and negative (punishment) incentives for citizens. There are cases where community hinders state authorities (police, some institutions) from carrying out their duties since they see the state as a taker and their fellows -who are formally criminals for the state- as their benefactors. Recent works moving away from state-led view on individual morality insist on the tension between individual, collective and state moralities (the initial Bourdieu argument, 1977, has been also used by Van Schendel and Abrahams 2005, Wanner 2005 and Werner 2002) referring to different values or even systems. Scott (1977) has highlighted the different codes weak and strong individuals might use and how rebellion can be explained through perceived unfairness. De Soto (2000) has made a very specific case of why capitalism is not working, nor will it in countries that have not contributed to construct the rules on which capitalism is nowadays based.

This leads to what can be called the cubic watermelon assumption. Informal organisational rules by communities and groups of citizens, just like a watermelon in a field, will be conceived and put into practice in any case, be there a state or an overarching entity or not. However, if we want a cubic watermelon, we need to use a structure that will help the watermelon grow into that shape. If the structure is too strict, the watermelon won't grow. If it's too loose, it might not take the cubic shape. Similarly, the success of an administration, claiming management of a given territory or aspect of life, depends on its capacity to direct and harmonise informal rules with formal ones. Or, better, to construct formal rules that are based on (what they perceive as their) real necessities, reckon with local rules and possible conflicts arising, and channel informal rules into formal ones putting everyone on the same level.

Capacity to ensure compliance in a given situation depends on the capacity to prize, punish but, also equally important, to propose solutions people can live with in the short term. Radical change is still possible in the medium term but people need to be educated and directed, not necessarily forced.

An assumption here is that informality is part of the human condition as much as sociality and other features that seem to be quasi universal. As much as there are efforts to formalise, regulate, channel, control and, in other words, to limit the power of human agency (Polese and Morris 2015) there is a reaction reasserting the power of informality. Even in the most transparent and meritocratic organisations there are little chances of career advancement if your line managers despise you; reputation in an office is directly linked to the person's reputation and, in turn, to the capacity to be respected and praised for one's work. Success in limiting the power of informality may not be measured by how much informality is present in a system but where informality is and how it is manifested. Anyone in the position of choosing their subordinates will chose people they like and they think they can find a common language, they will try to put through "their" people but there's a difference. One thing is to choose, among qualified candidates, someone with lower qualifications because they seem to have a more positive attitude or because the manager sees an advantage. A different thing is to tamper with the job market in a particular area or field by not allowing anyone else but your kin into prestige positions, a thing that in the long term might sink the organisation.

The cubic watermelon principle may be applied here also. Informality is part of every society and the role of a public administration, laws and instructions is to ensure that its agency does not affect state effectiveness or that can benefit from a certain degree of informality, whilst limiting the power and influence of human agency and subjective choices that can harm it in the long term.

Informality has played a scapegoat role in many cases so far, being the phenomenon to blame if things do not work properly in transition economies. Recent empirical studies have shown that some expression of informality may be challenged by the actors engaging with informality themselves. For instance, when companies understand that nepotism practices are harmful to the company in the long term (Chavdarova 2015), that forced monopolies resist formally, but are challenged informally by a myriad of actors unable to formally enter the sector but the facto having a role in it (Cieselewska 2014; Giordano and Hayoz 2014; Karajanen 2011, 2014) as several studies on border crossing have shown (Mueller and Migglebrink 2011; 2014; Polese 2006, 2012; Sasunkevich 2014). Informal payments to doctors or teachers mean a de facto privatisation that might be seen as limiting brain drain and total bloc of public services (Polese 2006; see also Osipian 2014; Stan 2012; Stepurko et al 2013, 2014; Wamsiedel 2013; Jingqing 2015) or create a new system even more embedded in social relationships than the previous one (Kovacs 2014; 2015).

Functionalists suggest that informality may be higher in systems with higher amounts of red tape but this might hold true only to a certain extent. I would suggest that the existence of certain types of informality depends on the bureaucratisation of institutions and rules but informality, in itself, is present everywhere, although in different forms and modalities in a range of situation that may go from informal economic practices up to insurgency (Polese and Kevlihan 2015). Organically speaking, informality is the (survival) instinct of a society, it is the intuition of a musician, the creativity of the educated artist. We can get rationally (regulate) to a certain point. Imagine someone who says: until this point I get thanks to my knowledge or skills but, after that, I have no idea how I managed to do that. That "last leap" is informality and there is a great deal to be gained in understanding it, as Ledeneva (1998, 2006, 2013) has been advocating for more than a decade.

Informal practices are present in the East as in the West, in the North as in the South, and one needs not to go far. Think of the cash-only diamond market in Antwerp, of trust relations regulating who works with whom in a stock exchange or of hiring practices in companies and universities. There are certainly overarching rules limiting the role of agency and abuse of power but there is also a margin of subjectivity that is used, and sometimes stretched to the edge of the legality. Formalisation and overregulation have also made it easier to accept whatever is legal, regardless of whether it may be seen as licit or not. Ambiguous financial or hiring practices, mobbing and other practices do not represent a problem until it becomes possible to demonstrate, before a court, that this was not illegal. A thing that could be possible to avoid, at a certain risk of high subjectivity, simply by having larger and stronger social control. The success of a state or a management board is not to limit informality, but to limit certain spheres that have a limited or no formal relationship with decision-making, effectiveness and functioning of a certain system. Informality is a tool and has no positive or negative connotation per se. It is the use of informality that can turn out positive or negative, depending on what you use it for.

Cited works

Aliyev, H. (2014) The Effects of Saakashvili's Era Reforms on Informal Practices in the Republic of Georgia. Studies of Transition States and Societies, 6(1), 19–33.

Aliyev (2015) Institutional Transformation and Informality in Azerbaijan and Georgia in Morris, J. and A. Polese (eds) Informal Economies in Post-Socialist Spaces: Practices, Institutions and Networks. London: Palgrave

Bovi, M. (2003) The Nature of the Underground Economy-Some Evidence from OECD Countries. JIIDT 7:60–70.

Bourdieu, P. (1977) Outline of a Theory of Practice. Cambridge: Cambridge University Press

Carothers, T. (2002) 'The End of the Transition Paradigm', Journal of Democracy 13(1): 5–21.

Chavdarova, T (2015) Perceptions vs. Practices: Nepotism in Small Businesses in Bulgaria, in Morris, J. and A. Polese (eds) Informal Economies in Post-Socialist Spaces: Practices, Institutions and Networks. London: Palgrave

Cieselewska, A. (2014) From shuttle trader to businesswomen: the informal bazaar economy in Kyrgyzstan. In Morris, J. and Polese, A. (eds.). 2014. The Informal Post-Socialist Economy: Embedded Practices and Livelihoods, London and New York Routledge, 121–134

Cizakca, M. (2011) Islamic Capitalism and Finance: Origins, Evolution and the Future, Cheltenham: Edward Edgar.

De Soto, H. (2000). The Mystery of Capital: Why Capitalism Triumphs in the West and Fails Everywhere Else. NY: Basic books.

De Soto, H. (2002) The Other Path: The Economic Answer to Terrorism. New York: Basic Books.

Davies, T. and A. Polese (2015) Informality and Survival in Ukraine's Nuclear Landscape: Living with the Risks of Chernobyl, Journal of Eurasian Studies 6(1): 34–45

De Mesquita, B. (2005). The Logic of Political Survival. Boston, MA: MIT press.

Dixit, A. K. (2007). Lawlessness and Economics: Alternative modes of governance. Princeton University Press.

Fogarty, P. (2005) "We all do it and we all think it's bad": Discourses and Practices of Corruption in Moldova, paper presented at the Workshop: Emerging Citizenship and Contested Identities between the Dniester, Prut and Danube Rivers, 10–11 March, Max Planck Institute for Social Anthropology.

Geertz, C. (1963) Peddlers and Princes: Social Development and Economic Change in two Indonesian Towns (Vol. 318). Chicago: University of Chicago Press

Gibson-Graham (1996) The End of Capitalism (As We Knew It): A Feminist Critique of Political Economy. Oxford UK and Cambridge USA: Blackwell Publishers.

Gill, S. (1998) The Pathology of Corruption. New Delhi: HarperCollins Publishers India.

Giordano, C. and N. Hayoz (eds.) (2014) Informality in Eastern Europe: Structures, Political Cultures and Social Practices, Bern: Peter Lang

Granovetter, M. (1984) Economic Actions and Social Structures: The Problem of Embeddedness, American Journal of Sociology 91(3): 481–510

Gudeman, S. (2001) The Anthropology of Economy: Community, Market and Culture. Malden, MA and Oxford: Blackwell Publishers.

Hann C. (2010) Moral Economy. In: Hart K, Laville J-L and Cattani AD (eds) The Human Economy. Polity: Cambridge, and Malden, pp. 187–199.

Hann, C. and K. Hart (eds) 2009 Market and Society: The Great Transformation Today. Cambridge University Press, Cambridge

Harboe, I. (2015) Fighting the Shadows Lithuania's Informal Workers and the Financial Crisis. In Morris J. and Polese, A. (eds.) (2015) Informal Economies in Post-Socialist Spaces: Practices, Institutions and Networks. Palgrave

Harboe, I. (2015) Grey Zones of Welfare, Journal of Eurasian Studies 6(1): 17–23

Hart, K. (1973) Informal Income Opportunities and Urban Employment in Ghana, Journal of Modern African Studies, 11(1): 61–89.

Helmke, G. and S. Levitsky (2004) Informal Institutions and Comparative Politics: A Research Agenda. Perspectives on Politics 2(4): 725–740

Humphrey, C. (2002) The Unmaking of Soviet Life: Everyday Economies after Socialism. Ithaca, NY: Cornell University Press.

ILO (1972) Employment, Incomes and Equality: A Strategy for Increasing Productive Employment in Kenya. Geneva: ILO

Isaacs, R. (2011) Party System Formation in Kazakhstan: Between Formal and Informal politics. London: Routledge.

Isaacs, R. (2013) 'Bringing the "Formal" Back in: Nur Otan, Informal Networks, and the Countering of Elite Instability in Kazakhstan', Europe-Asia Studies 65(6): 1055–1079

Jancsics, D., and I. Jávor (2012) Corrupt Governmental Networks. International Public Management Journal, 15(1), 62–99.

Ledeneva, A. (1998). Russia's Economy of Favours: "Blat", Networking and Informal Exchange, Cambridge: Cambridge University Press.

Ledeneva, A. (2006) How Russia Really Works: The Informal Practices That Shaped Post-Soviet Politics and Business, Ithaca, N.Y: Cornell University Press.

Ledeneva, A. (2013) Can Russia Modernise: Sistema, Power Networks and Informal Governance, Cambridge: Cambridge University Press.

Leff NH (1964) Economic Development through Bureaucratic Corruption. American Behavioural Scientist 3(8): 8–14.

Lewis, A. (1959). The Theory of Economic Growth. London, Allen and Unwin.

Karajanen, D. (2011) Tracing Informal and Illicit Flows after Socialism: A Micro-Commodity Supply Chain Analysis in the Slovak Republic, International Journal of Sociology and Social Policy, 31(11/12): 648–663.

Karajanen, D. (2014) When is an Illicit Taxi Driver More than a Taxi Driver? Case Studies from Transit and Trucking in Post-socialist Slovakia, in Jeremy Morris and Abel Polese (eds.), The Informal Post-Socialist Economy: Embedded Practices and Livelihoods, London: Routledge.

Kovacs, B. (2015) Managing Access to Full-time Public Daycare and Preschool Services in Romania: Planfulness, cream-skimming and 'interventions', Journal of Eurasian Studies 6(1): 6–16

Kovács, B. (2014) Nannies and Informality in Romanian Local Childcare Markets. In Morris, J. and Polese, A. (eds.). 2014. The Informal Post-Socialist Economy: Embedded Practices and Livelihoods, London and New York Routledge.

Millington, A., Eberhardt, M., & Wilkinson, B. (2005) Gift Giving, Guanxi and Illicit Payments in Buyer–supplier Relations in China: Analysing the experience of UK companies. Journal of business ethics, 57(3), 255–268.

Misztal, B.A. (2000) Informality: Social Theory and Contemporary Practice. Routledge, London.

Mollica, M. (2014) A Post-War Paradox of Informality in South Lebanon: Rebuilding Houses or Destroying Legitimacy? Studies of Transition States and Societies 6(1): 34–49

Morris, J. and Polese, A. (eds.). 2014. The Informal Post-Socialist Economy: Embedded Practices and Livelihoods, London and New York Routledge.

Morris, J. (2013). Beyond coping? Alternatives to consumption within a social network of Russian Workers. Ethnography 14 (1): 85–103.

Morris. J. (2012) Unruly Entrepreneurs: Russian Worker Responses to Insecure Formal Employment, Global Labour Journal 3 (2): 217–236

Morris, J. (2011) Socially embedded workers at the nexus of diverse work in Russia: an ethnography of blue-collar informalization. International Journal of Sociology and Social Policy, 31(11/12): 619–631.

Morrison, C. (2007). A Russian Factory Enters the Market Economy, London:. Routledge.

Müller, K and Miggelbrink, Judith (2014) 'The glove compartment half-full of letters' - informality and cross-border trade at the edge of the Schengen Area" in Morris, J. and A. Polese The informal post-socialist economy : embedded practices and livelihoods. New York : Routledge, 152 – 164

North, D. (1990) Institutions, Institutional Change and Economic Performance. Cambridge and New York: Cambridge University Press

Osipian A. (2012) Education Corruption, Reform, and Growth: the Case of post-Soviet Russia, Journal of Eurasian Studies 3(1): 20–29.

Özcan, G.B. (2010) Building States and Markets: Enterprise Development in Central Asia, Palgrave Macmillan.

Palmier L (1983) Bureaucratic corruption and its remedies. In: Clark M (ed.) Corruption: Causes, Consequences and Control. New York: St. Martin's Press, pp. 207–220.

Parry, J. and M. Bloch (eds). (1989) Money and the Morality of Exchange, Cambridge MA: Cambridge University Press.

Polese, A. (2012) Who has the Right to Forbid and Who to Trade? Making Sense of Illegality on the Polish-Ukrainian Border, in B. Bruns and J. Miggelbring (eds.) Subverting Borders: Doing Research on Smuggling and Small-Scale Trade, Leipzig: VS Verlag

Polese, A., & Kevlihan, R. (2015) Locating insurgency, informality and social movements on a spectrum: is there a theory linking them all. In 9th Pan-European Conference on International Relations, Giardini Naxos, Sicily, Italy, September

Polese, A. and J. Morris (2015) My name is legion. The Resilience and Endurance of Informality Beyond, or in Spite of, the State, in Morris, J. and A. Polese (eds.) Informality in Post-Socialism. London: Palgrave

Polese, A. J. Morris, B. Kovacs, I. Harboe (2014) 'Welfare states' in Central and Eastern Europe: Where Informality fits in? Journal of Contemporary European Studies 22(2): 184–198

Polese, A. (2014) Informal Payments in Ukrainian Hospitals: on the Boundary between Informal Payments, Gifts and Bribes, Anthropological Forum 24(4): 381–395

Polese, A. (2009) Informal Networks and Illegal Actions in the Former Soviet Spaces: the Case of Ukraine, Paper presented at the Workshop: Gouverner le local a l'est de l'Europe, Centre Marc Bloc, Berlin, 26–27 November 2009

Polese, A. (2008) 'If I Receive it, it is a Gift; if I Demand it, then it is a Bribe' on the Local Meaning of Economic Transactions in Post-Soviet Ukraine, Anthropology in Action 15(3): 47–60

Polese, A. (2006) Paying for a Free Education, Transitions Online (7 August).

Rasanayagam, J. (2011) Informal Economy in an Informal State in Surviving Post-Socialism, International Journal of Sociology and Social Policy 15(11/12): 681–696.

Rose-Ackerman, S. (1978) Corruption: A Study in Political Economy. New York: Academic Press.

Routh, S. (2011) 'Building Informal Workers Agenda: Imagining "Informal Employment" in Conceptual Resolution of "Informality"', Global Labour Journal 2(3): 208–27. Online. Available: <http://digitalcommons.mcmaster.ca/globallabour/vol2/iss3/3> (accessed 31 March 2013).

Sharp, G. (1973) The politics of nonviolent action, 3 vols. Boston: Porter Sargent.

Sasunkevich, O. (2015) Informal Trade, Gender and the Border Experience: From Political Borders to Social Boundaries. Ashgate Publishing, Ltd..

Sasunkevich, O. (2014) Business as Casual': Shuttle Trade on the Belarus-Lithuania Border. In Morris, J. and Polese, A. (eds.). 2014. The Informal Post-Socialist Economy: Embedded Practices and Livelihoods, London and New York Routledge.

Scott, J. (1985) Weapons of the Weak: Everyday Forms of Peasant Resistance, New Haven and London: Yale University Press.

Scott, J. (1977). The Moral Economy of the Peasant: Rebellion and Subsistence in Southeast Asia. Yale University Press.

Scott J. (1976) The Moral Economy of the Peasant: Rebellion and Subsistence in Southeast Asia. New Haven, CT; London: Yale University Press.

Stan, S. (2012) Neither Commodities nor Gifts: Post-Socialist Informal Exchanges in the Romanian Healthcare System. Journal of the Royal Anthropological Institute 18(1): 65–82

Stepurko, T. and Pavlova, M. and Gryga, I. and Groot, W. (2013) Informal payments for health care services – Corruption or gratitude? A study on public attitudes, perceptions and opinions in six Central and Eastern European countries. Communist and Post-Communist Studies 46(4): 419–431.

Stepurko, T. and Pavlova, M. and Gryga, I. and Groot, W. (2015) Informal payments for health care services: the case of Lithuania, Poland and Ukraine, Journal of Eurasian Studies 6(1): 46–58

Stieglitz, J. (2002) Globalisation and Its Discontents. New York: Penguin.

STSS (2014) Individual and State Morality: What if They do not Overlap, Studies of Transition States and Societies 6(1): 1–2

Temple, P. and G. Petrov (2004) Corruption in Higher Education: Some Findings from the States of the Former Soviet Union. Higher Education Management and Policy 16(1): 83–99.

Thomas, N. (1991) Entangled Objects: Exchange, Material Culture and Colonialism in the Pacific. Cambridge MA and London: Harvard University Press.

Smith A. and Stenning A. (2006) Beyond household economies: articulations and spaces of economic practice in postsocialism. Progress in Human Geography 30 (2): 190–213.

Urinboyev, R., and M. Svensson (2013) Living law, legal pluralism and corruption in post-Soviet Uzbekistan. Journal of Legal Pluralism and Unofficial Law 45 (3): 372 –390.

Urinboyev, R., and M. Svensson. (2013) Corruption in a Culture of Money: Understanding Social Norms in Post-Soviet Uzbekistan, in Social and Legal Norms, edited by Matthias Baier. Farnham: Ashgate, 267–284.

Urinboyev, R., and M. Svensson. (2014) Rethinking Corruption in Post-Soviet Uzbekistan: Ethnography of 'Living Law' In Eugen Ehrlich's Sociology of Law, edited by Knut Papendorf, Stefan Machura, and Anne Hellum.. Zürich/Berlin: LIT Verlag, 207–238

van Schendel, W. and I. Abrahams (eds). (2005) Illicit Flows and Criminal Things: States, Borders, and the Other Side of Globalization. Bloomington: Indiana University Press.

Wamsiedel, Marius. (2013) Non-monetary informal practices and their concealment in a Romanian hospital. Conference paper "Informal practices and structures in Eastern Europe and Central Asia", Fribourg (November 23); organised by The University of Fribourg (Switzerland)

Wanner, C. (2005) Money, Morality and New Forms of Exchange in Postsocialist Ukraine, Ethnos 70(4): 515–537.

Werner, C. (2002) Gifts, Bribes and Development in Post-Soviet Kazakhstan, in Economic Development: an Anthropological Approach edited by J. H. Cohen and N. Dannhaeuser Walnut Creek, Lanham, New York, Oxford: Altamira Press, 183–208.

White, R. and C. Williams (2014) Anarchist Economic Practices in a 'Capitalist' Society: Some Implications for Organisation and the Future of Work, Ephemera 14(1): 951–975

Williams, C., and A. Martinez (2014) Explaining Cross-national Variations in Tax Morality in the European Union: an Exploratory Analysis. Studies of Transition States and Societies 6(1): 5–18.

Williams, C. (2005) A Commodified World? mapping the limits of capitalism, Zed: London.

Yalçın-Heckmann, L. (2014) Informal Economy Writ Large and Small: From Azerbaijani Herb Traders to Moscow Shop Owners. In Morris, J. and Polese, A. (eds.). 2014. The Informal Post-Socialist Economy: Embedded Practices and Livelihoods, London and New York Routledge.

Yang, J. (2015) Governing informal payments in healthcare: lessons from China. In Informal Economies in Post-Socialist Spaces. London: Palgrave Macmillan, 245–269.

Informality and the (welfare) state[1]

With Jeremy Morris, Borbála Kovács, Ida Harboe

1 Introduction

Debates on the role of the state, and its relationship with its citizens, in the former socialist region have pointed at two possible directions. Transitionalists have tended to predict a convergence into Western European patterns (Deacon 1993; 2000) influencing scholars in several disciplines (Esping-Andersen 1996; Fenger 2007) and at various stages analysed the 'Europeanisation' of social policy paradigms in post-socialist countries (Deacon and Stubbs 2007; Lendvai 2008). In contrast, a growing number of scholars examine welfare provision or geographic regions and conclude that post-socialist states might follow non-traditional paths and constitute *sui generis* cases (Cerami and Vanhuysse 2009; Draxler and van Vliet 2010; Fajth 1999; Hacker 2009; Haggard and Kaufmann 2008; Kevilhan 2013; Manning 2004)

This debate has been recently enriched by two more elements. First, the view that changes in post-socialist welfare states reflect neoliberal ideology—policy paradigms characterised by (1) the 'individualization' of social risks (Ferge 1997); (2) privatization in provision; (3) the monetization of benefits; and (4) the partial devolution of social welfare provision to local authorities (Bratic 2008; Cerami 2009; Haggard and Kaufman 2008; Isaacs and Whitmore 2013; Popescu 2004; Szikra and Tomka 2009). The implication of these developments is the residualisation of CEE welfare states across the board, country- and programme-specific variations notwithstanding. Residualisation is apparent not only in the greater emphasis on cash transfers rather than universal (or close to universal) welfare services, but also in the reshuffling of the state's responsibility in social welfare programme financing. Direct payments to public providers of social welfare have increased; citizens participate directly in the financing of

---

1   First published as Abel Polese, Jeremy Morris, Borbála Kovács, Ida Harboe (2014) "Welfare States' and Social Policies in Eastern Europe and the Former USSR: Where Informality Fits In?" *Journal of Contemporary European Studies* 22 (2). London: Taylor & Francis (http://www.informaworld.com). Reprint with kind permission.

the welfare benefits they make use of (Haggard and Kaufman 2008; Tambor et al. 2011). Not least, weakened state capacity during the early phase of post-socialist transformations (Cook 2007) undermined welfare states' regulatory capacities on the one hand and prevented the proper implementation of new social policy provisions on the other (Deacon 2000). While the state, which monopolised social welfare provision, financing and regulation during the socialist era, withdrew from the provision and financing of social welfare programmes, it remained incapable of creating the regulatory framework in which non-state welfare providers, particularly market and non-profit welfare actors, could emerge and legitimately take on the welfare functions that post-socialist states were shedding.

Second, discussions about welfare state futures in CEE have also been marked by the re-discovery and application of the structure-agency debate in the social sciences. Emphasis on the role of individual agency has, on the one hand, enabled the study of the particularities of the region. At the same time, this focus has also pointed to new directions for research. In particular, attention has moved from structural factors to the study of welfare actors and the dynamics of mixed economies of welfare. The theoretical shift to actors and agency has brought into focus a diversity of welfare actors alongside public or state ones and the various ways in which they engage in welfare provision, financing and, much less frequently, regulation in mixed economies of welfare. As this article demonstrates, often welfare actors are informal, i.e. unacknowledged and undocumented by the state, and the welfare they provide, finance and, much less frequently, attempt to regulate is also informal.

Drawing on ethnographic material from Lithuania, Uzbekistan and Romania, this article explores actors and dynamics of welfare provision in post-socialist milieux and, in doing so, documents the existence of an informal welfare system that complements or even replaces the public one. In particular, three cases are discussed here about how different types of welfare—in particular old-age security through pensions, healthcare and childcare—may by produced and exchanged informally. The main agrument here is that when the state withdraws from the provision of protection from social risks that citizens expect or need, a bottom-up process of welfare provision and financing replaces formal welfare provision, citizens 'creating' an informal system of welfare that is independent from the state, but which fulfils the functions that the state should perform, in Wood and Gough's (2006) words an 'informal security regime'.

In the remainder of this chapter, first the context of welfare state change in CEE is explored with a focus on the individualisation of social risks, privatisation of provision and the importance of cash transfers in these countries. The discussion that follows focuses on the re-emergence of individual agency and its relevance for the understanding of bottom-up welfare provision in post-socialist spaces. Finally, three cases of mutual aid or self-help in the face of the failure of welfare provision in post-socialism are presented to then discuss how the high level of informality around welfare needs that are usually seen as the purview of the state in social democracies of Western Europe suggests that the very debate about welfare states and social policies should be revisited in order to also consider informality as a major element of social policy-making. The perception that welfare states have withdrawn from many fields of social welfare provision is widespread in post-socialist context, something that policy actors need to both acknowledge and address.

2 Welfare and the role of the state in post-socialism

Scholarly discussions about welfare state change in transition countries have been dominated by debate on old versus new models (Adascalitei 2012: 60). One strand has focused on whether CEE countries constitute a welfare regime in their own right (a new model) or whether they converge on Western European welfare models over time (Deacon 1993; 2000). In fact a diversity in newly emerging post-socialist welfare arrangements has been recognised, including a 'unique hybrids' perspective (Draxler and van Vliet 2010; Hacker 2009; Haggard and Kaufman 2008; Manning 2004), Cerami (2009: 51). Eastern Europe and the former USSR are divided into two broad welfare types: former USSR type (Belarus, Estonia, Latvia, Lithuania, Russia and Ukraine) and developing welfare state type (Georgia, Romania and Moldova) (Fenger 2007). Authors studying the Baltic republics have suggested that these have a particular pattern (Toots and Backman 2010) and that CEE countries have, overall, shown a wide degree of commitment to the welfare state (Orenstein and Haas 2005). A more careful conceptualisation of the main variables for welfare state analysis, it has been argued, should allow for adaptation to the Eastern European case (Toots and Bechman 2010).

The discussion on welfare regime types, and sub-types, has been matched by equal interest in mapping (Haggard and Kaufman 2008, Ó Beacháin *et al 2012*) and theorising patterns and specificities of welfare state change and post-socialist restructuring (Cerami and Vanhuysse 2009; Hacker 2009). There is some consensus in the literature that post-socialist countries have, by and large, exhibited a range of commonalities in the way in which social policy transformations took place, amounting—overall—to the residualisation of underfinanced and institutionally fragmented, but universalist welfare states.

The first of these generic trends has been what Ferge (1997) called 'the individualisation of the social', i.e. the state's abandonment of social objectives such as equality through state-led redistribution or social cohesion and the welfare state's withdrawal from the direct provision and the financing of (some) interventions protecting against certain social risks (Cerami 2009; Hacker 2009). Although the recasting of the role of the state in welfare provision, financing and regulation may not necessarily amount to the individualisation of social risks, the institutional legacies of state socialism and the politics of post-socialist social policy changes created an environment in which social risks proliferated and risk profiles diversified (Fajth 1999; Deacon 2000; Manning 2004). Socialist welfare states, despite the embedded universalism of social protection programmes, were institutionally fragmented ones. Social services, e.g. childcare, primary healthcare, housing etc., were often provided through state-owned enterprises (Szikra and Tomka 2009). Social insurance schemes were also fragmented, and sectorally organised (Haggard and Kaufman 2008). The early years of post-socialist welfare state adaptation were deeply affected by these institutional legacies.

Secondly, the macroeconomic transformations of post-socialist economies affected different sectors and industries differently, mobilising newly unemployed groups at different points in time. Fragmented social insurance systems were undergoing piecemeal changes not only pressurised by successive waves of unemployment and other risks affecting different sectors and industries to different extents (Cerami 2009; Deacon 2000; Haggard and Kaufman 2008; Szikra and Tomka 2009). The inheritance of state-centric social welfare provision prevented the legitimation—through legislation—of new ways of providing and financing welfare needs (Deacon 2000). In the absence of a regulatory framework enabling the participation of non-state welfare providers and financers (e.g. market and non-profit actors), social needs had to be tackled individually, through family and other informal relationships.

A second trend has been the privatisation of social protection, Private provision encompasses the family, the market and the non-profit sector. In the absence of proper markets and appropriate governance mechanisms (Deacon 2000), Wood and Gough (2006) argue that *people* engage in more diverse strategies of risk avoidance, uncertainty management, but most importantly security provision than in countries with developed markets and responsive and effective governance institutions. During the 1990s especially, CEE countries may be seen as satisfying all the principles that Wood and Gough (2006: 1697–1698) argue are essential to understand welfare regimes outside advanced welfare states: (i) weak state legitimacy and the marginality of well-functioning capital and labour markets; (ii) the limitations these pose on welfare states' capacity to compensate for social inequalities; (iii) social policy needs to account for non-state actors; (iv) social rights / entitlements may arise from domains other than formal state provision, i.e. familial and other informal relationships; (v) these phenomena and relationships are path-dependent and reproduce social stratification, inequalities and power asymmetries. Familial relationships and informal market exchanges between individuals became an important currency of protection against social risks (Hacker 2009; Haggard and Kaufman 2009; Hrzenjak 2012; Pascall and Manning 2000; Williams and Martinez 2014). Although market actors and non-profit organisations have also become key participants of post-socialist welfare mixes over time, they have done so without replacing informal welfare exchanges.

Thirdly, the social policy transformations have put greater emphasis on cash transfers and become less service-rich than during the socialist decades. This paradigmatic change in post-socialist welfare states has recast the financing and provisions of social welfare services in particular, transforming social service provision into a partially commodified good, available unequally through public, private, non-profit and familial channels (Hacker 2009; Hrzenjak 2009).

Finally, welfare state transformations in post-socialist locales have also meant the provision and financing devolution, although not regulation, to the local level, without providing sufficient financial resources or access to local revenues in order to ensure equal coverage and/or quality of services (Bratic 2008; Cerami 2009). One key implication of this has been growing inequality in the coverage of and access to a range of social services especially. Together, these structural changes in CEE welfare regimes have meant the emergence of informal welfare arrangements through which families, households and entire communities try to cope with the social risks that post-socialist welfare states claim to insure against, but fail to do so, or not even articulate and legally provide for.

3 Individual agency and bottom-up welfare provision

Agency has been emerging as a major focus of study in post-socialism (Cook 2007) as opposed to state-led policies (Majone 2002) and debates on the challenge to the Weberian state by post-communist transformation (Darth 2006). A 'non-monolithic' coneptualisation including a wide range of actors critiquing Esping's social and welfare policy approach (Kasza 2002). This concept is partially drawn from previous studies on regions like W. Europe, where a mixture of ideological consensus, centralized politics, and complex bargains among interest groups created a balance of forces (Katzenstein 1985) to preserve certain mechanisms and in some cases even democratic values.

The reintroduction of the agency variable suggests that no convergence less of a given due to the resolutely place/time specificity of models (de Soto 2002) or that such models are themselves more a construct than a reality (Carothers 2002). In turn, a reconceptualisation of the results of the role of the modern state and marketised economic relations, entwisted with (more or less) neoliberal models of intervention and laissez faire has purportedly propagates and upholds (Gibson-Graham 1996). Scott (1998) has engaged with a broad range of state projects worldwide to show that the desire to unify, standardise or find rules regulating a whole means to introduce a series of simplifications lacking legitimacy. Informality, in this respect, may be seen not only as a 'weapon of the weak', of the marginalised, but an instrument widely used in society. Informality, one may say, can be regarded as complementary to formality or even 'replacing' formal processes and structures. In other words, where the welfare state does not penetrate, welfare might be spread also through informal channels and redefine the very dynamics underpinning a society (Davies and Polese 2015). De facto 'privatisation' of certain sectors (Polese 2006) generates a potential conflict of competencies between the state and the citizens dealt with in a legal-illegal framework where payments are seen as bribes and corruption, as some empirical studies have already suggested (Polese 2008, 2012, 2013 Polese and Rodgers 2011).

Kasza argues that welfare policies are the result of negotiations and compromises between very diverse forces that might define a result very distant from the original plan or intentions. Other theorists of the state, although not necessarily of the welfare state, reach a similar conclusion. Migdal (2001) suggests that state and society mutually constitute, and contribute to transform, each other. The main point here is that in a complex system, where initiators do not always see, or even directly influence, the result of their choices, the final effects of an input may be very distant from initial intentions.

A number of current studies on welfare policies in Eastern Europe, but also in general, suffer from two deficiencies. First, it is generally assumed that legislation may be applied with no distortion to a whole country or region and that it is sufficient that a 'good' law be adopted for 'good' welfare policy to result. Consequently, the role of disruptive elements in the path between the conception, definition and implementation has been largely underestimated. Policy adopted at the national, or even regional level, may be 'boycotted' or even 'sabotaged' by street-level bureaucrats or other interest groups, even ingrained cultural norms (Cook 2007; Haggard and Kaufmann 2008). Scholars have explored the effects and consequences of rules conflicting with the local ethos, or simply norms (Gill 2000, Morris and Polese 2013, 2014, van Schendel and Abrahams 2005). Conflict between a social and legal norm may eventually lead to a change in the policy rather than the norm.

This, however, may also happen in the opposite direction and parallel structures where the state fails may arise from below. In spite of a growing body of research on informality, a wide number of phenomena have gone largely unnoticed in the region. An example is the literature on civil society and social capital in former socialist spaces. Scholars have shown that social capital and civil society were weak in post-socialist spaces but Pichler and Wallace (2005) argued that even social capital could be informal, and thus not so visible as in the West. This eventually led to explanations of the apparently surprising growth in civil society in Eastern Europe linked to street protests and regime change (Ó Beacháin and Polese 2010, Polese 2009).

In the previous chapter informality has been defined as the space between two informal rules. If one considers the role of the state, however, informality can be seen as the area between what a state is doing (or claiming to do) and the needs of a society (Figure 1). Here private and community initiative to complement state policies and tools is acceptable and accepted by the state that establishes the borders and the limits on private initiative.

Figure 2   Visualising informal welfare

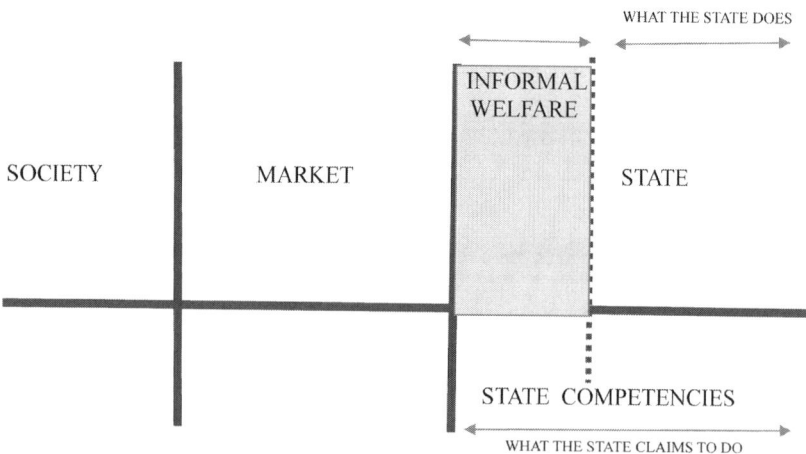

However, the area between what the state claims to do and what the state is doing in reality may be substantially large. Although *de jure* regulated by general state rules it remains *de facto* largely unregulated.

The state will claim that private initiative and actions not recorded by the authorities are breaking the law but the regulation of this contested zone may at least be the source of debate.

A relatively straightforward example is people squatting in public buildings. There is no obligation to provide housing for everyone but it may be assumed that the state should avoid misallocation of resources. If, because of red tape or bureaucratic hurdles, a building remains empty for a long time despite a shortage of housing, what should people do? On the one hand there is an empty building in disuse and potentially future disrepair. On the other hand people who cannot find affordable housing (this is always a subjective measurement) occupy the building, bring it back to life, renovate it and make it inhabitable again. This is unlawful occupation. The state, at this point, has two options: either it sends the police to reaffirm its power or let things be (at least until that building is needed and there are concrete plans for it) to avoid further tensions. In the second case the group of occupants has de facto influenced the state social policy.[2]

This chapter, and in general this book, focuses on areas where the state may be seen as ineffective, this resulting in the creation of alternative structures and institutions of welfare, social justice and many other socio-economic functions that remain unperformed or underperformed. The interpretation of state 'abandonment' of a broad layer of citizenry is widespread so that policy actors need to both acknowledge this and concentrate on policies that support the development of a renewed social contract, rather than relying on the welfare discourse of paternalistic relations that remains after socialism.

4 Reforms to the pension system from the bottom: Uzbekistan

Serdar is about to get married. When asked to whom he answers that he does not know but his parents are choosing for him and he is sure it

---

2   It has been suggested that squatters often come from privileged families so to question the social role of the squat (we should thank Lea Sgier for this and other useful observation on this paper). While acknowledging the need for a debate on the real function of squats, we have kept our example since its goal is to provide an alternative explanation on a social phenomenon rather than assessing to what extent this is useful to whom

will be a good match. His mother has been married for 25 years and allegedly knows what qualities are needed so she will pick a good one. His father is well connected and knows from which family, and milieu, a spouse has to be taken. As a result, he is confident that his wife will be a good one.

Behind this apparently anachronistic account of spouse selection lies a fundamental rule of welfare allocation in Uzbekistan that is possible to read only when knowing the context (Rasanayagam 2011; Urinboyev and Svensson 2013). The end of the USSR led to a crisis in the pension system in the country and, to make things worse, inflation has been eroding state pensions that were already meagre. As a result, it is not possible to think of 'making a living' out of state pensions. This situation is not unique to Uzbekistan but shared with all countries that have a weak pension system -the ultimate case being China, where the single child policy imposed for more than two decades has been recently questioned. With the current situation most Chinese couples are now responsible for four elders since each of them is the only single child of retired people.

It is not uncommon where the state is not providing a sufficient pension for the older generations to be supported by their children. Until a certain age—or the financial independence of their offspring- parents take care of the economic needs of children. After that the young look after the old. In the case of Serdar the other half of the story is as follows. In Uzbekistan, a breadwinner reaches maximum influence and earning power at around 50, which coincides with the time when his son finishes university and takes his first steps in the job market. It is in the interest of the parents to find both a good job and a good wife (meaning not only a good woman but the daughter of influential people). This is ultimately the ticket to a serene retirement with no need to do extra jobs as in some parts of the population.

The state is nominally fulfilling its functions, as it is not refusing to pay pensions. There is, however, a discrepancy between what the state claims to do—paying pensions—and what it is really doing—paying some token money that is not enough to 'make a living'. The space between what the state is doing and is claiming to do has been occupied by a 'privatised' pension mechanism. Pensions, in this case are paid by new generations as debt to the elders but can also be seen as reciprocation of a service received (the parents have helped to find a good job and good life).

We have started with the example of Uzbekistan because this is where 'privatisation' of pensions may be more visible. However, this situation is not very distant from the one observable in countries like Ukraine or Romania, where new generations have a phase of receiving, when their parent are in a stronger position than themselves, and paying back, when they have reached an influential position while their elders have seen their power and influence diminish.

A similar situation is observable in southern Europe, where new generations are known to stay and live longer with their parents. There is certainly a cultural component but the structural, and possibly more important one, is the difficulty in finding a job that gives long-term security. As a result, the older generation provides some kind of social support (de facto unemployment benefits or job seeking allowance) by granting free housing and possibly free food until the new generation decides to leave the family nest. It is nonetheless expected that, once the old generation is unable to take care of itself, the younger generation will reciprocate the assistance received.

5 Access (or lack thereof) to healthcare: Lithuania

Šarūnas is a bachelor in his late 30s who works in the construction business. Every year Šarūnas travels to Sweden during the summer where he works for a salary he only can dream of in Lithuania. In the autumn he returns to Lithuania where he resides with his elderly father while finding work here and there. Work in Lithuania gives him anything from 30 to 100 litas (€8.70–29) a day. The low Lithuanian salaries are a strong inducement to go to Sweden. Šarūnas pays tax neither in Lithuania, nor in Sweden. He works in 'the shadow', (šešėlyje) as Lithuanians express it. Šarūnas' maintains a life largely separate from official society and he is but one out of many Lithuanians doing so.

Šarūnas belongs to a group of Lithuanians referred to as *Invisible Citizens*: people who choose to avoid formal and institutional relations with the state due to a general skepticism towards such institutions and those maintaining them (Harboe Knudsen 2013). The *Invisible* do not register their employment and therefore pay no tax. As they largely maintain their lives on the margins of the state, many of them do not register as unemployed either. In the case of Lithuania this means that they are deprived of state support—most importantly public health insurance and economic and social support in case of unemployment—just as they will not receive an adequate pension when they reach retirement. Unregistered work is most frequent in areas of seasonal and mobile employment. Thus, construction workers, plumbers, agricultural workers and other crafts/tradesmen dominate the field. Šarūnas' story represents a general pattern in Lithuania. While he initially had high hopes after independence, he soon found general conditions to be too difficult, leading him into a spiral of different work experiments before finally settling for shadow employment as the best and most promising solution. While he in principle could receive health care if he registered as unemployed, a number of fines for motoring offencees prohibit this. As he cannot pay his debts, he avoids legal work (the income would be registered and state authorities would enforce payment of the debt), he cannot open a bank account (it would be registered and the state authorities would claim the money in the account) and he cannot own property, nor inherit from his parents (this would be taken as compensation for his debt). He is pushed into a marginal position in society, and it seems close to impossible for him to get 'back in'. Thousands of *Invisible* like Šarūnas bear witness to a problem for the state in terms of lack of participation and lack of tax payment, partly produced by the unsettled economic and social circumstances after independence.

Although 'shadow work' and increased marginalization have been problems since Lithuania regained independence in 1990, the *Invisible* and their implicit criticism of the postsocialist compact have to a great extend been ignored by the Lithuanian authorities. Indeed, only after the financial crisis struck in 2009—a little later than in Western Europe—did the *Invisible* become an explicit point on the political agenda due to the state's need for cash, something which partly could be helped by restoring tax payments among the country's many shadow workers. In 2010 Lithuania's shadow economy was estimated to account for between 27 and 33 percent of the country's GDP.[3] National campaigns were launched, which both highlighted the criminal

---

3   Source: http://www.scribd.com/doc/48801903/Swedbank-Analysis-Lithuania-December-2011 (accessed 9 July 2012).

aspect of the act of shadow working, and strove to appeal to the shadow workers' feelings of solidarity and civic obedience, just as law-abiding citizens were encouraged to report about illegal work if they knew about such cases.[4] However, as the continued high frequency of shadow work testifies, the campaigns had little success.

In a seemingly contradictory manner, the aspect of *insecurity* plays an important role, not with reference to one's own ability to make it through, but with reference to the unsettled situation of the state. Indeed, the continuously social and economic unstable situation marked by unfulfilled promises in the 1990s has reinforced a general feeling of insecurity and distrust of the system, leading people to approach institutional solutions and options with skepticism (Torsello 2003). As the state cannot employ citizens and provide the same guarantees as it could formerly, opportunities outside the state seem to be the most promising. In this regard we witness what Stenning *et al.* have coined as a 'domestication' of neoliberalism as people coped with the new system by filtrating it through their own daily practices (2010). In the case of Lithuania, this was done by turning down interaction with the official version of the economic system and engaging in the widespread 'shadow economy'.

Conversely from the previous case, where there is no mechanism for a decent state pension (there are pensions but they are too low) the welfare mechanism is here provided by a desire to opt out. In this case the mechanism is more complex; it is not in place to make up for a deficiency in the same field but opting out results from misconception of citizens about the function of protection the state had during socialism and has no longer. There is a denial of the social contract that makes people prefer total isolation to having a contractual relationship with authority.

6 Welfare as childcare: Romania

The case of household-level paid childcare solutions in the Romanian context is the final example illustrating the complexities of micro-level tactics and transactions. Undocumented cash-for-care transactions in

---

4 See the homepage of the Lithuanian Labor Control: http://www.vdi.lt/index.php?-1371079622 (accessed 9 July 2012).

post-socialist countries is a particular form of citizen-to-citizen welfare provision arising in the context of underdeveloped public childcare services, unaffordable and few market-based services and, on the supply side, easily accessible local women who complement regular incomes with 'bespoke' childcare for non-relatives (Hrzenjak 2012; Kovács forthcoming).

Childcare and other domestic services have been described as gendered involuntary informal employment (Parlevliet and Xenogiani 2008). In wealthy countries, such work is often carried out by illegal migrants in live-in situations that undermine their control over working hours, privacy, and chances for exiting employment relationships and incomes (Ehrenreich and Hochschild 2003; Lister et al. 2007; Lutz 2007). However, in CEE countries nannies are usually local citizens with some regular income, performing childcare and other domestic services in live-out situations (Hrzenjak 2012; Kovács forthcoming). Although unskilled, often temporary, flexible, sometimes part-time, therefore constituting sub-optimal employment, home-based paid childcare is neither poorly remunerated, nor necessarily exploitative.

Home-based childcare services for pay in post-socialist Romanian urban contexts have arisen due the complex interactions between the demand side (parents and their childcare needs) and the supply side (local women available for informal cash-for-care transactions to secure higher standards of living) in *local* mixed economies of childcare. The undeclared character of these services has arisen from the ways in which the local supply of *all types* of childcare services and the local demand for quality childcare play out, shaped by structural factors. The perceived low quality and insufficient supply of public childcare services, labour market status differentials with high occupation rates among the highly educated and low occupation rates among the less educated, relatively high local income inequalities, the burdensome character of the regulatory framework regarding early years childcare services provision and, not least, a history of informality in the purchase of domestic services have jointly created an environment in which early years childcare is habitually sought out and purchased from private individuals through informal channels, in undeclared transactions.

Zita, the informant of this case study, illuminates this process eloquently. Zita successfully used her precarious job as a cleaner in a bank as a springboard for informal employment as a trusted domestic worker doing both cleaning and childcare for several years. Working as a domestic secured Zita an income three times higher than her post-tax salary as a cleaner, but also enabled her to cultivate a professional persona and exercise control in her informal employment relationships (e.g. when putting down her employer for her arrogance or refusing her services when encountering humiliation), both of which gave her a sense of (differentiated) equality and self-respect. Zita's informal employer, Dorina, the managing partner of a successful local business and the mother of two boys, organised her competing round-the-clock demands in the family business and the family home by hiring an extension of herself for her domestic responsibilities. The undeclared character of the cash-for-care relationship was seen by both Zita and Dorina to fit perfectly with the flexibility of the job description and its intensity. According to Zita's account, neither party wished to formalise the cash-for-care exchange while Zita also worked as a cleaner at the bank on a permanent contract.

For Zita, working as an informal carer brought a significantly higher income than her formal job, which she could keep due to the flexibility of her care responsibilities at Dorina's. In addition, the undeclared character of her caring position enabled her to exercise significant control in her employment relationship, something she could not do as a cleaner. Because her caring was indispensable, but not bound to any formal employment rules, Zita felt she had substantial leverage in her relationship with Dorina. She felt she could easily exit her informal employment if she chose to and therefore did not shy away from voicing her criticisms, objections and frustrations. The informality of the cash-for-care transaction Zita was part of enhanced her professional identity and also empowered her in her dealings with Dorina.

For Dorina and many other parents in her position, the reliance on paid help with childcare most often served to bridge the care gap between the time when the paid parental leave came to an end, usually around children's second birthdays[5], and when kindergarten could commence, i.e. around children's third birthdays. As cheap as a full-time nanny sometimes came—prices ranging between 400 RON/month

---

5   The Romanian paid parental leave is available until children's first or second birthdays, depending on the parents' choice.

(~ €96) and 1.200 RON/month (~€270) –, even wealthier Romanian parents regarded nannies as a 'luxury' when compared to the costs of public preschool services (between 60–120 RON/month, i.e. ~15–30€). . For many parents, however, it was a desired and affordable luxury. For some, this luxury was also part of a particular middle class repertoire that some couples chose to adopt. Functionally and symbolically, hired help was indispensable to being part of a local middle class and to being able to choose good quality childcare for one's child(ren) on one's own terms.

Part of the reason for hiring a nanny without a contract was the evident reduction in the costs of services. No contract meant no taxes and social contributions. It also meant saving the burdensome legwork and paperwork of registering a contract. Furthermore, parents wishing to hire a nanny would enter a local nanny market that invariably operated informally. Parents who employed paid help did so informally because this is 'how it was done'. Furthermore, as informality permeates most sectors of the Romanian economy and the entire workforce, everyone was comfortable with this situation (Parlevliet and Xenogiani 2008). Not least, with the quality of purchased childcare services seen to emanate from the chemistry between child and nanny, and not the generosity (or lack of generosity) of the pay, many parents saw no motive to insist on the formalisation of the cash-for-care exchange. What could a contract add to a care relationship that was proving ideal anyway? Nothing. And what improvements could a contract make to the services of a bad carer? None.

The informality of early years childcare services in Romania originates and is reinforced by a set of institutional and symbolic factors. The informality of local nanny markets endures due to families and would-be nannies feeling compelled to make household-level, personal arrangements in the absence of the state's ability to provide good quality and readily available childcare services or an accessible legal framework through which cash-for-care transactions might be easily formalised and lawfully conducted. The demand for early years childcare services, the supply of women participating in 'multiple economies' to avoid poverty (Rose 1994) and the absence of incentives to formalise personalised economic transactions creates a context in which citizens, acting without coordination, take responsibility for bridging the gap between the welfare needs that the state claims to be tackling and the welfare needs that it actually tackles.

7 Conclusion

A wide range of transactions and practices may be seen falling within the area of state welfare failure and they are often classified as illegal, or at least illegitimate, whether citizens' action is overlapping state action or simply complementing it. Ultimately, this can point at the need to reconceptualise the allocation of roles between state and society in situations where the state is absent or inadequate in terms of welfare distribution and social policies. This also suggests the possibility that social policies in a number of countries is de facto privatised or depends on the agency of citizens, despite an official narrative stating that the state is the sole welfare distributor. Citizens care with little help from the state, the only problem is that they did not ask for permission and the state responds to such action as an infringement of its sovereign sphere.

Whilst it is impossible to deny negative impacts of certain informal practices, such as uneven access to resources, there are also possible positive effects of a 'system' that replaces and complements the formal one, especially in a situation where the difference between what the state does and claims to do is wide. While the moralism of political economy results in an unacknowledged normative approach to corruption, this chapter's interpretive standpoint, indebted to both the concepts of moral economy and reciprocity, allows a more differentiated and nuanced understanding of the mechanism of informal payment practices in post-socialist countries.

This also possibly inform the argument that practices that may be seen as harming the state may have micro-level positive or at least non-negative effects. It is problematic to blanket-label such practices as unequivocally 'harmful' (see Van Schendel and Abraham 2005 on the distinction between illegal and illicit), an assumption that seems implicit in most anti-corruption literature. While reciprocity has been linked to enduring notions of justice, there is nonetheless a potential risk given by how easily arrangements such as informal payments can slip into rent-seeking that cements itself as 'hierarchical inequality' (Graeber 2011: 115).

Going beyond the transitional-alternative paradigm, and locating in the structure-agency debate, however, allows to show how welfare policies are renegotiated by domestic and local actors and come to form something approaching a systematised form of mutual aid and self-help welfare, but which exists beyond the purview of the state and is therefore anything but systematic. In some cases the state clearly benefits from such actions by citizens and turns a blind eye or makes policy accordingly (for example, informality of 'pension' arrangements in Uzbekistan could be seen to perpetuate inadequate policy). Current accounts of welfare partially miss the role of informal welfare policies and informal renegotiations of welfare policies. This means that, rather than seeing welfare from below in the former socialist region as an exception, the high level of informality around coping and caring suggests that the very debate about welfare state and welfare policies should be revisited in order to consider also informality as a major element of social policy-making.

Cited works

Adascalitei, D. (2012) Welfare State Development in Central and Eastern Europe: A State of the Art Literature Review, Studies of Transition States and Societies 4(2): 59–70.

Baran, P. and E. J. Hobsbawm (1961). The Stages of Economic Growth, Kyklos 14(2): 234–242.

Bourdieu, P. (1977) Outline of a Theory of Practice, Cambridge University Press.

Bratic, V. (2008) Local Self-Government in Central and Eastern Europe: a Strong and Independent Local-Level Management Tool or Just a Paper Tiger?', Financial Theory and Practice 32(2): 139–157.

Carothers, T. (2002) The End of the Transition Paradigm, Journal of Democracy 13(1): 5–21.

Cerami, A. and P. Stubbs (2011) Post-communist Welfare Capitalism: Bringing Institutions and Political Agency Back in, EIZ Working Papers 1103.

Cerami, A. and P. Vanhuysse (eds) (2009) Post-Communist Welfare Pathways: Theorizing Social Policy Transformations in Central and Eastern Europe, London: Palgrave MacMillian.

Cerami, A. (2009) Welfare State Developments in the Russian Federation: Oil-Led Social Policy and the Russian Miracle, Social Policy and Administration 43(2): 105–120.

Cook, L., J. (2007) Postcommunist Welfare States: Reform Politics in Russia and Eastern Europe, Ithaca, NY: Cornell University Press.

Deacon, B. (1993) Developments in Eastern European Social Policy, in C. Jones (ed) New Perspective on the Welfare State in Europe, London: Routledge.

Deacon, B. (2000) Eastern European Welfare States: the Impact of the Politics of Globalization, Journal of European Social Policy 10(2):146–161.

Deacon, B. and Stubbs, P. (eds) (2007) Social Policy and International Interventions in South East Europe, Cheltenham: Edward Elgar.

Deacon, B. Lendvai, N and Stubbs, P. (2007) Conclusions in Deacon and Stubbs (eds) Social Policy and International Interventions in South East Europe, Cheltenham, UK and Northampton: Edward Elgar, 221–242

De Soto, H. (2000) The Mystery of Capital: Why Capitalism Triumphs in the West and Fails Everywhere Else, London: Black Swan.

Draxler, J. and van Vliet, O. (2010) European Social Model: No Convergence from the East, Journal of European Integration 32(1): 115–135.

Ehrenreich, B. and Hochschild, A. R. (2003) Global Woman: Nannies, Maids and Sex Workers in the New Economy, London: Granta.

Esping-Andersen, G. (1990) The Three Worlds of Welfare Capitalism. Cambridge: Polity Press & Princeton: Princeton University Press.

Esping-Andersen, G. (ed) (1996) Welfare States in Transition: National Adaptations in Global Economies, London, Thousand Oaks and New Delhi: Sage.

Esping-Andersen, G. (1999) Social Foundations of Postindustrial Economies, Oxford: Oxford University Press.

Fajth, G. (1999) Social Security in a rapidly Changing Environment: The Case of the Post-communist Transformation, Social Policy & Administration 33(4): 416–436.

Fenger, H. J. M. (2007) Welfare regimes in Central and Eastern Europe: Incorporating Post-communist Countries in a Welfare Regime Typology, Contemporary Issues and Ideas in Social Sciences 3(3): 1–30.

Gibson-Graham, J. K. (1996) The End of Capitalism (As We Knew It): A Feminist Critique of Political Economy, Oxford: Blackwell Publishers.

Gill, S. (1998) The pathology of corruption. New Delhi: HarperCollins Publishers India.

Graeber, D. (2011) Debt: The First 5,000 Years, New York: Melville House.

Hacker, B. (2009) Hybridization instead of Clustering: Transformation Process of Welfare Policies in Central and Eastern Europe, Social Policy & Administration 43(2): 152–169.

Haggard, S. and R. R. Kaufman. (2008) Development, Democracy, and Welfare States: Latin America, East Asia, and Eastern Europe. Princeton, NJ: Princeton University Press.

Hall, P. and Soskice, D.(eds.) (2001) Varieties of Capitalism. The Institutional Foundations of Comparative Advantage, Oxford: Oxford University Press.

Held, D. (1999) Global Transformations: Politics, Economics and Culture, Stanford, CA: Stanford University Press.

Hrzenjak, M. (2012) 'Hierarchisation and Segmentation of Informal Care Markets in Slovenia', Social Politics 19(1): 38–57.

Isaacs. R. and Whitmore, S. (2013) The Limited Agency and Life-Cycles of Personalized Dominant Parties in the Post-Soviet Space, Democratization 21(4): 699–721.

Jackson G. and R. Deeg, (2006) 'How Many Varieties of Capitalism? Comparing the Comparative Institutional Analyses of Capitalist Diversity', MPIfG Discussion Paper No. 06/2.

Kasza, G. (2002) The Illusion of Welfare Regimes, Journal of Social Policy 31(2): 271–287.

Katzenstein, P. J. (1985) Small States in World Markets: Industrial Policy in Europe, Ithaca, NY: Cornell University Press.

Kevlihan, Rob. (2013) Designing Social Inquiry in Central Asia: A case study of Kyrgyzstan and Tajikistan, Studies of Transitional States and Societies, 5(1): 56–66.

Kovács, B. (2013) A Child Carer in Romania, in Morris, J. B. and Polese, A. (eds.) The Informal Post-Socialist Economy, London: Routledge.

Lane, David and Marting Myant (eds) (2007) Varieties of Capitalism in Post-Communist Countries. Basingstoke: Palgrave MacMillian

Lendvai, N. (2008) EU Integration and the Transformation of Post-communist Welfare: Traversing a 'Quantum Leap'? Social Policy & Administration 42(5): 504–523.

Lister, R., Williams, F., Anttonen, A., Bussemaker, J., Gerhard, U., Heinen, J., Johansson, S., Leira, A., Siim, B. Tobio, C. and Gavanas, A. (2007) Gendering Citizenship in Western Europe: new challenges for citizenship research in a cross-national context, Bristol: Policy Press.

Lutz, H. (2007) Migration and domestic work: a European perspective on a global theme, Aldershot: Ashgate.

Majone, G. (2002) Regulating Europe: Problems and Prospects, London: Routledge.

Manning, N. (2004) Diversity and Change in pre-accession Central and Eastern Europe since 1989, Journal of European Social Policy 14(3): 211–232.

Megginson, W. L. and J. M. Netter. (2001) From State to Market: A Survey of Empirical Studies on Privatisation, Journal of Economic Literature 39(2): 321–389.

Migdal, J. (2001) State in Society: Studying How States and Societies Transform and Constitute One Another, Cambridge: Cambridge University Press.

Morris, J. and A. Polese. (201X) Informal Health and Education Sector Payments in Russian and Ukrainian Cities: Structuring Welfare from Below. European Urban and Regional Studies (forthcoming)

Morris, J. and Polese, A. (eds) (2014). The Informal Post-Socialist Economy: Embedded Practices and Livelihoods. London and New York: Routledge

Morrison, C. (2007) A Russian Factory Enters the Market Economy, London: Routledge.

Ó Beacháin D., V. Sheridan and S. Stan. (eds) (2012) Life in Post-Communist Eastern Europe after EU Membership, London: Routledge.

Ó Beacháin, D. and Polese, A. (eds). (2010) The Colour Revolutions in the Former Soviet Republics: Successes and Failures. London: Routledge.

Orebstein, M. A. and M. E. Haas. (2005) Globalisation and the Future of Welfare State in the Post-Communist East-Central European Countries, in Miguel Glatzer and Dietrich Rueschemeyer (eds) Globalization and the Future of the Welfare State, University of Pittsburgh Press, 130–152

Parlevliet, J. and Xenogiani, T. (2008) Report on Informal Employment in Romania, Working Paper no. 271, OECD Development Centre.

Pascall, G. and N. Manning. (2000) Gender and social policy: comparing welfare states in Central and Eastern Europe and the former Soviet Union, Journal of European Social Policy 10(3): 240–266.

Pichler F., Wallace C. (2007) Patterns of Formal and Informal Social Capital in Europe. European Sociological Review 23(4): 423–35.

Polese, A. (2012) Who has the right to forbid and who to trade? Making sense of illegality on the Polish-Ukrainian border, in Subverting Borders: Doing Research on Smuggling and Small-Scale Trade, Bettina Bruns and Judith Miggelbring (eds.). Leipzig: VS Verlag.

Polese, A. (2008) If I Receive it, it is a Gift; if I Demand it, then it is a Bribe, on the Local Meaning of Economic Transactions in Post-soviet Ukraine, Anthropology in Action 15(3): 47–60.

Polese, A. (2006) 'Border Crossing as a Daily Strategy of Post Soviet Survival: the Odessa-Chisinau Elektrichka", The Anthropology of Eastern Europe Review 24(1): 28–37.

Polese, A. and P. Rodgers. (2011) Surviving Post-Socialism: The Role of Informal Economic Practices, International Journal of Sociology and Social Policy 31(11/12): 612–618

Potucek, M. (2009) Welfare state transformations in Central and Eastern Europe, in Hayashi, T and A. Ogushi (eds) Post-communist transformations: the countries of Central and Eastern Europe and Russia in comparative perspective. Sapporo, Japan: Slavic Research Center, Hokkaido University, 99–144.

Przeworski, A. (1991) Democracy and the market: Political and economic reforms in Eastern Europe and Latin America, Cambridge: Cambridge University Press.

Rasanayagam, J. (2011) 'Informal economy, informal state: the case of Uzbekistan', International Journal of Sociology and Social Policy 31(11/12): 681–696

Rose, R. (1994) Who Needs Social Protection in East Europe? A Constrained Empirical Analysis of Romania, in Ringen, S. and Wallace, C. (eds) Societies in Transition: East-central Europe Today, vol. I, Aldershot: Avebury – CEU.

Scott, J.C. (1985) Weapons of the Weak: Everyday Forms of Peasant Resistance, New Haven and London: Yale University Press.

Scott, J. C. (1998) Seeing Like a State: How Certain Schemes to Improve the Human Condition Have Failed, New Haven and London: Yale University Press.

Sengoku, M. (2009) Welfare State Institutions and Welfare Politics in Central and Eastern Europe: the Political Background to Institutional Diversity, in Hayashi Tadayuki, Ogushi Atsushi (eds) Post-Communist Transformations: The Countries of Central and Eastern Europe and Russia in a Comparative Perspective, Sapporo, Japan: Slavic Research Center

Sharafudinova, G. (2011) Political Consequences of Crony Capitalism inside Russia, Notre Dame: University of Notre Dame Press.

Standing, G. (2000) Social Protection in Central and Eastern Europe: A Tale of Slipping Anchors and Torn Safety Nets, in Gøsta Esping-Andersen (ed) Welfare States in Transition: National Adaptations in Global Economies, London, Thousand Oaks and New Delhi: Sage.

Stenning, A., Smith, A., Rochovská, A. and Swiatek, D. (2010) Domesticating Neo-Liberalism: Spaces of Economic Practice and Social Reproduction in Post-Socialist Cities. Malden MA and Oxford: Wiley-Blackwell.

Tambor, M., Pavlova, M., Woch, P. and Groot, W. (2011) Diversity and Dynamics of Patient Cost-sharing for Physicians' and Hospital Services in the 27 European Union Countries, The European Journal of Public Health 21(5): 585–590.

Toots, A. and J. Bachman. (2010) Contemporary Welfare Regimes in Baltic States: Adapting Post-Communist Conditions to Post-Modern Challenges, Studies of Transition States and Societies 2(2): 31–44.

Torsello, D. (2003) Trust, Property and Social Change in a Postsocialist Slovakian Village. Lit Verlag.

Urinboyev, R. Svensson, M. (2013) Living Law, Legal Pluralism and Corruption in Post-Soviet Uzbekistan, The Journal of Legal Pluralism and Unofficial Law 45(3): 372–390

Van Schendel, W. and Abraham, I. (2005) Illicit Flows and Criminal Things: States, Borders, and the Other Side of Globalization, Bloomington: Indiana University Press.

Williams, C. and Martinez, A. (2014) Explaining Cross-national Variations in Tax Morality in the European Union: an Exploratory Analysis. Studies of Transition States and Societies 6(1) (in press)

Wood G.D. and I. Gough. (2006) A Comparative Welfare Regimes Approach to Global Social Policy, World Development 34(10): 1696–1712.

Informality, borders and boundaries[1]

Limits to human action and interaction are detectable everywhere in a state (and not only). The state does not necessarily have a direct role in setting them, but they exist nonetheless. A local trader, from a village or another city, wishing to sell some products in another place must face a number of obstacles: finding the right place, entering a new zone, facing new competitors, finding new connections and in general affording new costs. Likewise, somebody wishing to move from one city to another, temporarily or definitively, has to face a number of issues such as finding a place to sleep, earning the necessary amount of money, finding and trusting the right people. Even somebody simply wishing to visit a relative has to face issues like finding the way to the other town, affording the ticket and in general moving away from a comfortable environment to enter the unknown.

Borders, acknowledged or not, indicate separation between different geographical, administrative, social unities and actors; they also limit circulation of goods, people, ideas or money. In this respect, instead of using dualistic categories such as 'borders' (places where there is a real and tangible limitation to circulation) and 'non-borders' (place where there is no limitation to circulation) we could see a continuous line between different administrative entities and see that the number of obstacles to human action grows from a non-border, village to village, city to city, to a state one. As an intermediate situation we could think of de facto states with their hybrid status (O'Beachain 2014, 2015) where borders do not exist but some control is applied, like on the Moldovan-Ukrainian border (see Polese 2006a).

Even in the case of 'non-borders', or former borders, like those among EU states, the end of a territorial competency generates some discrepancies that people are willing and able to exploit, the borders between Germany and Poland, where in theory free circulation of goods should level down differences, are an example. Price differences

---

1 First published as Abel Polese (2012) "Who has the right to forbid and who to trade? Making sense of illegality on the Polish-Ukrainian border". In: Bettina Bruns and Judith Miggelbrink (eds.). *Subverting Borders. Doing Research on Smuggling and Small-Scale Trade.* Wiesbaden: VS Verlag für Sozialwissenschaften/Springer. Fachmedien Wiesbaden GmbH. Reprint with kind permission.

and labour costs are such that people move regularly across the border to buy cheaper goods or simply buy what is not available on the other side.

There is, however, a substantial difference between non-state and state borders. Whilst with non-state borders the state tends not to put any direct limitation to the circulation of people or merchandise (there are of course exceptions), in state borders the state's claim to a monopoly of regulated predation (taxation, state expenditure) is based on the delegitimisation of other forms of predation (see van Schendel and Abraham 2005: 7). The state is the ultimate judge and has the right to set limits, to decide what is good and what is bad. Where its territorial competence comes to an end, the state feels the need and the right to regulate, to adopt a moral code, to suggest or better impose, what is right and what is wrong. What is legal on the one side of the border might not be on the other. If good relations with a neighbour state may be improved by tackling smuggling or migration, the state may be interested in finding an agreement with the neighbour state that will put local citizens' direct needs on a secondary level. When too many goods are smuggled through a border a state might come under pressure from neighbour countries. This may lead to a situation in which the state harms the citizens twice: first, by not creating the conditions for employment it prompts citizens to engage with illegal actions, such as smuggling, in order to survive; on the top of that it punishes the activities generated by state mismanagement. In that case not only the state cannot create the conditions to develop this area, but it is also punishes private initiatives that make up for state ineffectiveness or absence. In this respect the border is an interesting case, being the place where it is possible to see the potential conflict between the citizens and their state amplified to the maximum, thanks to the explicit limitations for the circulation of people, goods, capital, or even services.

Regional inequality is difficult to correct by national laws and people living in peripheral places, like border regions, might have to search for new resources and sources of income and borders will be a major opportunity for two reasons. The first is that borders, being points of discontinuity, provide opportunities for mediators, people matching a demand and supply on the two sides of the same border and earning money out of it. The other is that restrictions and prohibitions generate new demands. What becomes forbidden sees its price increase and the more a state prohibits a good, the more a good will be in demand. This generates new tensions on the one side, and new opportunities on the other. State morality might not overlap people's morality and socially backed rules (see Polese 2006a; van Schendel and Abraham 2005; Wanner 2005). This makes borders places where people cross to buy cheaper tobacco and spirits, to get a cheaper and nicer haircut to places where such practices are consolidated and constitute a strategy of daily survival for many people, to situations in which such borders are a source of extremely high incomes and high economic interests.

It would be extremely difficult to find a moral threshold in such cases, and anthropologists have already warned about the difficulty to generalize moral standards everywhere and for everyone (see Humphrey 2002; Patico 2002; Polese 2008, 2010; Rasayagan 2005; Wanner 2005) so that the border between actions aimed at survival and those aimed at profit may be more fluid than one can imagine. If somebody decides to earn money by selling tobacco on the other side of the border because this may generate a profit there are two options. If s/he brings only one carton s/he is within the law, if two, this is already unlawful. However what is the difference between somebody bringing two cartons and somebody carrying one and asking a friend to carry the other carton through the border for him? And if somebody crosses the border 3 times per day with a single carton? They are still 'within the law' but what is the difference to one person taking 3 cartons at once? We tend to think in terms of lawful (bringing one carton) and unlawful (crossing in a car with 300 cartons) but there are millions of intermediate situations.

Whilst one may be more sympathetic towards those crossing the border with ripped clothes trying to make a living rather than somebody in an expensive car with gold chains and bracelets, both actions, in the end, are unlawful. The difference is that small traders use deception as a first method, whilst wholesalers may attempt deception but might also have the money to buy their way into or out of the country. The questions about the functions, and uses, of a border, and the consequent switch in people's attitude, that move from a generalized moral standard to a contextual one is the main object of this paper. To do this the chapter is centred around the case study of a border region, the L'viv, where dozens of people cross the Polish-Ukrainian border every day to make a living. The aim is to examine some of the issues related to business in border crossing from a closer perspective. We will look at them as forms of resistance, political participation but also as starting points to try to further blur the dividing line between legal and illegal, lawful and unlawful, to distinguish the legal and social approach to restrictions. How often should we buy tobacco for ourselves on the other side of the border to be lawful? If I buy for my neighbour is it illegal? Even if I buy it as a present? And if I accept a favour in exchange? It is all too easy, in the name of good governance, to condemn gift exchange and equate it to corruption. But what should be one's position if 'unlawful actions' are indirectly prompted poverty that may be seen as a direct result of state mismanagement?

1 Redefining borders and their morality

Borders are places of great economic interest where goods are demanded and supplied. They are also areas of tension, not only physically but also symbolically, between the citizen and the state, and the ultimate evidence of limits of control over space by the modern state (see Lefebvre 1974). For the state, violation of the boundaries of legality becomes acute when we approach the political limits of the law or the geographic limits of the state (see Newman 2001). They are also places where individuals can renegotiate state policies that are not tailored for a given context in a way recalling the individual daily resistance conceptualised by Scott (1985). Starting from a perspective that borders, like all state institutions, are "peopled" (see Jones 2007), they are an area of tensions between individuals, and their agency, and the state. Central to this discourse is the idea of representation. On a border some people may claim to represent the state and others not. However to draw a line between who is the state and who is not seems difficult. Availing the Foucauldian (1980) idea that power is everywhere, one can see not only border officers but also common citizens as acting on behalf of the state and showing its multi-facetedness that makes it difficult to distinguish between those acting and those acted in the production of the political (see Navaro-Yashin 2004).

The border, the borderland and the way of living it (see Gavrils 2005; Nugent 2002), become places for the production of the political, of actions that go beyond the mere economic interest of the actors (see Abbink 2001; Bruns 2009, 2010; Hoehne and Feyissa 2008) but have a political relevance and contribute to reshaping an economic policy. By studying the central role of the border in making and breaking ties between individuals one can shed some light on the way borders reshape human, social and economic relations in transitional countries. In doing so it becomes possible to challenge the notion of borders as monolithic entities to show their permeability and how their function may be affected by human agency. As border officers are also individuals with desires and needs not all decisions imposed from the top might suit them. They are part of a community and are, like others, subject to the social understanding of rules and impositions, of a local understanding of licit and illicit, suggesting that "what determines legality and illegality depends on the origin of regulatory authority, allowing the distinction between political (legal and illegal) and social (licit and illicit) origins of regulatory authority" (van Schendel and Abraham 2005: 17).

In many cases people, and transactions, are not confronted with state morality until they come across it. Moving a good to sell it from a city to another is not a crime. But crossing a border with the same good might be, if the good is illegal somewhere else or if the quantity transported exceeds the permitted one and no declaration is filled. As a result, people living in places where the state has less influence might find easier to live according to their rules and engage with illegal actions without being aware of it. A teacher living in a remote village may offer private classes to his weakest students, helping them to pass the final test, and being rewarded with money or commodities. The same action in the capital city, where relationships are less personal and that is more under scrutiny from the international community is more likely to be perceived as illegal. Despite a recent ban, teachers continue accepting gratifications in the form of cognac or chocolates, at least until the state outlaws it. Those commodities, it has been shown, can be recycled and provide revenue so that they are not very different from money, which in turn is officially banned and morally unacceptable. On borders, however, there is a direct confrontation with the law, things are either legal or not and this has to be decided quickly, to allow, forbid, or find a price for actions, goods, favours, connections. Due to this direct confrontation between individual morality, state laws and norms that are perceived as socially acceptable (or unacceptable), borders are a good environment for further investigating informal economies. However, because the concept and use of informal economies does not only depend on facts but on perceptions, the interest of borders is twice as high. On the one hand it is important to define what happens at the border and why it happens and on the other it is the perception of what happens, that is whether people think that 'it is wrong' but they do it nevertheless (see Fogarty 2005) or simply do not see this as wrong because a little corruption does not harm anybody (see Rasanyam 2011). Or perhaps they think it is wrong towards the state but they also feel the state is incapable of taking care of their needs and this is their response (see Polese 2006a, 2008).

Space may be conceived as folded into social relations through practical activities (Harvey 1996), paving the way to an idea of space as undergoing continual construction as a result of the agency of things encountering each other in more or less organised circulations. Space is no longer viewed as a fixed and absolute container, where things are passively embedded, but as a co-production of those proceedings, as a process in process and this is useful to understand the evolution of border relations and dynamics (see Thrift 2009: 86). As a result, one can be spaces as fulfilling at least two functions, one is to create a place for human interaction, the other to create a space for resistance to state measures. This interpretation of space is due to a misunderstanding between the state and the citizen. A state, to be respected, must not only be a state but also act as a state, that is to fulfil the functions its citizens expect them to (see Polese 2007). Should it fail to do so, people would act accordingly.

However, space may be limiting as a concept because it is often conceived in geography as a setting and scale for people's daily actions and interactions (see Castree 2009). This definition has geographical limits, not only given the role of place based agency, but also given that it varies from place to place (see Gregory 1982; Pred 1986). Such limits have been acknowledged to suggest that the global, the international and people's place based agency are interrelated in what Giddens calls 'structuration' (see Giddens 1984), shifting attention from an overemphasized historical dimension of phenomena to a more conscious awareness of how deeply dynamics of power, especially those created in capitalism, are inscribed in spatial relations (see Smith 1984; Soja 1989).

By concentrating on the social relations generated by the use of space, one can try to contextualize 'illegal' or 'extra-legal' practices that sometimes become legal in a different context (see de Soto 2001; Polese 2010). Recent empirical work from economists has highlighted the need to look behind informal payments to suggest that they depend, at least in part, on the incapacity of the state to act as a welfare dispenser (see Peter 2005). If state salaries are too low to secure the survival of public workers, they will look for an alternative source of income and this will most likely be in conflict with what the state rules, although it is generated by the fact that the state itself is unable to regulate such situations (see Polese 2006a, 2006b). What if unlawful actions are prompted by poverty that is, in turn, generated by state mismanagement? Informal transactions are strictly dependent on the very action of a state, its management and the kind of coercive power it may exert. This, in turn, also depends on the perception of the state, whether people agree with the devolution of power that many states (or rather their governments) take for granted, forgetting that, to be perceived as a state, one has to act as a state and fulfil its moral and material obligations.

State authority lies on a compromise, *a do ut das* between the authorities and the citizens. If the state does not honour the contract, people might not be willing to respect it. As Bourdieu (1977) suggested, individual morality is also a matter of opportunities and people might be willing to forget 'state morality' in some occasions if they can see a benefit in this attitude. The fact that borders are places of high economic interest reshapes human relations. In the case of the border citizens may switch identities and identify with public zealous workers or with unsatisfied and underpaid officers depending on the situation. Some people tend to often change sides and boycott the state only when it is convenient, otherwise they simply exploit the state, and the power derived from it, for personal benefits.

Never in history has a black market been defeated from the supply side (Naylor 2006: 11). In our case, once petty smuggling on the Polish-Ukrainian borders reached a worrying level for the EU, a decision was made not to allow more than 2 packets of cigarettes (instead of the internationally agreed 'one carton') through the border. This may work in the short but not in the long run as repression may liquidate some mechanisms but not a demand for income by people living in the border region, but it has changed the rules of the game.

2 Scenes from a border

L'viv bus station 8am. Groups of people are getting organized to head towards the Ukrainian borders, car drivers offer lifts, people negotiate with bus drivers and discuss among themselves. There are three main ways to cross the Ukrainian-Polish border: the slowest and most expensive is the train, where the wheels have to be changed to adapt them to the USSR railway size, differing from the Central European ones. Another way is to take a bus going to a main city, generally Lublin or Warsaw. The most exotic is to take a minibus to the border and cross it on foot. Those wishing to continue may take another minibus to the closest Polish city, Rzeszow, from where they continue their journey. The three ways are main channels of informal trade, though of different nature and modalities.

In many respects the Polish-Ukrainian border looks like a time boundary, with black leather jackets on the Ukrainian side and coloured sport coats on the other. Despite the EU recently investing a large amount of money in border security, also to increase the capacity of Ukrainian border officers, there is still a big difference in attitude between the two sides of the border and the amount of goods smuggled through the border is unknown to many.

The border is a sensitive one, in the sense that huge political and economic interests are at stake. On the one hand we have the European Union, with its desire to control the flux of people, and goods, through their borders, on the other we have the Ukraine that is seeking good relations with the EU, as this means assistance and support, in financial and material terms, and is willing to follow the EU's instructions. This means, conversely from the Moldovan-Ukrainian border, that the official version of the authorities matters. The border is not a no-man's land like Transnistria, on the contrary reports are filed, data recorded and the flux between the two countries monitored. With no responsibility (or even complicity) towards the neighbour country,

Ukrainian border officers can allow themselves to simply ask for money, but with the EU controlling, petty negotiations are not in place here. Still, there is a way for most people to benefit from the border.

3 A false bottom train

There are few trains in Europe that offer such different conditions to the passengers, depending on the direction of the travel, other than the Berlin-Warsaw-Kiev. Passengers travelling from Berlin will enjoy a relatively smooth trip with Soviet courtesy at the Ukrainian border and elegant business manners from the train inspector to the Ukraine. The point here is not quantity, but quality. Few things are easily sold cheaper in Poland or Germany than in Ukraine so that trade is sporadic, if compared to the other way. Until a few years ago there was an agreement between travel insurance sellers and border officers, that they would send the sellers to compartments hosting foreigners, then compel them to buy medical insurance to enter Ukraine. The habit seems to no longer exist and the worse annoyance now is the insistent offer of *vareniki*, fish or other eatable products. Smuggling in this direction is discrete, and one could say elitist, with computer accessories or some other small packets passed through the border.

What is more relevant for the researcher, and even more for border officers, is the petty smuggling starting from Kiev and continuing all the way to the Polish border. In that case passengers might face a sleepless night, with energetic ladies jumping across the car, hiding goods and moving them from place to place until the border has passed. They first have to convince the Ukrainian border officers that they are not worth paying attention to. After all, it is known, everyone starting from the *provodnik* (train inspector) is involved in some kind of business. The mere fact of going onto the other side of the border is a potential gain so every chance has to be used. Who does not need some extra money? This is why the train is the festival of short-term benefits.

Ladies aged from 30 to 60 show their vitality and move boxes as big as they are before getting to the Ukrainian border. The kind of movements varies depending on how tough they expect Ukrainian, and then Polish officers to be. To this we can add the variable unemployment and inflation, with people happier to engage in transactions once they need more money. Professional 'traders' have a key to open most doors and a screwdriver to open walls and ceilings like a tin can. The Ukrainian side of the check is normally made by the nose by officers seeking extra revenue in exchange for a blind eye. Thanks to the need to change the wheels time is not short, but never enough to check everybody. Officers might want to look for bigger businessmen, those who expect most of the gain from the trip, often leaving people with small quantities of goods alone. Occasionally, they might want to detain someone just to fill the reports with something.

People who expect big gains from the border crossing, on their side, also know that such gains do not happen without taxes and partial losses and they will be more than happy to negotiate with Ukrainian border officers.

For this reason the traders have to pack their goods in a way that they seem harmless, dividing big boxes into small bags, distributing them among several compartments or hiding them in other places. The compromise is for traders not to bring 'too much', in the eyes of border officers. The *provodnik* will then negotiate a price with them or the conditions to have a light inspection. Custom officers have to find a way to integrate their income and also have a certain plan to fulfil but, conversely from their Polish counterpart, their main concern is their superiors, who will demand a part of their extra incomes. Thus their task is to check the right people, who can present them with enough money, for money needs to be shared with their superiors. There seems to be little of the civic engagement to the state and the sense of duty that pushes them to act. This 'uncivic' approach has been explored by anthropologists like Roitman (2005) redefining the way people live their citizenship and engage in civic actions or their denial like in the case of fiscal disobedience. Likewise Kyle and Siracusa (2005) also show how failed-to-meet expectations can alter the relationship of citizens with domestic and international laws, prompting them to break laws in search of welfare their country is unable to grant. In such cases social rules come to overlap legal ones and the border between the legal and the licit becomes fluid. Control over the situation is not assured by laws but by informal norms like in the case of traffic police fines that regulate the behaviour of drivers. In the West it would be 'if you do not want to pay a fine, drive consciously' whereas in the Ukraine 'if you want to lower the risk of being harassed by traffic police drive consciously'. The result might be very similar (see Polese 2008) with the difference that in this second case the state loses the extra revenues coming from fines.

The level of prohibition and control the state imposes does nothing but alter the supply-demand relationship and the income of the actors involved. Tougher border controls will not discourage the daily traders but change the prices to be paid at the border, with seasonal higher revenues for custom officers or traders, depending on the context. The only hope for the state may be that controls become so tough that it will not be economically convenient for traders to smuggle cigarettes or alcohol and cease. However, even if this becomes highly burdening, if traders have no other option can they really let things be? Not only their income, but also custom and border officers' income as well as that of their superiors and their families depend on their activity. Border smuggling does not end at the border but benefits a whole set of people from those buying goods to those selling to those who accept bribes and smuggling and corruption will not be eliminated by stopping the trader. This will just change the rules of the game. If smuggling is tackled the state will have to face the issue of low salaries for border officers and unemployment in border regions, which might make things even worse.

Once the Ukrainian side has been passed, the train becomes even more evanescent as the Polish officers are supposed to come and they will apparently show no mercy for petty smugglers. Immune from any bribe attempts, they have a reputation of being insensitive to personal problems and have a black and white approach: either you pass or not. Despite being a common perception among petty traders, this is only half of the picture. True that EU pressure on external borders is such that Poland has seen itself implementing a number of reforms unthinkable some years ago. True also that internal control is such that small bribes will not buy your way into the country. Also true perhaps that custom officers have become much worse since 2004, when Poland joined the EU. In this respect, seeing so many possibilities to earn easy money and not being able to take advantage from might affect their attitude towards petty smugglers.

However Polish custom officers might not be as bad as they are depicted in the account of many Ukrainian 'border traders'. The Polish-Ukrainian border is a hot spot, it is well-known that smuggling passes through it and the EU has asked for effective measures to be taken. Due to the level of control, officers are more reticent to accept bribes, although this does not mean that there are no informal agreements. If one has to take a risk at this border, they will not do it for 5 USD as on the other side. They would go for more substantial sums.

Polish officers have something in common with their Ukrainian counterparts. They have to confiscate a quantity of goods big enough to make their superiors happy but will not be rewarded financially. They, in turn, can use the records of confiscated material to show that their controls are effective and they are indeed fighting smuggling through the border. There are no official figures on how many goods are smuggled through the border (if they were available the EU or Poland would be happy to use them to crash such flows) so that a good way to show zealous inspection is to confiscate enough goods. This means no bribes at the Polish borders but tributes to the EU. Custom officers may also understand that those traders have children, need revenue, and not necessarily all of them might be willing to show scorn for their poorer neighbours but also custom officers need to eat, and to do this they need to show some results. The compromise is to confiscate enough goods to show some work has been done, but leaving enough to the traders to make their border crossing worthwhile. Time at the border is also limited, especially on a train, but the quantity of goods found is also seasonal, depending on the expectations of high-level officers and the EU. The train might be opened as a bean can, checking ceilings, walls, toilets or rubbish bins and all parts that could be used to hide goods, or the control will be a fast one, supposing the period of the year, or day of the week, is a quiet one.

Border officers, like other people, seem to incarnate the drama of dual identities. They are individuals and fellow citizens, but also representatives of the state and this demonstrates a conflict between professional tasks and individual choice that is proper to the state-citizen relationship (see Jones 2007).

4 Alternative ways of crossing

Besides the train, one can cross the border on foot and by bus. Walking through the borders is difficult and not worthwhile for the case study. First of all it is harder to find alliances at the border and everything is done on a personal basis, people are searched individually and they have few places to hide the goods, in addition, they prepare themselves well before the border, so it is more difficult to observe the dynamics that are otherwise shown clearly in a space safe from state officers. The second hurdle is that this is physically proving. One has to work one's way through using elbows and knees and the concept of a line is an abstract one here. Once you cross you see a settlement grown on informal trade, where people buy the cheapest cigarettes and alcohol in Poland. There is a service for the next city, from where you can reach most Polish destinations, but many people stop here, sell, and return to their place on either side of the border. Not only Ukrainians go to Poland to sell, also Polish cross the border and return to Poland to sell, crossing the border as many times as they can during the day.

Informal trade is all the more visible when crossing by bus. On the way to the border the ladies in the bus start rushing around and open the cigarette cartons to hide single packets wherever they can. Some squeeze 3 or 4 of them into black stockings and hide this 'black sausage' behind the bus curtains. Some others remove the pillow from the seat and hide some underneath it. All places with little light are particularly appreciated, be this the overhead compartment (where the black stockings are hidden as deeply as possible) or other small sections between a seat and the bus walls. Almost everybody changes their clothes to be able to hide some cigarettes under the new, and wider, ones and everybody only keeps the maximum quantity of alcohol and cigarettes allowed in their hand bags ready for inspection.

The border approaches and we queue for inspection. The ladies make their final checks to make sure the cigarettes will not fall out at the wrong moment. Once the time has come, passengers may be asked to leave the bus and take out their personal belongings. The inspection has two dimensions. On the one hand they check every passenger and how many goods they have with them. On the other they check the bus full of nobody's goods, cigarettes that nobody will claim back and that will be confiscated without punishing those trying to pass them through the border. Controls on people and hand luggage have got tougher so the strategy has evolved to become impersonal with teams working together. Everybody hides goods in the bus and remembers where. Some bags are eventually found and taken away. Once back in the bus, traders check who has lost what for the good of the community. Having to find a quantity of cigarettes means the Polish officers will not look at whose they are but go for a certain quantity. Those who have the highest losses will find consolation in that next time it might not be their turn to lose that much and their profit will be higher. I talk of teams because, especially in some buses (like the L'viv-Lublin one) people get into the bus at the same point and come from the same village, showing solidarity with each other. The question of whether what they were doing was acceptable or never arose. As in other cases (see Fogarty 2005; Rasayam 2004; Polese 2006a; van Schendel/Abraham 2005) the boundary was between licit and illicit, leaving the judgement on legality to the officers. As long as we have children, need money and the state does not provide us with enough access to resources, what we are doing is simply to make up for a lack of action of the state. Local moralities overlap, conflict, and partially replace state morality. However local moralities are also subject to certain rules, as the follow-up of this case shows.

Passengers go back into the bus and wait. Only one young lady is sent for and disappears into a custom barrack. Along with alliances and rivalries, sometimes also love, hand in hand with money, is a main feature of daily survival. One of the ladies turns out to have a lover at the border crossing point and is with him while everybody waits for them. Thanks to this asset, other say, she is the bravest one in the bus, carrying far more goods than she would be allowed and securing much higher revenues than the others. This has allowed her to buy some land and build a house where she lives comfortably enough, whilst her village mates struggle to survive.

Most ladies acknowledged that team work is needed to cross the border. Belonging to the same village was another reason to cooperate and no one ever mentioned what they were doing as something they perceived as 'illegal'. However, the relationship with the young border officer put this lady in an ambivalent position. She seemed to be outside the team, able to carry more things but being only partially accepted as part of the village, as some people considered she was selling her body for money. The fact that she enjoyed a higher economic status in some cases was not enough to justify her 'low moral level' and some ladies mentioned they would not do this even if they had the possibility.

There seems to be a dividing line between what you are allowed to do and what is socially acceptable and the above lady seemed to have crossed it. Whilst engaging in an activity widely justified by local norms, she was deliberately violating some principles of her community. The question is what the border was. Was she judged because of making much more money than the others and thus envied? Or because she was mixing love and money? What principles was she violating? They were all going beyond legality but she seemed the only socially stigmatisable. Apparently she was not only violating legal rules but also the principle of licitness existing among her fellow villagers.

After the border was crossed nobody hurried to retrieve their goods. There was still a chance of a hidden control before the first village. Once the chances lowered, they set out to check who had lost what and changed back into "normal" clothes. Normally the driver stops the bus and they buy huge nets of onions, that for some reason are cheaper in Poland than in the Ukraine and can be sold back home. Meat is another of the goods to buy in Poland and sell in the Ukraine but it is riskier. First of all transporting meat is not permitted across the border, secondly meat is a perishable good and it might go off (especially in the summer) or be confiscated whereas onions are more innocent in many respects.

Such buses and ways to cross the borders are quite frequent along the Polish-Ukrainian border and people do this on a regular, often daily, basis. A question that is still puzzling is the gender dimension, for most of the traders were ladies. To conduct a study on the gender dimension of this trade would be extremely interesting. At this stage I can only speculate on the fact that this job requires little physical efforts (although high levels of stress), whereas men can be employed in construction or agricultural works. Another point might be the social status of those women and that they only engage in such transactions if their husbands' revenues are not enough, this may imply that the husband is not working, has problems with alcoholism, or is gone.

5 Concluding remarks

The trade in the proximity of the Polish-Ukrainian border described in this paper seems in contrast with the values a state, and in this case the Ukraine, is willing to propose and accept. However, despite an official discourse condemning contraband, the petty trade in which people engage is often perceived as something socially acceptable by the traders themselves and, in some respect, even by border officers. The Bourdieuan (1977) gap between state and individual morality finds empirical application in this research, where people choose to subscribe to a state or individual moral code depending on the opportunities they offer. A weak state means uncontrolled revenues, no income taxes paid and, even more importantly, a distorted perception of the role of the state. In such cases the state may be perceived as limiting initiative and activities whilst bringing no real advantage to the loyal citizen. As Bovi (2003: 67) and Layoza (1996) noticed, where the state is able to protect its citizens and offer some advantages, or at least perspectives of change, people would be more willing to act in the frame of legality. In the case above people might not want to abide because control is only partially enforced. However, this also happens because allowing people to survive on the verge of illegality is a way to make up for ineffective economic reforms that affect some regions in particular. Owing to necessity, people seem to have constructed a grey area between legality and illegality in their narrative when they use expressions already present in other geographical contexts such as 'signs of attention' (see Patico 2002), 'little corruption' (that does not hurt anyone; see Rasanayagam 2003, 2011) or construct social norms to survive legal impositions (see Harrison 1999).

In such a context informal payments are not necessarily an example of the degradation of society. On the contrary, they participate in creating an independent—and possibly uncontrollable—economic system in which the state officially forbids, but in reality allows, and the people officially abide by the rules, but also know how to increase their revenues. All actors are satisfied, limiting economic discontent and avoiding social tensions. Such petty trade may be seen as the solution, rather than the cause, to problems such as high unemployment and low revenues. When few people are willing—or allowed—to invest in domestic companies, goods are hard to find and money scarcely circulates, informal payments, networks, *blat'* seem a possible solution. This situation is also convenient for political elites, especially when they are unable to engage in effective reforms. Border officers will not object since they can top up their salary and ordinary people can break up a vicious circle preventing them from earning money and access some goods at a price cheaper than the domestic one.

Cited works

Abbink, J. (2001) Creating Borders: Exploring the Impact of the Ethio-Eritrean War on the Local Population, Africa 56(4): 447–458.

Abraham, I. and W. van Schendel (2005) Introduction: The Making of Illicitness, in: W. van Schendel and I. Abraham (eds.): Illicit Flows and Criminal Things: States, Borders, and the Other Side of Globalization. Bloomington: Indiana University Press, 1–37.

Bovi, M. (2003) The nature of the underground economy—some evidence from OECD countries. Journal for Institutional Innovation, Development & Transition 7:60–70.

Bourdieu, P. (1977) Outline of a Theory of Practice. Cambridge: Cambridge University Press.

Bruns, B. (2009) Grenze als Ressource: Die soziale Organisation von Schmuggel am Rande der europäischen Union. Wiesbaden: VS Verlag für Sozialwissenschaften.

Castree, N. (2009) Place: Connections and Boundaries in an Interdepent World, in: N. Clifford, S. Holloway, S. Rice and G. Valentine (eds): Key Concepts in Geography. London: Sage, 153–172.

Fogarty, P. (2005) 'We all do it and we all think it's bad': Discourses and Practices of Corruption in Moldova. Paper presented at the Workshop: Emerging Citizenship and Contested Identities between the Dniester, Prut and Danube Rivers, 10 and 11 March, Max Planck Institute for Social Anthropology.

Giddens, A. (1984) The Constitution of Society. Cambridge: Polity Press.

Gregory, D. (1982) Regional transformation and industrial revolution: A Geography of the Yorkshire Wollen Industry. Minneapolis: University of Minnesota Press.

De Soto, H. (1989) The Other Path: the Economic Answer to Terrorism. New York: Basic Books.

De Soto, H. (2000) The Mystery of Capital: Why Capitalism Triumphs in the West and Fails Everywhere Else. New York: Basic Books.

Foucher, M. (1991) Fronts et frontiers. Paris: Fayard.

Gavrilis, G. (2008) The Dynamics of Interstate Boundaries. Cambridge: Cambridge University Press.

Gorodnichenko, Y. and K. S. Peter (2006) Public Sector and Corruption: Measuring Bribery from Micro Data. IZA Discussion Paper No. 1987, URL: http://www-personal.umich.edu/~ygorodni/private-public-Gorodnichenko-Peter-2006-01-25.pdf (last accessed: 13 March 2010).

Gupta, A. (1995) Blurred Boundaries: The Discourse of Corruption, the Culture of Politics, and the Imagined State, American Ethnologist 22(2): 375–402.

Harrison, G. (1999) Corruption, Development Theory and the Boundaries of Social Change, Contemporary Politics 5(3): 207–220.

Harvey, D. (1986) Justice, Nature and the Geography of Difference. Oxford: Basil Blackwell.

Herzfeld, M. (2005) Cultural Intimacy. Cambridge: Harvard University Press.

Hoehne, M.V. and Feyissa, D. (2008) Resourcing state borders and borderlands in the Horn of Africa. Working papers, Max-Planck-Institute for Social Anthropology.

ILO (1972) Employment, Incomes and Equality: A Strategy for Increasing Productive Employment in Kenya. Geneva: ILO.

Jones, R. (2007) People, States, Territories. Oxford: Blackwell.

Lefebvre, H. ([1974] 1991) The Production of Space. Oxford: Blackwell.

Miller, W.L., A. B. Grodeland and T. Y. Koshechkina T.Y. (2000) Victims or Accomplices? Extortion and bribery in Eastern Europe, in A. Ledeneva and M. Kurkchiyan (eds.): Economic Crime in Russia. London: Kluwer Law International, 113–128.

Navaro-Yashin, Y. (2002) Faces of the State. Princeton, NJ: Princeton University Press.

Naylor, R.T. (2002) Wages of Crime: Black Markets, Illegal Finance, and the Underworld Economy. Ithaca/NY: Cornell University Press.

Newman, D. (2001) Borders and Barriers: Changing Geographic Perspectives on Territorial Lines, in M. Albert, D. Jacobsen and Y. Lapid (eds.): Identities, Borders, Orders: Rethinking International Relations Theory. Minneapolis: University of Minnesota Press, 137–151.

Nugent, P. (2002) Smugglers, Secessionists and Loyal Citizens on the Ghana-Togo Frontier. Athens: Ohio University Press.

Papava, V. and N. Khaduri (1997) On the Shadow Political Economy of the Post Communist Transformation, an Institutional Analysis, Problems of Economic Transitions 40(6): 15–34.

Patico, J. (2002) Chocolate and Cognac: Gifts and the Recognition of Social Worlds in Post-Soviet Russia, Ethnos 67(3): 345–368.

Polese, A. (2006a) Border Crossing as a Daily Strategy of Post Soviet Survival: the Odessa-Chisinau Elektrichka, Eastern European Anthropology Review 24(1): 28–37.

Polese, A. (2006b) Paying for a Free Education. Transitions On Line, Prague (08 August).

Polese, A. (2007) Ukraine: the State is Public, the Private Sector is Private, the Public Sector is? Presented at the Workshop on Property in Eastern Europe, New European College, Bucharest 14 and 15 June 2007

Polese, A. (2008) 'If I Receive it, it is a Gift; if I Demand it, then it is a Bribe': On the Local Meaning of Economic Transactions in Post-Soviet Ukraine, Anthropology in Action 5(3): 47–60.

Polese, A. (2010) At the Origins of Informal Economies: Some Evidence from Ukraine (1991–2009). Friedrich Schiller University of Jena, Working Paper.

Pred, A. (1986) Place, Practice and Structure: Social and Spatial Transformation in Southern Sweden. Cambridge: Polity Press.

Rasanayagam, J. (2003) Market, State and Community in Uzbekistan: Reworking the Concept of the Informal Economy. Max Planck Working Papers no.59.

Roitman, J. (2005) Fiscal Disobedience: An Anthropology of Economic Regulation in Central Africa. Princeton, NJ: Princeton University Press.

Scott, J. (1985) Weapons of the Weak. Heaven, London: Yale University Press.

Soja, E. (1989) Postmodern Geographies: The Reassertion of Space in Critical Social Theory. London, New York: Verso.

Smith, N. (1984) Uneven Development: Nature, Capital, and the Production of Space. Oxford: Blackwell.

Temple, P. and G. Petrov (2004) Corruption in Higher Education: Some Findings from the States of the Former Soviet Union, Higher Education Management and Policy 16(1): 83–99.

Thrift, N. (2009) Space: The Fundamental Stuff of Geography, in G. Valentine, S. Holloway and N. Clifford (eds.): Key Concepts in Geography. London: Sage, 85–95.

Wanner, C. (2005) Money, Morality and New Forms of Exchange in Postsocialist Ukraine. Ethnos 70(4): 515–537.

Border crossing, petty trade and the role of informality in breaking artificial monopolies[1]

1 Introduction: a running bazaar

Odessa railway station, 11.30 a.m. The sun is shining on people and trains while a crowd overloaded with luggage has gathered on the last platform, leaving the rest of the station almost empty. Despite the heterogeneity of the crowd, one main type of character is immediately noticeable: the *babushka*. These old ladies jump back and forth with unexpected vitality, carrying huge quantities of goods. Bags full of coffee, flour, cucumbers and cabbages are tied down on improvised trolleys and thrown onboard. People cry, argue, or even fight for a place. This unexpected phenomenon awoke curiosity in me as a casual observer (which I was at that time) and this only increased as I discovered that it was the train I had to take: the *elektrichka* travelling from Odessa to Chisinau.

An *elektrichka*, in Soviet terminology, is a small train, with only fourth class carriages (still, by paying the equivalent of 10 cents one gains access to a coach equipped with a TV showing old-fashioned action movies for five hours), covering a short distance very slowly. In this case it covers the 180 km separating Odessa from Chisinau in about five hours. What was an internal train commuting between two Soviet cities is nowadays, as a result of the collapse of the USSR, an international train that several hundred people use everyday. The train goes to Chisinau via the Transdnistrian Republic. For this reason Russian and Romanian speakers are evenly distributed but hardly anybody seems to be travelling for any other reason apart from "business". Actually, trade is the quintessence of the *elektrichka*, whose function is that of feeding people on both sides of the border.

---

1 This chapter was originally published as Abel Polese (2006) "Border Crossing as a Daily Strategy of Post Soviet Survival: the Odessa-Chisinau *Elektrichka*". Anthropology of East Europe Review 24(1): 28–37; and as Abel Polese (2013) "The Ambiguity and Functions of Informality: Some Notes from the Odessa-Chisinau Route". In: C. Giordano and N. Hayoz (eds.) *Informality in Eastern Europe: Structures, Political Cultures and Social Practices*. Bern: Peter Lang. Reprint with kind permission.

Few things are more indicative of the drama of the post-Soviet transition than the Odessa–Chisinau train, where a "separate" world with its own economic system has developed spontaneous institutions, making up for the lack of state assistance. The *elektrichka* train travelling between Odessa and Chisinau is a microcosm that incorporates many relevant aspects of post-Soviet societies, from the political struggle for power, corruption and ethno-political clashes, to the shadow economy and border problems. The peculiarities of this train are numerous. First of all there is the geographic location of the railway line that unites Moldova and Ukraine, passing through the separatist republic of Transdnistria (not recognized at an international level but *de facto* a state between Moldova and Ukraine). Secondly, the border crossing itself: apart from some administrative changes, at the time of the research Moldovans still considered Odessa the place to go for purchasing goods, as they did in the past, when Odessa was the largest Soviet port on the Black Sea. Finally, there is the informal economy, reigning supreme due to a lack of a strong state to provide security to those needing a more secure income besides their meagre or nonexistent wages.

The aim of this chapter is to use the case study of the *elektrichka* to discuss some of the most important issues of the region. The first part examines the impact of an unrecognized state, the Republic of Transdnistria, with Tiraspol as capital, on the economic dynamics of the region. It will describe the train trip to highlight major issues related to border crossing between Ukraine and Moldova and the ambiguity of the Transdnistrian border. The fluidity of the physical border between the two countries will serve to introduce the main focus of this chapter: informal economic practices. We will look at the exchanges of favours and money on the border between Moldova and Ukraine to explore the ambiguity of actions that may be condemned by anticorruption and antismuggling organizations and their official narratives, but which have the function of helping people survive. The two case studies that supplement the discussion examine the trade and the shadow economy in the context of the *elektrichka*, using previous literature and my own analysis of fieldwork data. Finally, the controversial issue of corruption will be described in its local forms, including its positive and negative aspects. I suggest that, before stigmatising corruption as an evil to eradicate, one should reckon with the fact that a "little" corruption may guarantee an equilibrium and an even distribution of money. In this respect petty smuggling might be seen as a market regulator able to elude the protectionist policy of local monopolists who operate to the detriment of consumers and prevent new investors from entering the market. At the end of each trading trip, a relatively positive effect is achieved: officers and traders make financial gains and consumers have access to better quality goods.

Methodologically, this chapter is based on participant observation carried out in the spring of 2004, completed by informal interviews with local informants. Given the sensitivity of the issue I have preserved the anonymity of informants and omitted any information that could be dangerous to the individuals concerned. I had initially planned an update of the study in 2010 but, once I arrived there, I discovered that the train had been phased out in an attempt to put illegal practices under control. This gave me the chance to visit some other places and get material to compare the situation with other cases. Only border crossings by bus or car now remain but I still believe this study can help understand some peculiarities of the region.

2 Hum, I am Sorry. . . Where is the Border?

Less than 2% of the European borders determined during the twentieth century are the result of a plebiscite (Foucher 1991), and the Ukrainian–Moldovan border most definitely does not belong to this 2%. Ruré reports that a "Socialist Soviet Republic of Moldova was born on the 2nd of August 1940 merging Central Bessarabia and a large part of the Moldovan SSR. The other part was attributed to Ukrainian RSS, that incorporated the north and south of Bessarabia, the Hertza District and the north of Bukovina" (Ruré, 1999: 228, translated by the author). The line separating Ukraine and Moldova has very little in common with a "traditional" border and it is much more imaginary than real. On the Ukrainian side control procedures are quite normal—for a former Soviet Republic; the train arrives in Razdelna, passports are checked, custom officers screen people and the train starts again.

The question is: where is the Moldovan border? After the Ukrainian border the train stops again in Kuchurgan, situated on the territory of the Republic of Transdnistria. The Republic pledges a Soviet identity, many citizens still travel on Soviet passports as the Transdnistrian passport -if ever issued- would have no international value, and strives to continue the Soviet tradition of territorial continuity and open borders. No customs officer shows up and people literally jump out of the train and rush out of the station. I discovered the reason behind this during an informal interview with a border official in Chisinau: to check on people entering the administrative territory of Moldova would mean further official recognition of the separatist republic, something Moldova is not prepared to do.

Nonetheless, in order to fight the contraband problem, the Chisinau government decided, on 1 June 1999, to establish 17 permanent custom posts and 30 mobile posts along the inner Moldovan administrative border and also along the border with Ukraine but, as Neukrich (2001) reported, these posts did not seem very effective. The fact that various political groups/classes in Chisinau profit from contraband and illegal trafficking might be an additional incentive for not having rigid customs control between Transdnistria and Moldova.

To complicate the whole issue, whilst international efforts are made to solve the situation (Ó Beacháin 2013), sporadic actions to regularize the situation were unsuccessful. The economic sanctions imposed by Chisinau on Transdnistrian goods for failure to respect minimal standards of quality resulted in a blockade of the railway, the closure of Romanian schools in Transdnistria and the cutting off of gas and electricity supplies to Moldova (the main supplier is the plant in Kuchurgan in Transdnistria) (Dogaru, 2004).

A palliative faced by Chisinau was to place customs officials along the train line to control, if not people, at least goods. From the first Moldovan station, officials are liable to enter the train and check anyone, though they might not be officially allowed to carry out a complete border control—and actually passports are not always checked – on my first trip my visa was not even stamped.

How many borders does one have to cross on the route Odessa-Chisinau? The answer depends on the means of transport. The Chisinau–Odessa trip by coach shows a different version of the borders from that experienced when crossing by train. In the case of a bus, the bus driver collects the money and hands it to a border official obtaining unofficial permission to pass the border. The impression I gained during my border crossings is that, even at the checkpoint, a sort of jungle law exists. Those who are able to get the money from travellers will do it, regardless of hierarchies and role. I was once stopped by an official who did not want to let me pass as I refused to pay a bribe. Then I met somebody less important who allowed me to pass for a much lower amount of money (8 euros). As he was starting the procedure, other people became interested and I heard another one saying "*Ya tozhe khochu babki*" ("I want the money too"). The translation of the word "*babki*" is not literally money but gives the sense). Bribery has its specific rules in this part of the world; for instance officers never put the money into their pocket until they are alone so that they can always drop it on the floor if caught.

The fact that even fixed entities like borders are experienced in a mobile way is indicative of the weak role of the Moldovan state after independence, as locals are able to manipulate it for their own benefits. No official control to leave the Moldovan administrative territory exists but, to enter Tiraspol, the capital of Transdnistria, people have to pass an "imaginary" border not recognized on any world map. Then they will have their passports checked but not stamped, because their country does not enjoy international recognition. However, people will be asked to buy a *talon,* in this case a piece of paper with an unofficial stamp on it, for the price of seven lei (half a euro) to be presented when leaving the "country" as evidence that a "tax" has been paid.

A border official checks the passports[6] and orders all those not living in the Republic or travelling on a Russian passport to buy a talon. The diligent traveller has to go to the nearby office, pay seven lei and get the piece of paper that is produced when passing the border again—be that the border leading to Ukraine or the one back to Moldova. Failure to produce the talon might result in a "Soviet fine", that is a request to pay some money.

On the Ukrainian side there is another paradox. Ukraine has waived registration for foreigners, a procedure still practised in other former USSR countries. But it has introduced a registration (immigration card) at the border. Foreign passport holders must declare their destination and address of stay. I have witnessed several times the awkwardness of both border officers and passengers as the latter indicated the length of their stay at the train station as "a few hours".

Foucher also suggests that the border marks the point where the territorial competences expire (1991 :47). If there is an exception to this statement, it is represented by the Transdnistrian border. The starting point of Transdnistrian and Moldovan territorial competence is unclear or even mobile depending on several factors but even the existence of territorial competence is challenged by the current situation.

The shock of the collapse of the USSR is still perceivable in the former Bessarabian region. The repartition of power from Moscow to local centres (Kiev, Chisinau) was not accepted by some elites, especially in the Tiraspol region, where Russian elites had been forming since the 1970s and proposed themselves as an alternative to the Moldovan elites in Chisinau. This resulted in armed conflict in 1992, the presence of the Russian army and an informal division of Moldova that boosted the economic crisis of postsocialist societies in the 1990s while generating new borders not recognized by the international community but affecting the life of locals who, despite the conflict, have to find the means to survive. The next section is dedicated to the way locals organized themselves to make up for the lack of state provision of security and stability.

3 Smugglers or Traders?

As Papava and Khaduri (1997) remarked, external border controls in communist countries were tight, but the controls were designed primarily to detect political and criminal activities (such as involvement in drugs and arms dealing). In countries that have undergone postsocialist transformations, the type of smuggling has changed—increasingly including ordinary commercial and seconded goods[2], which have plagued the Soviet economy for many years.

The result was a huge volume of trade between and inside post-Soviet countries. This is to say that Moldovans are not alone in this cross-border strategy. For one thing Malinovskaya (2003) noticed a similar pattern in Ukraine. A common reaction in the region has been to initially punish manifestations of illegal trade as individual asocial inclinations.

---

2 [seconded goods] are inferior, substandard and even unsafe products . . . by offering these pseudoproducts for lower prices, they [businessmen] capture considerable segments of the market and receive significant incomes, to the detriment of consumers' interest (Papava and Khaduri 1997: 30)

Sometimes they were given political importance, as in the Khrushchev era when reports of corruption increased. Illegal trade was also ignored as "beneficial" for the economy, during the Brezhnev era (Werner, 2002). Few raised questions concerning the roots of the problem.

Odessa, the biggest commercial port in Ukraine, has always provided its inhabitants with a strong local identity, fostered by the economic opportunities offered by the city's location and climate. It has always been considered the quintessence of the city of opportunities, where people could feel at home regardless of their status and nationality and Odessians are proud of the fact that the city, even in its darkest moments, was the best refurnished city in Ukraine. The expression "Odessa mama" means that the city would feed anybody living in it, like a mother, and the popular quote "*Mama grechanka, papa turek, ya Odessity*" ("my mother is Greek, my father is Turkish, I am Odessian") highlights the fact that "Odessian is not a status, it is a nationality" (personal communication). For a more detailed description of the economic opportunities provided by the city see Herly (1986).

Odessa was home to some of the most prestigious Soviet champagnes (*Frantsuskyj Bulvar, Odessa*), considered an elite present; it was also the place where the biggest open-air market in Ukraine (*Sedmoj Kilometer*, Seventh Kilometer) operated (Polese 2006, 2009). Given its dimension as a port and its high networking potential, at the end of *perestroika* it was common knowledge that anything, from meat to guns and bombs, could be found at the legendary Odessa bazaar (*Privoz*).

Odesskyj vorovanyj chaj (literally: stolen tea from Odessa) was another expression of this tendency. In countertendency with the spread use of Georgian black tea (gruzinskij chaj) that was considered of dubious quality, at the beginning of the 1990s it was possible to find a slightly better quality of tea, prepared mixing Georgian tea with some varieties that were shipped (and allegedly stolen) to Odessa.[3]

Odessa's markets were, and are, the place where any item can be found for sale if you are willing to pay. I have heard of Japanese cars and motorcycles shipped for a few dollars and this is just the tip of the iceberg.

Odessa–Chisinau has always been a route of intense—and not necessarily legal—trade and its importance has been developing in the

---

3 I am grateful to Viktor Stepanenko for sharing with me this information.

course of the years as a result of the economic evolution (and involution) of the two countries. Even though official figures are hard to find and, to my knowledge, no research on such a topic has been carried out, one can put together a picture of the evolution of trade between the two cities from the history of Odessa's markets. For instance, *Sedmoj Kilometer*, was established as a local market situated in the centre of the city. Eventually it was moved out to the Moldavanka, one of the oldest parts of Odessa and later, when it reached its current size, was relocated once more, this time to outside the city. This allowed for expansion enabling the trading of a higher quantity of goods but also made it easier to escape strict state control. As a result, after 1960 *Sedmoj Kilometer* became practically illegal but it kept active and functioned as the biggest smuggling market of the USSR (Nikolski, 2005). It is therefore conceivable that, given the short distance, Moldovans have a long history of trading with Odessa in order to obtain what was lacking in the rest of the region and what Odessa sailors and traders were able to ship into their city through their networks.

In recent times, two phenomena have increased the variety of goods purchasable in Odessa: the opening up of Ukraine to foreign imports, which started with *perestroika* and overproduction in some neighbouring countries, especially Turkey, of clothes that could easily be shipped across the Black sea.

Although nowadays Ukraine cannot be considered an economic paradise, the city of Odessa is a completely different story. The market *Sedmoj Kilometer,* named so because it is situated seven kilometres outside of Odessa, is by far the biggest trading centre in Ukraine. It hosts 2000 sellers and around 8000 people buy goods there daily. It is open 24 hours a day; during the daytime normal goods are traded while at night time the typology of goods traded is unknown to most. Low-cost goods are received mainly from Turkey and China but also from Russia and Poland, allegedly Italy and Slovakia (Nikolski, 2005).

The rental of a container to store goods can cost from 1500 US dollars upwards. As a result, although numerous people go to the markets simply to shop, there are others –and this is more relevant to this analysis—who live on the daily export and smuggling of goods.

The *Sedmoj Kilometer* market provides many of the wares that are transported by the *elektrichka*. From the first moment one climbs on, the train shows the features of a moving bazaar. At the Odessa railway station the congestion is so bad that railway officials have to filter the passengers approaching the train and to divide them into several waves. Everybody has at least one trolley overloaded with boxes filled with recent purchases. Once people reach the train they run for the best places to put down their heavy luggage; aggressive behaviour and even petty physical confrontation –sometimes culminating in a slap or a little more—are common at this time. As the train leaves, repacking procedures begin. From the departure of the train until it reaches the Ukrainian border (the station of Razdelna) most people mix up, hide and change the composition of their boxes. The aim is to hide valuable things purchased under food or socks. Normally, people trade in clothes as they are easier to transport and allow a higher profit, given that the choice on the Moldovan market is very limited. But the boxes might contain any other item.

The typology of goods and the way of smuggling has changed with time. One of my informants reported ". . . we used to trade boots and there was a moment, at the border, when all the doors of the train got blocked [by us] (he smiles) so that officials were unable to come onboard to check us...then the train simply started again . . ."

One of my informants, whom I met several times during my trips spelled out some of the products he intended to buy in Odessa— margarine, *krabovy palochky* (crab meat) and mayonnaise—because he could find them at lower prices in Odessa. He used to travel every other day to Odessa and already had a retailer in Chisinau so that, once he returned, he could sell everything immediately and rest for the remaining part of the day. This activity is completely beyond state control but limited in size and therefore of little interest to Moldovan officers. Nevertheless the man took the precaution of getting off one station before the main Chisinau station in order to avoid possible customs control officers.

The types of goods introduced into a country varies according to which particular border is being crossed. The Polish–Ukrainian and Polish–Belorussian trains are opened like tuna cans as officials search for cigarettes. The buses running between Ukraine and Poland operate on a system of sharing out the goods, although also there are strategies for hiding items in the usual ways (Polese, 2012). In the

Ukraine–Moldovian–Transdnistrian case neither alcohol nor tobacco is involved and trains are not searched. The system is simpler and everything takes place during daylight hours. After passing the Ukrainian border, as mentioned, there is no real Moldovan border but officials may jump on the train anytime.

The first exodus happens in the Moldovan (actually Transdnistrian) station of Kuchurgan, the first station after the border. Here people leave the train and run out of the station, which is quite small (the street is some 30 m away from the train). There is general concern that, should local officials have had a bad day, they might want to stop to check somebody; this is why the sooner one leaves the station, the better. At the same time some other people, without luggage, remain seated in the train. Most of them are relatives or simply partners of those carrying the goods. They pretend to be together and divide the quantity of goods being carried amongst four or five persons.

From this moment until Chisinau it is a matter of negotiation. People will have to play "the poor", "the ignorant", and "the naïve" and pretend that the quantity of goods they carry with them is fair -though there is no official definition of "fair". Otherwise they will be obliged to leave the train and negotiate with the officer.

It may be interesting to note that, in this process, with several officials going around the train several times, neither I nor my passport were ever checked.

The first way to categorize this phenomenon may be to see it as smuggling, but the situation is more complicated. When recalling the concept of informal economy firstly used by Hart (1973) to refer to the irregular income earning opportunities of the urban poor in Ghana, Rasanayagam (2003) warns us of the difficulty of making a distinction between state and shadow economies particularly in the ex-USSR. This is because, depending on one another, the state and shadow economy form two aspects of a single economy and each operation may involve both legal and illegal aspects. Indeed, it is impossible to operate completely within the law all the times (Rasanayagam, 2003:6). The boundary between legal and illegal is often blurred (Morris 2012, 2013; Morris and Polese 2013, 2013b), especially in the former USSR. The perception people have of what is legal and illegal is determined by morality and often localized. Therefore any such phenomena should be contextualized and Western definitions avoided.

To further complicate the picture, there is the political and economic function covered by the *elektrichka*. Papava and Khaduri (1997: 30–31) remark that amongst those who call themselves entrepreneurs in post communist countries, many are former Party figures and former directors in whose behaviour it is very difficult to find the merits possessed by Western type entrepreneurs. They are able to carry out political lobbying to obtain favourable conditions for their work; they are able to hamper competition in the country aware that this would entail the arrival of quality goods on "their" market, which is dominated by "their" seconded goods.

Papava and Khaduri (1997: 31) continue that competition and the welfare of customers is harmed by such entrepreneurs. In a "healthy" market environment they should either lower the prices and improve the quality of goods produced. Unfortunately, very few postsocialist businessmen consider this option. It is much easier to persuade authorities to pursue a strong protectionist policy (erect a "Great Wall of China"), using calls to patriotism as a basis for justification.

Smugglers address this discrepancy, making up for the low quality of goods and improving choices for customers by breaking the circle of a seconded goods economy run by local entrepreneurs.

In addition, trade smuggling on the *elektrichka* has the function of making up for the failure of the state. The *elektrichka* is a breath of fresh air in the failure of post-MSSR (Moldovan Socialist Soviet Republic) politicians to take care of their citizens. Thanks to the *elektrichka*, people can still earn money despite unemployment. People can still find goods, despite shortages. Barely legal actions have the function of cooling down the social climate and avoiding an extreme level of discontent that could cause further unrest.

Despite the fact that the shadow economy is negatively perceived by economists who see it as a loss for state finances and by those who see it as fiscal fraud, contextualization shows the specificities of the *elektrichka* case. In this case, the shadow economy is the response of local traders to an imposed monopoly by local businessmen, characterized by a deficit of quality goods, a shortage of goods, high prices and a lack of jobs.

4 Do you have a Tomato?
Scenes of "Legal" Corruption

Social scientists do not always agree on a definition for corruption. In anthropology there is the recent tendency to contextualize the exchange of goods or favours before labelling them as "corrupt" acts since, in many non-Western cultures, gift exchange is basic to everyday relations and paves the way for economic networks. It is not always easy to distinguish gifts from bribes (Werner, 2002; Polese, 2008), in whatever form they are presented. This is also the case with the *elektrichka*, which supports trading activities in the context of a Moldovan state that is tacitly to blame for a lack of interest in the concerned regions and for living conditions that are so low that supplements to the salary or pension are necessary for survival.

Both state officials and ordinary people expect to benefit from the *elektrichka*. In examining widespread and explicit corruption it is useful to recall a case study analysed by Temple and Petrov (2004). They found that, contrary to the norm (where corruption is discovered, and people and institutions who are implicated are discredited), in Russian educational institutions, for example, the "transparency" of the process of corruption, including sometimes even the setting of an official price list, is "not harmful" for the corruption process. This is also the case with the *elektrichka*: the fact that everybody knows how things work is far from a hindrance.

As wages are very low on both sides of the border, the situation is comfortable for the government and its employees: by tolerating widespread corruption, the Ukrainian and Moldovan states do not have to allocate more from the budget for the salary of state officials but, at the same time, as it is well known that the meagre salary will be topped up with additional "provisions", it is still possible to recruit people to work on such a low wage.

On the Ukrainian side of the Ukrainian-Moldovan border everything is relatively calm. If success in smuggling things into Poland depends on the mood of the officers and the quantity of goods (Polese, 2011), here it is more simple, it depends on the price. It has been remarked that, whilst in the Western world bribes are given for actions that the law does not allow, in the post-Soviet case bribes in the great majority of cases are given for entirely lawful actions (Papava and Khaduri, 1997: 25).

The customs officer goes back and forth handling out a customs declaration to those with luggage. The form will remain blank; its only function is to envelope the five *Hryvnia* bills. A newcomer is rapidly integrated; he just has to ask what the price is and he will be updated by more experienced colleagues. One bill for small luggage, more as the load increases. Everybody hides most of the valuable goods under petty items such as paper or pencils. The trick here is to move objects around and convince officials that one has little (in value) in order to pay as little as possible.

Passport control moves along smoothly too but, as the holder of the only EU passport in the train, I had the honour of dealing with officers and speaking with them. Normally they simulate a problem with the documents and expect you to offer money to "regulate" the matter but on one occasion the officer called over a colleague and they took me into an empty corridor and, while stamping my passport, asked for a present (*prezent dlya pogranichnykh*). I grabbed my stamped passport and returned to the carriage, not responding to the repeated requests that followed my retreat, *a prezent?* in a mixed tone of surprise and rage. The routine practice of "giving and taking" under communism has turned into often institutionalized, widespread corruption, suggest Temple and Petrov (2004). Whatever name we want to use for such practices, it remains the case that payments to officers are acceptable, not to say expected, in Ukrainian society, even though every new president promises to eradicate it.

The Moldovan side is more complicated. There is no checkpoint and people have to be ready to be checked at any time. Boxes are distributed around the train with the hope that they remain unnoticed. A further common strategy is to invite the whole family to share the purchases after the first Moldovan station. The family beside me included the grandmother, a relative who was not introduced to me and two nephews of around 16 years. They probably had different surnames in their passports in order to pass themselves off as strangers. Nevertheless, the officer in this case understood that they were together and, after long negotiations, directed them off the train.

The *elektrichka* is, surprisingly, the safest and cheapest way to run this kind of business. Transdnistrian officials are not involved in the process and this lowers the costs. The trip by car is perhaps more interesting as it opens different possibilities. Several informants reported the level of corruption of Transdnistrian officers as extremely high—this is why most of those going by bus to Odessa come back by train but do not risk travelling by bus with full bags.

As suggested, institutionalized corruption helps to regulate the system. Nevertheless sometimes it may go too far, falling into a paradox and revealing the mere (and very human) wish to get easy extra money from the casual traveller. As one informant complained, border officers were capable of asking for anything they could take, and another reported the following conversation:

> "Do you have, by chance, a dollar?"
> "No!"
> "A tomato?"
> "No!"
> "A cucumber?"

Finally, I experienced, as have others, the threat of "pay or we will not let you pass". In this game, is it possible to find out who is the victim and who is the perpetrator? Using the threefold classification—victims, sources of corruption and accomplices—used by Miller et al. (2000) and the judgement of Temple and Petrov (2004) for the case of corruption in higher education institutions, citizens are not at all "victims" rather, given the existence of a price list, they should be seen as accomplices.

According to Palmer (1983), we can define corruption as the "use of public office for private advantage". Whilst this prompted Temple and Petrov (2004: 86) to refuse to acknowledge a grey area existing between legality and illegality, even "petty corruption" is able to bring a nation to its knees, other scholars have a more relative approach, suggesting that a "little corruption" does not hurt anyone (Rasanayagam, 2003) or that different moralities may apply to different contexts (Wanner, 2005). Moreover we have a moral justification developed out of necessity, which is quite common to a number of cultures (some would argue to many cultures). In southern Italian cultures, for instance, moral justification is given for all sorts of illegal acts on the basis that the concerned person has children to feed (*chill e' pat' e' creature*—he is a father). This highlights similarities that Putnam (1993) has also explored. Evidence suggests a fruitful comparison can be made with Putnam (1993), who shows how the functioning of civil society may be hindered by pre-existing kinship structures.

To support this argument one can call upon Harrison (1999), who reported that corruption in Africa was considered by some social scientists as a mere infusion of a culture of traditional gift giving into the bureaucracy following the logic of family, village, or tribal loyalty. In the same way, corruption is not an example of the degradation of society; rather, in the case of the *elektrichka* it has a function of generating an independent—and uncontrollable—economic system in which all the actors are happy, with the result of limiting economic discontent and avoiding social tensions. The contextualization of "corruption" leads to the understanding that the way the system is organized—informal exchanges, bribing, favours—is the best option given the national political and economic context, especially in the Transdnistrian republic. In a country where the state and economic elites are more interested in the preservation and creation of their profits than in the welfare of people, where there are not enough jobs and where wages are extremely low, condemning corruption has little meaning. In this case, the state failing to protect its citizens from what, from a Western standpoint, is labelled "corruption" can be viewed as one way for a population to survive. Ukrainian, Moldovan, and Transdnistrian governments are unable to guarantee decent standards for their citizens who therefore have to work out their own ways to survive.

5 Conclusion

In a situation of stalemate, where international actors are unable to intervene and local elites are glad to preserve the current *status quo*, the *elektrichka* may be understood as an example of "the best we can do given the current political situation" (Polese and Rodgers, 2011). In this respect, the *elektrichka* seems to be a theatre for a play with few losers. Border officers are also quite happy as they can receive some benefits and top up their salary, something they do of necessity, living in one of the most depressed areas of the region. Finally ordinary people can break up the vicious circle of the crisis and introduce new goods and earn some money.

Nevertheless, as Bovi (2003) remarked, the shadow economy is generally related to institutional failure. Hence, in this case, there is a loser and this is the state itself. A weak state means uncontrolled revenues, no taxes paid on income and, even more importantly, a distorted perception of the role of the state. The state is perceived as limiting initiative and activities and bringing no real advantage to the loyal citizen. Where the state is able to protect its citizens and offer some advantages and perspectives in exchange for loyalty, people would be more willing to act in the frame of legality (Bovi, 2003: 67). Given the present situation in the region, this is still a distant option in Moldova and Ukraine. In a region with strong emigration, the *elektrichka* is to be seen as another strategy of survival for Moldovans (as well as for the Ukrainian officials) who cannot count on their state institutions.

In countries such as Ukraine and Moldova, the dynamics analysed here offer themselves to different interpretations. In the view of Western political analysts, the weakness of the state (its inability to control economic and social processes) encourages the shadow economy, which in turn feeds corruption. This is viewed as problematic in that it brings no revenue to the state and prevents the state from securing decent living standards for its citizens. In an alternative vision, the weak state is a facilitator of a circle of smuggling and corruption, and can challenge the traditional vision of the state—as welfare dispenser—since it gives birth to a circle of functioning transactions where people themselves are the dispensers of welfare without passing through the state channels: traders can earn what they need to eat, customs officers can round up their wages and future purchasers can have access to goods that otherwise they would never get. Whether these should be classified as "illegal" or "necessary" actions is for the reader to decide.

Cited works

Bovi, M. (2003) The nature of the underground economy—some evidence from OECD countries. Journal for Institutional Innovation, Development & Transition 7: 60–70.

Crowter, W. (1995) Moldova: caught between nation and empire, in Bremmer, I. And R. Taras (eds.) New States, New Politics. Cambridge, Cambridge University Press.

Dogaru, V. (2004) Moldova, and economic arm wrestle, Transitions Online, 8 September. Available at http://www.tol.org/client/article/12702-an-econo mic-arm-wrestle.html (last accessed 25 April 2013)

Foucher, M. (1991) Fronts et frontiers. Paris: Fayard

Harrison, G. (1999) Corruption, development theory and the boundaries of social change. Contemporary Politics 5(3), 207–220.

Herly P. (1987) Odessa: a History, Cambridge, MA, Harvard University Press

Malinovskaya, Elena (2003) Poezdki za granitsu kak strategiya vyzhivaniya v usloviyakh perekhodnogo perioda: opyt Ukrainy. In Trudovaya Migratsiya v SNG. Sotsiyalnie i ekonomicheskie effekty. Russian Academy of Sciences, Moscow, 197–210

Miller, W., Grodeland, A. and Koshechkina, T. (2000) Victims or Accomplices? Extortion and bribery in Eastern Europe. In Economic Crime in Russia (eds A. Ledeneva and M. Kurkchiyan). London, Kluwer Law International.

Morris, J. and A. Polese (201X) Informal Health and Education Sector Payments in Russian and Ukrainian Cities: Structuring Welfare from Below European Urban and Regional Studies. Online first at: http://eur.sagepub.com/content/early/2014/03/30/0969776414522081.abst ract

Morris, Jeremy and Polese, Abel (eds.) (2013) The Informal Post-Socialist Economy: Embedded Practices and Livelihoods, London and New York: Routledge.

Morris, Jeremy (2013) Beyond coping? Alternatives to consumption within a social network of Russian workers. Ethnography 14(1): 85–103.

Morris, Jeremy (2012) Unruly Entrepreneurs: Russian Worker Responses to Insecure Formal Employment, Global Labour Journal 3(2): 217–36. Online. Available: <http://digitalcommons.mcmaster.ca/globallabour/vol3/i ss2/2> (last accessed 31 March 2013).

Nikolskij, K. (2005) 7-j vykhodit iz teni. Korrespondent, 4 June.

Palmer, L. (1983) Bureaucratic corruption and its remedies. In Corruption: Causes, Consequences and Control (ed. M. Clark), London, Pinter.

Ó Beacháin, Donnacha (2013) The Role of the EU and the OSCE in Promoting Security and Cooperation in the South Caucasus and Moldova' in Ayca Ergun and Hamlet Isaxanli (eds) Security and Cross-Border Cooperation in the EU, Black Sea Region and the Southern Caucasus (NATO Science for Peace and Security Series, IOS Press), 42–57

Papava, V. and Khaduri, N. (1997). On the shadow political economy of the post communist transformation, an institutional analysis. Problems of Economic Transitions 40(6): 15–34.

Polese, Abel (2006) Border Crossing as a Daily Strategy of Post Soviet Survival: the Odessa-Chisinau Elektrichka, The Anthropology of Eastern Europe Review 24(1): 28–37.

Polese, A. (2008) If I receive it, it is a gift; if I demand it, then it is a bribe: on the local meaning of economic transactions in post-Soviet Ukraine. Anthropology in Action 5 (3), 47–60.

Polese Abel (2009) "The guest at the dining table: economic transition and the reshaping of hospitality, reflections from Batumi and Odessa", Anthropology of Eastern Europe Review 27(1): 65–77.

Polese, A. (2012) Who has the right to forbid and who to trade? Making sense of illegality on the Polish-Ukrainian border. In Borders as Resources (eds B. Bruns and J. Miggelbring). Leipzig: VS Verlag.

Polese, Abel and Peter Rodgers (2011) Surviving Post-Socialism: The Role of Informal Economic Practices, International Journal of Sociology and Social Policy (with P. Rodgers) 31(11/12): 612–618.

Putnam, R.D. (1993) Making Democracy Work: Civic Traditions in Modern Italy, Princetown, NJ, Princetown University Press.

Rasanayagam, J. (2003) Market, state and community in Uzbekistan: reworking the concept of the informal economy. Max Planck Working Papers no.59.

Rure, A. (1999). Ukrainiens et Roumains, IX-XX siecle, Paris, l'Harmattan.

Temple, P. and Petrov, G. (2004) Corruption in higher education: some findings from the states of the former Soviet Union. Higher Education Management and Policy 16(1): 83–99.

Tomiuc E. (2004) Moldova: mass migration threatens the country's future. RFE, 29 October, available at http://www.rferl.org/content/article/1055583.html (last accessed 25 April 2013)

Wanner, C. (2005) Money, morality and new forms of exchange in postsocialist Ukraine. Ethnos 70(3): 515–537

Werner, C.A. (2002) Gifts, bribes and development in post-Soviet Kazakhstan. In Economic Development: an Anthropological Approach (eds J.H. Cohen and N. Dannhaeuser). Walnut Creek, CA, Altamira Press.

Informality and grey areas: introducing the "brift"[1]

1 If I receive it, it is a gift.
If I demand it, then it is a bribe.

This chapter starts from Gudeman's two-fold view of the economy where 'the market realm revolves about short-term material relationships that are undertaken *for the sake of* achieving a project or securing a good. In the communal realm, material goods are exchanged through relationships kept *for their own sake*' (2001: 10). This dual approach allows us to emphasise the embeddedness and social significance of economic transactions (Granovetter 1985, Hann and Hart 2011, Mauss 1966, Malinowski 1921, Sahlins 1978) suggesting that transactions are suitable only if it is possible to measure the gain expected (Andreoni 1988, Becker 1976, Egbert 2006).

In the Global North, the excessive attention to money-driven transactions has come under criticism from a number of scholars, and perspectives (Gibson-Graham 1998; Williams 2005), in an attempt to rediscover the role of intangible bonds and long term mutual dependence relations (Ledeneva 1998, Morris 2012, 2013, Morris and Polese 2013). This has allowed some scholars to reject, or at least challenge, essentialist views that certain rituals and rules are universal values presents, perhaps in different forms, in most societies (Hann 2006). When it comes to informal payments, in the post-socialist world and beyond, it is possible to cluster them into three categories according to their function. They could be used to solve a problem that might not be solved through legal means (for instance, you need document A to get document B but cannot get document B without document A). They could, otherwise, be used to solve a hindrance that was created artificially (or of ineffectiveness, incompetency or simply

---

[1] This chapter is a rewritten and updated version of the following article: Abel Polese (2014) "Informal Payments in Ukrainian Hospitals: On the Boundary between Informal Payments, Gifts, and Bribes". *Anthropological Forum: A Journal of Social Anthropology and Comparative Sociology* 24(4): 381–395. London: Routledge.

because someone has decided to ask for money). Finally, they could be used to allow, or turn a blind eye on, something illegal or harmful.

This chapter deals mostly with the first two categories and sees them depending on the existence, or lack thereof, of an overarching entity that has, or claims to have, coercive power on the individuals under its control. Here, I will build upon two more concepts that I have elaborated on in my previous research. First, Migdal (2001) has shown that a state may claim to be a redistributor but fail to do so in a proper or equitable way. This concept has informed the ideas behind chapter one and our work on welfare (Polese et al 2014) that there might be a gap, that informality is likely to permeate, between what the state claims to do and what it does in the end. Second, I see the likelihood of tensions when state's instructions enter in conflict with local rules and norms (Gill 1998, van Schendel and Abrahams 2005). Relying on these works allows us to go beyond a mere defence of corruption as a socially embedded phenomenon (Scott 1969, quoted in Rose-Ackerman 2010, 128) to place allegedly corrupted practices into a broader category encompassing diverse economic systems (Gibson-Graham 1996, de Soto 2000) and views on corruption that stretch the category into a more blurred and complex one (Haller and Shore 2005; Polese 2014). In most, if not all, world societies it is possible to notice tension between legal and social norms, which becomes even more visible when some illegal practices turn out to be acceptable by a community, or even a society. This could draw from a distinction on whom the transaction is harming directly: the state (and thus, indirectly, the society) or fellow citizens (and, as a consequence, the state). As previously stated, payments from a bribe for illegal practices, such as selling drugs or trafficking, is harming to those who are the victims of such acts (the person trafficked or those who will buy hard drugs) and they are unlikely be accepted by their fellow citizens. However, fiscal fraud or smuggling of clothes are damaging state revenue first and only indirectly fellow citizens (they affect state income and thus the budget that can be spent on citizens-oriented services) and it is even possible to find local explanations and norms used by some segments of the population to justify non-compliance with tax rules. justify noncompliance with tax rules. Addressed in the empirical part of this chapter are some dysfunctional aspects of a state and the way civil servants and citizens address them, without necessarily harming directly other fellow citizens, which is briefly presented in the table below.

Table 1: Origins and effects of informal transactions (Polese 2014)

When you pay and whom you may harm	Harm citizens	Harm state (society)
Excessive red tape	Pay for a document denying property of another citizen	Pay for receiving a document "A" that you can only get with document "B"
Solve an invented problem (by a civil servant)	Not fighting such behaviour normalises it and it becomes impossible to escape extra payments	A police officer claims you have passed despite a red light. Bribe a police officer (no taxable revenue, encourage corrupted practice)
Being allowed to do something that goes against legal codes	Pay to dump toxic refuse into a living area; pay to sell heroin in a given area of a city	Fiscal fraud

2 Informal payments and the role of the state

Research on grey areas is becoming increasingly more popular and so the blurred boundary between a gift and a bribe has received a growing amount of attention (Harboe 2015; Harboe and Frederiksen 2015). If we accept that gifts and bribes can be connected by a continuous line, I have called "brift" the grey area between them (Polese 2008). To be able to place a transaction onto this spectrum of situations, it is possible to look at two variables. First, the power relationship between the two parties entering the exchange and, second, the existence—and role—of an overarching entity in these two parties' existence and, in particular, in the transaction.

An understanding of the power relationship between two parties can help us to predict whether an obligation of reciprocation, in the short- or long-term, arises from the transaction. It is possible that a favour between two long-term partners will not be reciprocated immediately but in the long-term, or that the transaction is just one in a pool of many where there is no obligation to reciprocate every single transaction but the two parties look for a balance between what they give and what they receive (see Ledeneva 2008 on blat' in this regard).

An exploration of the role of the overarching entity (a state taking care of its two citizens, a company employing both parties), in addition, will help us understand whether the transaction has been conceived to replace the entity or to supplement it in an area that is not sufficiently regulated to function properly without a little help from its subordinates, that is the role of a human agency in an apparently established system. If I depend on a state, it is possible that I have to pass through it to have access to a number of services and privileges. The state provides an army to defend my territory, a police force to guarantee my safety, doctors when I am sick and other services in exchange for a contribution (tax, military service in some countries). Normative approaches to the role of the state assume, by default, that limitations and services are fairly distributed and there is even access to them among citizens so that an uneven distribution of welfare may be seen as a temporary exception. In contrast, a growing body of empirical research has been showing that there are countries, or areas, where uneven access to state resources is the norm. Anthropologists, from Scott (1985) on, have suggested that informal transactions or actions may be a way to achieve what locals perceive a more even access to opportunities and resources or to participate in political processes from which they feel excluded (Gupta 1995).

Take two individuals, A and B, if one or both of them are representing an overarching entity C, their relationship should be regulated by that entity (doctor-patient, teacher-pupil but also finance manager of a bank and loan-seeker). When it is not, and they are acting on behalf of that entity without the entity being involved in the decision-making process, we have the situation that has generated the most widespread definition of corruption used so far (the use of a public function for a private advantage). However, there is also a case where individuals may be willing to acknowledge the role of the overarching entity and pass through it but this turns out very difficult. What happens in a situation where A needs to connect with B through the entity but this reveals impossible? A citizen needs a doctor but the doctor is not available because the citizen-doctor ratio is too high in a country or city; a company needs to register but the process is too costly or long (see de Soto 2000); someone wants to get a university degree but there are no available places in that country's universities.

The spectrum of possible solutions to the above-mentioned dilemma is wide and neoliberal reforms have provided an alternative by allowing private initiative to provide some extra services. Think of the parallel existence of private and public healthcare in some countries. It is possible that the same doctor will attend to you and you might even be hosted in the same hospital but, depending on whether you are covered by a private or public health insurance scheme, conditions might significantly vary. In economic terms, there is a demand and a supply that emerges to meet the demand. The state regulates the supply but also endorses it, happy to outsource some services and generate extra tax revenues. In this respect, the "naivety of informality" lies in the incapacity of certain countries to regulate supply and demand in some spheres of governance and "mask" informality as a private service. Lack of formal rules leaves no other option than to classify private payments to a hospital or its staff as bribes, contributing to produce evidence on how corrupt certain countries are.

This means that A wants access to B and is ready to pay extra money, B is willing to work extra hours and take extra money but the overarching entity (the state, or the hospital administration) is not creating the environment where this can happen. As a result, A connects with B directly. While this puts B in a power position (there are no official prices or ceilings to what could be demanded) the main difference with partial privatisation is the lack of a system enabling A to pay, B to receive and the state to tax this new revenue (or the institutions to tap from this payment). As a result, whilst in some countries regulated payments from A to B "in spite of the state" may be authorised by the state, by allowing the development of a private sector (to then tax it), in some other countries they regarded are the utmost expression of a corrupt society without distinguishing the situation where A and B do not inform the state because they do not want or because they cannot. Figure 1 below shows four possible options of payment between A and B.

Figure 3.1 The state (B) as an intermediary between citizens

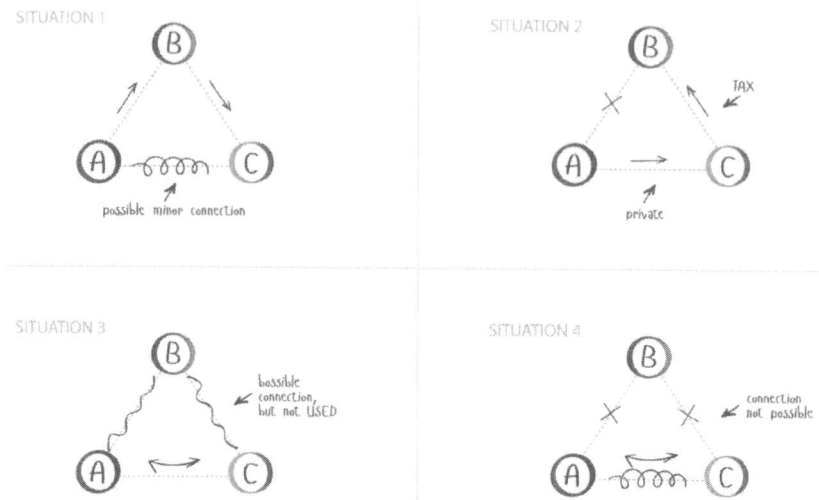

The figure above illustrates the different combinations in the relationship between two citizens (A and C) and the state (B). Four options are possible:

1. A connects with the overarching entity (C) that connects with B. This could be the case of A paying taxes that serve to pay B's salary or A purchasing a service from company C that then pays B a salary.
2. A connects directly with B but B informs C. This could be a consultancy case carried out by B as the employer of company C or of A going to a private company B for a service. B would then pay taxes on the income.
3. A could pass through C but prefers to connect with B directly. B, in turn, does not inform C about this. This could be a service delivered by a private company employee without their company being aware of it; a doctor accepting a private payment despite working for a state-funded institution or a private doctor not declaring their income.

4. A and/or B are unable to connect with C despite they might want to. This could be the case of state defective structures when A needs to be treated but C does not provide hospitals or makes it extremely difficult to use state-funded structures (overcrowded, not enough doctors). It could also be the case where there is a need for services from B but bureaucracy does not allow to register payments from A to B making it impossible for B to declare their revenues. A and B connect without C being aware in what can be seen as a grey zone.

All the situations above may be seen as connected to the Polanyian (1968) distinction between reciprocity (no dominant political force present), redistribution (there is some entity managing and redistributing some commodities) and market exchange (dominant in modern industrial societies). In situation one, A and B communicate through an intermediary C. Still, some small favours (or gifts) are possible. This is the case where B is a civil servant and speeds up a document that A urgently needs on the basis of sympathy for A or where a doctor spends more time than average to check A. This might simply be due to spontaneous sympathy or empathy for A. Small favours and gifts are at the basis of human interaction, A's gift could simply be a positive attitude that makes B feel appreciated or A's diplomatic skills in explaining why they need the document more quickly making B feel responsible for their case. In situation one, interaction between A and B could simply be a present for an employee who has been very helpful without expecting anything. I remember the case of an Italian bringing home-made sausage to an employee from the consulate who had been very zealous and helpful with his case. Whether such transaction, that to me is a gift, may be seen as a bribe depends on the internal rules of the administration. Help from the employee had come with no claims, possibly out of empathy for that person. Previous research on hospitality has shown that a guest may repay the host merely through interesting stories or making them feel respectable (Polese 2006b, 2009, Zanca 2003). On the other hand, A might have 'interested' B through a small material offer. This is, for instance, the case of Christmas gifts in some Western societies that can come to cost several thousands of euros.

A same transaction (informal payment, gift) between A and B has a different meaning depending on which of the four situations one is referring to. So where is the boundary between what can be seen as a gift and as a bribe? International institutions and administrations have a relatively simple approach. The European Commission asks its civil servants to report any gift (or series of gifts) that exceeds 150 euros in a year (if the same person bought me 150 coffees at 1 euro in a solar year, I need to report it to the ethics authorities).

In situation two, the overarching entity is aware and avails so that we normally name it privatisation: the state allows directs payments to B, who is taxed accordingly. Situation three seems clear, there is a functioning structure but A and B prefer not to pass through the overarching entity. This might be due to the fact that A is asking for an unlawful service but also that B prefers the entity not to be aware of such relationship. The most immediate example is fiscal fraud, where B reduces their taxable revenue but there might be a limit to this case since B does not want to charge A and keeps this transaction secret (to the state). Situation four is possibly more complex and reflects most transactions illustrated in this paper whose classification as a bribe or a gift may not be automatic. It is important to notice that situation four can happen when the overarching entity is absent, like in primordial (stateless) societies, or simply where the state is not regulating a certain aspect of people's personal or professional lives. Situation four does not cover only state dysfunction but also liberalisation of a service or delegation from the state and this is why I prefer the general word entity to state. Time banks manage a commodity that the state is unable to manage and has thus let it to the citizens to manage. Likewise, a private company replacing the state in providing a service can be an object of study as overarching entity, as shown in chapter five.

Because transactions between A and B are not necessarily monetary but could involve an exchange of services and commodities a distinction is necessary. While informal payment refers to a monetary transaction a gift, inspired by Mauss, refers to something inalienable, offered from A to B and purchased, or prepared, specifically for B.

While Mauss' gift categories can encompass a large variety of transactions, this chapter is limited to transactions of a 'present nature' to which people 'resort to' in the absence of the necessary network of friends (Humphrey 2002:129) as opposed to long-term relations and social networks that have been the object of study by other scholars (Ledeneva 1998, 2006; Lonkila 1998, 2010). In contrast to Rivkin-Fish (1997, cited in Patico 2002: 352), I do not consider that the order in which the exchange happens to be relevant since, as we will see in the case studies, this does not affect the very nature of the transaction. Finally, opposing Patico (2002), we shall not attribute a different meaning depending on whether the exchanged encompassed some monetary donation or not. Previous authors (Parry 1991, Thomas 1991) have shown the subjective character of goods and money—whose meaning is strongly defined by local culture, political use, and context. In line with Patico's (2002) discussions of 'chocolate and cognac', I would say that some specific objects take a special meaning when offered as 'signs of attention'. However, this argument alone is insufficient to explain the variety of cases one could encounter in the post-USSR region and beyond and this is partly due to them happening in a different historical moment. Although a tendency to offer chocolate and cognac—or brandy—is still present, money is largely gaining ground for the ever-increasing availability of what may be perceived as luxury goods (of questionable quality, see Patico 2003) to a growing amount of people. Wanner (2005), accounting for the particular socio-economic structures of Ukrainian life, has proposed a switch from objective to subjective morality in order to justify—albeit not fully and only in specific conditions—some actions such as bribe giving or not keeping one's word, things that in a Western context would be stigmatized. She maintains that in Ukraine, people might 'subscribe to a different moral order' (2005:14) suggested by *ad hoc* needs to which one might add the crisis of the modern state and its symbolic order analysed by Gupta (1995, 2005). In line with her thesis, I would like to propose a contextual morality that could ease the understanding of the perception locals have of some transactions otherwise stigmatized according to a Western—and often sold as objective—morality, forgetting that engagement in such transactions in the Ukrainian example is often not a choice but a necessity.

3 Switching moralities

Power is granted to the state from the citizens who, in turn, give up some of their freedom for the good of the community. But the state must not only be a state, it has to act like a state (Polese 2007) and protect its citizens and workers. Once the state fails to respect its obligations, there is a wide spectrum of 'acceptable' reactions by a public worker. One might accept, in certain cases, that the 'worker' feels no obligation towards the state and refuses to work but he has, in any case, the obligation not to damage his fellow citizens.

Gifts and corruption are not objective, but they do depend on the context and the same definition is not applicable everywhere. Offering a box of chocolates to a teacher, therefore, does not have the same meaning in Odessa and London. Harrison (1999) advises that, in African societies, monetary exchanges may just be the modern equivalent of a gift exchange. For this reason corruption in Africa has been considered by some social scientists as a mere infusion of a culture of traditional gift giving into bureaucracy. This follows the logic of family, village, or tribe loyalty and in this context the 'practice' of bribe giving [is] not...simply an economic transaction but a cultural practice that requires a great degree of performative competence (Gupta 1995: 217).

The switch from an objective—state—morality to a subjective one (Wanner 2005) requires consideration of all the peculiarities of the analysed context to better understand the values at stake in a given transaction. Most, if not all, studies on bribing in post-Soviet societies, present—implicitly or explicitly—the idea of a dual morality; a notion that is applicable to all sorts of exchanges. Locals are often ambivalent about monetary or commodity exchanges. When talking informally sometimes I heard people referring to those transactions as wrong, when informants present complaints about corruption at the level of the state. However, those same informants sometimes refer to it as 'thankfulness' (this is especially the case when talking of a doctor), the only way to ensure the survival of a particular category of people (mainly doctors or teachers).

Possibly, a further element of confusion comes from the etymology of the word in English, compared to other languages. In Russian, *vzyatka* comes from the verb *vzyat'*, to take, in some other languages it is the word used for money in another language (bakchich in French, para in Kazakh). In English, this word is translated with the morally sensitive word 'bribe'. Normally the word *vzyatka* in daily life is used to describe somebody's else action; when the story is told in first person people tend to use synonyms like 'present' or 'way of creating interest'. In some cases people may also decide not to use it since, as many informants' reported, petty payments to a doctor are rather seen as a sign of thankfulness rather than a bribe. The perception of those exchanges is strongly affected by the amount of money paid—people are much more sympathetic to petty payments than to significant ones, like the ones given for complicated operations; and the relationship with the person who offered the present.

As noted for other cases, a double standard is often applied. When talking about oneself, moral judgements are almost absent. However, when talking of doctors and people not close to them, people tend to be more prone to condemn informal payments and blame their country for the high level of corruption that they are obliged to bare. In many respects, the word '*vzyatka*' is not a taboo. The concept is so embedded in the society that the very act is sometimes perceived as fully normal, though the word is avoided in official discourses, which will be illustrated in the following sections.

4 The academic 'moral code'

Dimitry is a student in the Faculty of Medicine in Odessa. To pass his exam he 'gifted' the teacher with a 10-dollar bill. Svetlana, in the same situation, offered the teacher a bottle of 'kon'yak' (brandy) after passing the exam. Patico (2002: 355) maintains that there is a sharp difference between offering money and offering 'chocolate and cognac' since only those latter recognize the 'personhood' of the teacher. However, Wanner (2005), reports that sometimes teachers bring the chocolate back to the shop to get a refund. This implicitly lowers the difference between monetary exchange and offering consumable goods. From a legal point of view, there is also little difference: both donations in money or commodities are punished as corruption though a difference exists at a socio-cultural level.

Following Wanner (2005), who asked how present takers used the chocolates, I asked a doctor what he did with his 'gifts'. He told me that boxes of chocolate were recycled as presents for nurses or to celebrate birthdays. Simultaneously, he offered some chocolates from a box whose origins I think I can guess. There are several ways to receive money in a higher education institution; nobody dared to tell me how he accepted a gift but I collected quite a number of interviews with students describing the conditions to pass an exam. In some cases there are prices fixed by the professor and a bill in the student book will allow you to get a A, B or C according to the money paid, in other cases it is sufficient to attend the course to get the minimal grade.

When the money is paid (before the service is received or after) seems to alter the meaning of the transaction.

> 'Some of my colleagues require money or presents *as conditio sine qua* non to pass an exam, I agree that this is to blame and is ruining our country. But when a student [who has been bouncing around several exams] comes to me and wants to pass my exam, my reasoning is: I know that, sooner or later, he will pass and I also know that it is not his fault if he is obliged to get a degree to work afterwards, since in Ukraine it is unthinkable to get a job without university education. In this case, he will pass my exam; I see this as a personal favour. In return, if he offers a bottle of spirit or a box of chocolates I do not refuse, this is simply thankfulness for my action'.

Two things are to be considered. I collected this statement from a *dotsent* (associate professor) whose salary was around 200 dollars per month with a teaching load of 900 hours per year. A number of variables could be used to try and define the boundary between a gift and a bribe. The university staff paid attention to the regularity of the demands and the amounts demanded; was this a habit of the teacher or did they do it 'only' once or twice? Those with the worst reputation were known to regularly accept presents, whereas some others only accepted them sporadically. A very important element is the order of the exchange. Would a teacher offer a favour and hope to receive a payback or would the teacher refuse to provide a service until a payment was received? As one of my colleagues, now a friend, brilliantly put it: 'If I receive it, it is a gift. If I demand it, then it is a bribe'.

In a short article I wrote some years ago I suggested (Polese 2006c) that the utmost source of those strategies in the academic world is the weak role of the state, too slow to follow the evolutions of the educational sector and to suggest appropriate changes. On the other hand, by turning a blind eye on what teachers do, the state permits many things that are not allowed elsewhere. In a study by Dalton (1959) then cited in Granovetter (2007) turning a blind eye was a way to secure informal rewards to the employees who, at the end of the day would take away some food informally so that their salary was paid also with non-monetary perks.

In general, university staff have a limited amount of work that they can perform for other employers. In most UK universities professors can do some consultancy work upon condition that the majority of their income goes to their university. Exerting virtually no control on the university's staff extra activities it is possible to keep the salaries low while allowing extra freedom to integrate one's salary with a variety of unrecorded and uncontrolled activities that the staff finds and performs independently from their employer, as in the case of multiple economies (Pavlovskaya, 2004; Williams, Nadin and Rodgers, 2012). The side effect, however, is that those in search for a higher stability (that is to have one single job and one single salary instead of depending on many different sources) might either abandon academia or, if they have good connections abroad, abandon the country at once.

There are many and various situations in which informal payments are used that a few books could be written on the subject. This section only deals with payments to pass an exam. I have identified three main tendencies. The first, and least personal, is to go to the *metodist* (a sort of intermediary between students and teachers who plans lectures and takes care of practical questions, but also has teaching duties) and discuss 'one's situation'. A student may explain that, because of personal problems, could not prepare for the exam and whether "something can be done". The *metodist* contacts the teacher and gets back to the student with a price (normally in US dollars) that they will pay.

The same situation might happen without an intermediary. The students get to know the price of an exam and find a way to get the money to the teacher. For instance, by inserting it into the *studencheskaya knizhka*, the notebook where all the exams are recorded. During the exam the teacher will get the notebook, open it to supposedly check the student's previous exams and take out the money, after which the exam will only be a formality. Both transactions happen in the form of a contract and with mutual obligations, to pay and to provide a service. As often in business the payment has to be made before the service is rendered. This is not to say that such a situation happens always and everywhere, it normally applies to the students who have not been willing or able to prepare for an exam, as one informant reported:

> [[When I was a student there were two ways of passing an exam. Either study hard or pay and buy the exam. This choice, eventually, distinguished those who wanted to take advantage of the knowledge gained for their work from those simply willing to hang a degree on their wall. However, I have also seen excellent students who, after receiving their degree, started working in a different sector.]]

In many respects, the current situation echoes a market logic with a demand-supply curve. Given the symbolic status of higher education, and the legacy of the Soviet culture, even for non-intellectual jobs a higher degree will be preferred. Because parents, and students, know that a degree is a competitive advantage they will struggle to get into the best university they can. This is also fomented by the insufficient availability, and possibly lower reputation, of technical and vocational education institutions. A demand for university education is met by a demand for a higher income by the teachers, who are technically abusing their public function.

If we refer to figure 1 in this chapter, we might better understand the relationship between A (teacher), B (student) and C (the state in this case). Is the state accessible to both A and B? There are several elements to consider. The state has established and is funding institutions called universities. Teachers are paid by the state and the students' education is often state-subsidised. Not only does it not allow for the purchase of equipment and books, it also obliges teachers to take more than one job to be able to pay for their expenses.

A taxi driver taking me from the airport (this is a recurrent mockery in anthropology) told me that, he was sending his son to a university in Kherson because it was cheaper to pay enrolment than in Kiev (education in Ukraine should be free of charge according to the constitution) and confirmed a tendency that many other informants mentioned: if you do not have a degree, you cannot even work in a shop. The mechanism dictates that even for low level jobs people with a degree might be preferred. If someone wants to be competitive in the job market, then they need a degree regardless of whether they feel like continuing their studies or not.

In a state where there is a clear boundary between jobs that require a degree and jobs that do not, it is possible to make a choice: getting a degree gives you access to some segments of the job market, not getting it gives you access to other ones. In a context where a degree is a requirement a priori the failure of the state is not to set the boundary between requirements needed for different jobs. The demand for a degree is high but state-managed universities have limited resources and cannot let everyone in. Private universities are one of the solutions but cannot accommodate everyone and not spread out enough to meet the demand since they teach mostly business related subjects. B (teachers or even universities) work for the state but their salaries are insufficient to survive on and they need to find alternative sources of income. With inadequate communication (between A and B with C) we are very close to situation four, the one that highlights the grey zone between a gift and a bribe. There are, however, sets of situations that can be seen as more or less close to a bribe (or a gift), for one thing one needs to distinguish the case where a teacher asks systematically for something or sporadically.

Once they have agreed to pay for their education, students add extra income to universities (or some of its members at least). If a teacher is failing a student, they might feel pressurised by the administration who are in fear that the student might drop out (and stop paying the fees) so they duly adapt to this. Another informant diplomatically stated: 'I am very bad at mathematics. At the end of the semester, thus, I assume that everyone has done their job and I pass them'. This informant was lecturing in several universities because she could not afford to be dismissed from one of her jobs simply because she had decided to fail a student. In addition, she also highlighted that failing a student is something unpleasant because she might be preventing him or her from getting a job and have a normal life, given that even for unspecialised jobs people with a degree are preferred.

Teachers are not always interested in student-originated income. Notwithstanding this, they might still face pressure from the administration not to fail students. I know of cases where the teacher asked, how much money students were "budgeting" to pass their exams, which was to be spent to provide the university library with some extra books. According to the informant, there were three advantages: 1) students who are not used to studying learn that there is a library, and where it is; 2) they have to learn which books are lacking and 3) the library grows offering more of a choice of books.

The meaning of bribing depends on a local legal code, whether such donation is allowed by law or not. Even more, they depend on cultural settings. A colleague, who had agreed to give a catching-up lecture on Saturday, was rewarded with some flowers.

Flowers are a common offering in Ukraine, and most of the former USSR world—but according to recent adopted anti-corruption laws it could be equated to bribing. In a non-functioning economy, where people are obliged to abide to certain unwritten rules (getting a degree, for students; passing students, for teachers) in addition to state ones, one can observe two embedded and parallel systems that pressure citizens to follow instructions from the state and from the environment they work or live in. By force of this, the gap between a gift and a bribe may become blurred and it is possible to suggest the existence of a grey area that most anti-corruption regulations and strategies tend to ignore.

5 'Survival techniques' of hospitals

A friend of mine got injured during a football match. We had to go to the hospital to check his eye. The doctor saw us (it was after midnight), thoroughly checked him and gave us a prescription. While leaving, another friend slipped the equivalent of 2 euros into the doctor's pocket saying 'thank you'. Once back home, we were asked whether we had 'paid' for the service or not. Medical assistance in Ukraine is free of charge so the payment was technically a bribe. However, in the word of a doctor:

> I earn [the equivalent of] 90 euros per month, from which I also pay taxes. If a patient comes to see me at the hospital and needs assistance I will certainly provide it. It is my job. In turn I also expect to be thanked afterwards. To become a doctor you have to study ten or more years, then you provide specialised advise and treatment, but we [doctors] do not get enough to survive on our state salary.

When this person was looking for a job in Odessa, after she completed her degree, she was asked for 3000 dollars by a local doctor to get a post. In the end, she was able to get a job 'for free' in Ilichovsk (a city 30 minutes from Odessa) where she is currently working. Births and surgery are special cases and handled differently. The normal procedure is to find a doctor who one judges able and helpful and 'interest him (or her)' so that they will take your case. But this is not the end of the story, the amount paid in the end will be redistributed among doctors, nurses and the hospital depending on their roles, responsibilities and hierarchy. Once you secure a doctor, they will look for auxiliary staff to help them with the delivery and will have to "contract them", which means sharing some of the money with them. This also means that, with no money, it will be more difficult for doctors to convince nurses and hospital staff to help them. Free of charge births are certainly possible, but in the choice between a paid one and a free one what would the staff prioritise? If you have no time or money to get a deal with a doctor, you can still go to the hospital but you will not be able to know, in advance, who is going to take care of you and risk being treated as a second level patient or being ignored. Who wants to run this risk when delivering a baby?

This is not to say that attendance with no payment is not possible. Retired and poor people will possibly try to avoid paying but this comes down to personal negotiation skills and the sensitivity of the doctor. A sanatorium in Mirgorod (Poltava oblast') changed bribes into payments by simply allowing its personnel to work extra hours and receive money from the patients they treated. This was feasible because it offered an elective service but when Kiev's mayor introduced an obligatory payment for hospital treatment it complicated life for many elders seeking medical assistance on their meagre pension.

One informant was asked for money for a blood analysis. He first protested that medical assistance is free of charge in Ukraine and then that he had no money that month (which was true). As a result he did not pay. Unexpectedly, his analyses were processed and he received medical treatment for free.

Money redistribution works just like any other hospital with the differences that: 1) the amounts are negotiated informally and depend on the doctor's relationship with their subordinates and 2) this money will never officially transit through the hospital. The result is that in Ukraine, *de facto*, all hospitals are private. Patients pay for what they get, sometimes they even have to buy the pen with which the nurses will take notes on their conditions. Doctors will not have to pay taxes on their revenue, nor will they be willing to invest 'their' money to buy new equipment for the hospital—actions that would ultimately ease their work.

Informal payments are also subject to a "professional code" that has been perfected over the years. Sometimes, when receiving the money the doctor will just open their pocket, refusing to touch the money. Payment can also be left on the desk but the patient should ensure that the doctor sees them paying so to guarantee that the amount was enough. Patients cannot ask for change and should, ideally, pay a small amount of cash using one single bill (if you give 20 hryvna you need to use a 20 hryvna bill, not 2 smaller 10 hryvna notes). Money, however, is not only leading to a service, it can also create a social bond, ending up having a function different from the initial one. One of my informants reported paying her gynaecologist more than she should have. She was happy to pay a bit more (1–2 euros) so that she did not feel in debt when calling her late in the evening or simply asking for advice on the phone (that could not possibly be charged). It was like accumulating a credit towards the person. This doctor-patient relationship, however, eventually evolved into a quasi-friendship so that payments and advice become eventually almost disjointed. She would pay knowing that the doctor would advise her even if not, but she felt responsible to contribute to the doctor's income.

This gap between the demand for treatment and the offer by state structures has generated a niche that private hospitals are trying to occupy. A growing number of people, in Ukraine as in other former USSR republics, are now going to private hospitals and a number of jobs with private companies provide employees with a private insurance and access to private hospitals. However, this is still a limited portion of the population. Those unable or unwilling to go to a private hospital might want to offer some type of reward to the doctor, a thing that I would put in three different categories.

Option 1: you know the doctor (are in a relationship of mutual dependency)
Option 2: you know someone who knows the doctor
Option 3: you do not know the doctor.

Option 1: if the doctor is a friend or a good acquaintance, they might not expect anything from you. The doctor will visit you for free and you know that you owe the doctor something. Reciprocation might happen but also might not. If you decide to offer a gift, however, you should choose something that is more personalised than standard money, cognac or chocolate.

Option 2: you do not know the doctor but someone recommended him to you. Depending on your relationship with this person you will choose to offer something or not. In general, if you are introduced to them, the doctor will become an "extension" of your friend and you will come from your friend's part (so if you owe something to your friend, or are in a subordinate position, you will pay the doctor and if your friend owes you something, you might not have to pay).

Option 3: the patient offers a gift (chocolate or money depends on the doctor's preference but it is easy to learn from other patients) to compensate the lack of connections with the doctor.

There is, of course, a role of the state in all this. The state will suggest how things should work in theory. However, if the state is perceived as weak or marginal actors by the two parts, or at least one of them, the relationship between them will be reshaped by the (Bourdieu-like) social capital they have access to. In option 1, the payment is made in social capital, in option three money is offered to make up for the lack of social capital and option 2 is an in-between case.

6 Concluding remarks

Informal payments and gifts may harm social and economic structures of a country but they can also be regarded as a "little help" to a system that does not guarantee even distribution of welfare. Current normative understandings of corruption is so wide as to encompass most of the aspects of the social life and social exchanges. However, a possible incapacity to concentrate on some essential phenomena, and therefore to focus on what it really worth fighting for, results in wasting government energy and money. In addition, by preventing doctors from accepting gifts while keeping wages low the state may generate tension that might not be solvable by any other means, which in turn can push the best doctors out of public service consequently and further worsening the already poor hospital conditions.

All the rest being equal, what would happen should the executive power succeed in stopping all the above mentioned transitions? What doctor would agree on working in a public hospital and what teacher in a public university? Using corruption to define the systematic thankfulness of the patient to the doctor seems to ignore the Ukrainian context and its peculiarities. Corruption, in cases like these, may be seen as the solution rather than the problem (Polese 2010) just as informal practices might be seen as the only way to make a system work (Ledeneva 2012). In contrast to Temple and Petrov (2004), one could suggest that the practice of taking and giving has allowed this society to survive, in the face of a budgetary policy that seems to ignore some needs of the public sector.

Informal payments, monetary and in goods, have sometimes much more in common with Maussian gifts than with bribes: reciprocity, spontaneity and inalienability of the gift as a social fact starting up a relationship. Mauss maintained the reciprocity of a gift, but reciprocity may be perpetuated in different ways. In some cases (Tanzi 1998), this reciprocity has even been associated with bribing. Literature on bribing in the former Soviet Union distinguishes a long term economic relationship (Ledeneva 1998), called 'blat' from those transaction with a character of immediate reciprocity of a bribe—*do ut das*. However, this model fails to gauge the meaning of an economic exchange with partial spontaneity aimed at a personal benefit that is hard to classify as a mere bribe or as a gift.

Spontaneity is closely linked to reciprocity. We cannot know when somebody is going to offer a gift but most of the time a return is expected. Perhaps we can say that we are dealing with a gift when the return is expected but not demanded. If it is laid claim to, then the character of spontaneity is lost. But in some cases, the enigma of the gift (Gerard 1998) can also be the enigma of the bribe. Not all informal payments in hospitals, universities and police posts are anticipated and one should learn to understand when—and how—to pay and when not.

In this regard, I have collected as many cases of unpaid consultations as I have of paid ones.

Therefore when dealing with corruption and gift giving, attention should be paid to a) an analysis of local context, reckoning with local culture and understanding of local, or even contextual, concepts of morality and gifts and b) the fluidity of the border between bribes and gifts and the existence of a grey zone in between, that can host some hybrid phenomena. If so, then gifts and bribes do not suffice as categories to explain the complexity of the socio-economic relations in a modern transitional society. It might help if we consider both gifts and bribes as results of the same phenomenon of human economic and social interaction. Putting those phenomena on a line, we could have gifts and bribes as the left and right extremes, and a continuum line between them. Slowly moving from the left (gift, spontaneous with no obligation of reciprocity) towards the right (bribe, lack of spontaneity and obligation of reciprocity) we have a number of exchanges that are neither a pure gift and whose spontaneity and lack of obligation are not pacific, nor a pure bribe, but something combining features of a gift and a bribe that we could call 'brift' (half bribe half gift).

Cited works

Andreoni, J. (1988) Why Free Ride? Strategies and Learning in Public Goods Experiments, Journal of public Economics, 37(3): 291–304.

Becker, G. (1976) Altruism, Egoism and Genetic Fitness: Economics and sociobiology. Journal of Economic Literature 14: 817–26.

De Soto, H. (2000) The mystery of capital: Why capitalism triumphs in the West and fails everywhere else. New York: Basic Books.

Egbert, H. (2006) Cross-border Small-scale Trading in South-Eastern Europe: Do Embeddedness and Social Capital Explain Enough? International Journal of Urban and Regional Research, 30(2): 346–361.

Gerard, Marc (1998) Essai sur le don, Humanités Modernes 113 :67–72.

Gibson-Graham. (1996) The End of Capitalism (As We Knew It): A Feminist Critique of Political Economy. Oxford UK and Cambridge USA: Blackwell Publishers.

Gill, S. (1998) The Pathology of Corruption. New Delhi: HarperCollins Publishers India.

Granovetter, M. (2007) The Social Construction of Corruption, in Victor Nee and Richard Swedberg (eds.) On Capitalism, Stanford University Press, 152–172

Granovetter, M. (1985) Economic Action and Social Structure: The Problem of Embeddedness, American Journal of Sociology, 481–510.

Gudeman, S. (2001) The Anthropology of Economy: Community, Market, and Culture. Oxford: Blackwell.

Gupta, A. (2005) Narratives of Corruption: Anthropological and Fictional Accounts of the Indian State, Ethnography, 6(1): 5–34.

Gupta, A. (1995) Blurred Boundaries, American Ethnologist 22(2): 375–402.

Haller D. and C. Shore (eds) (2005) Corruption: Anthropological Perspectives, London: Pluto Press.

Hann, C., & Hart, K. (2011) Economic Anthropology, London: Polity Press.

Hann, C. (2006) The Gift and Reciprocity: Perspectives from Economic Anthropology. Handbook of the Economics of Giving, Altruism and Reciprocity, 207–223.

Harboe I., and M, Frederiksen (eds.) (2015) Ethnographies of grey zones in Eastern Europe: relations, borders and invisibilities. Anthem Press.

Harboe, I. (2015) Grey Zones of Welfare. Journal of Eurasian Studies, 6(1): 17–23.

Harrison, G. (1999) Corruption, development theory and the boundaries of social change. Contemporary Politics 5(3): 207–220.

Ledeneva, A. (2012) Cronies, economic crime and capitalism in Putin's sistema. International Affairs, 88(1), 149–157.

Ledeneva, A. (1998) Russia's Economy of Favours: "Blat", Networking and Informal Exchange, Cambridge: Cambridge University Press.

Ledeneva, A. (2006) How Russia Really Works: The Informal Practices That Shaped Post-Soviet Politics and Business, Ithaca, N.Y: Cornell University Press.

Lonkila, M. (2010) Networks in the Russian market economy. London: Palgrave Macmillan.

Lonkila, M. (1997) Informal Exchange Relations in Post-Soviet Russia: A Comparative Perspective. Sociological Research Online 2(2), available at http://www.socresonline.org.uk/2/2/9.html (last accessed 29 July 2014)

Malinowski, B. (1921) The Primitive Economics of the Trobriand Islanders. The Economic Journal 31 (121): 1–16.

Mauss, M. ([1924] 1966) The Gift: Forms and Functions of Exchange in Archaic Societies, London: Cohen and West LTD.

Migdal, J. (2001) State in Society: Studying How States and Societies Transform and Constitute One Another. Cambridge: Cambridge University Press.

Morris, J., & Polese, A. (2014) The informal post-socialist economy: Embedded practices and livelihoods. Routledge.

Morris, J. (2013) Precarious Work, Entrepreneurial Mindset and Sense of Place: Female Strategies in Insecure Labour Markets: a Response to Hanna-Mari Ikonen. Global Discourse, 3(3–4), 482–485.

Morris, J. (2012) Beyond coping? Alternatives to consumption within a social network of Russian Workers. Ethnography, 1466138112448021.

Parry, J. (1986) The Gift, the Indian Gift and the 'Indian Gift, Man 21: 453–473.

Patico, J. (2003) Consuming the West but Becoming Thrid World: Food Imports and the Experience of Russianness. Anthropology of East Europe Review, 21(1), 31–36.

Patico, J. (2002) Chocolate and Cognac: Gifts and the Recognition of Social Worlds in Post-Soviet Russia. Ethnos 67(3): 345–368.

Pavlovskaya, M. (2004) Other transitions: Multiple economies of Moscow households in the 1990s. Annals of the Association of American Geographers, 94(2), 329–351.

Polese, A., Morris, J., Kovács, B., & Harboe, I. (2014) 'Welfare States' and Social Policies in Eastern Europe and the Former USSR: Where Informality Fits In? Journal of Contemporary European Studies, 22(2), 184–198.

Polese, A. (2010) At the Origins of Informal Economies: Some Evidence from Ukraine (1991–2009), Fredrick Schielling University of Jena Working Paper

Polese, A. (2009) The guest at the dining table: Economic transition and the rshaping of hospitality, reflections from Batumi and Odessa. Anthropology of East Europe Review 27 (1): 65–77

Polese, A. (2008) 'If I Receive it, it is a Gift; if I Demand it, then it is a Bribe' on the Local Meaning of Economic Transactions in Post-soviet Ukraine, Anthropology in Action 15(3): 47–60.

Polese, A. (2007) Ukraine: the State is Public, the Private Sector is Private, the Public Sector is...?, Presented at the Workshop: Property in Eastern Europe, New European College, Bucharest, 14–15 June

Polese, A. (2006a) Border crossing as a daily strategy of post Soviet survival: The Odessa-Chisinau elektrichka. Eastern European Anthropology Review 24 (1): 28–37.

Polese, A. (2006b) Paying for a free education, Transitions Online (7 August). Available at http://www.tol.org/client/article/17426-paying-for-a-free-education.html (last accessed 1 August 2014).

Polanyi, K. (1968) Primitive, Archaic and Modern Economies. Garden City: Anchor Books.

Rose-Ackerman, S. (2010) Corruption: Greed, Culture and the State, the Yale Law Journal 125, http://yalelawjournal.org/2010/11/10/rose-ackerman.html

Sahlins, M. (1978) Culture and practical reason. Chicago: University of Chicago Press.

Scott, J. C. (1985) Weapons of the Weak: Everyday Forms of Peasant Resistance. New Haven: Yale university Press.

Tanzi V. (1998) Corruption Around the World: Causes, Consequences, Scopes and Cures, IMF Working Paper (Washington DC: International Monetary Fund) 45 (4): 559–594.

Temple, P. and G. Petrov (2004) Corruption in Higher Education: Some Findings from the States of the Former Soviet Union. Higher Education Management and Policy 16(1): 83–99.

Thomas, N. (1991) Entangled Objects: Exchange, Material Culture and Colonialism in the Pacific. Cambridge MA and London: Harvard University Press.

van Schendel, W. and I. Abraham (eds) (2005) Illicit Flows and Criminal Things: States, Borders, and the Other Side of Globalization. Bloomington: Indiana University Press.

Wanner, C. (2005) Money, Morality and New Forms of Exchange in Postsocialist Ukraine, Ethnos 70(4): 515–537.

Williams, C. C., Nadin, S., & Rodgers, P. (2012) Evaluating Competing Theories of Informal Entrepreneurship: Some Lessons from Ukraine, International Journal of Entrepreneurial Behavior & Research 18(5): 528–543.

Williams, C.C. (2005) A Commodified World? Mapping the Limits of Capitalism, Zed: London.

Zanca, R. (2003) "Take! Take! Take!" Host-Guest Relations and All that Food: Uzbek Hospitality Past and Present. Anthropology of East Europe Review, 21(1): 8–16.

Informality between private and state initiative[1]

With Thom Davies

1 Introduction

In post-socialist spaces, beneath the shadows of the neon-lit signs of marketization, the informal economy remains acknowledged and vital, yet largely 'invisible'. Beyond the more obvious street-level traders and the like, most informal activity—for a variety of reasons—occurs beyond the 'panoptic gaze' of the state (Foucault 1977). The seemingly invisible nature of this economy is suggested in the various names it is given; from "shadow", to "underground", to "hidden" or "black". This underlying assumption that informal activity is unseen, that it takes place in "other worlds" (Gibson-Graham 2008, 1), is often put in contrast with the Western world where, it is assumed, visibility of the economy is secured by the fact that market forces have penetrated almost every sphere of modern society (Hann and Hart 2009, Williams et al. 2011). This has been reflected in the wide literature starting from either Polanyi (1941) or from developmentalist approaches suggesting the next alignment of new emerging powers with standards set in industrialised countries (Haller and Shore 2005, Pieterse 2010).

On the uphill struggle through post-socialism, however, there is an emerging school of thought suggesting that the route is no longer planned by neo-liberal ideas of 'transition' from *a* to *b*, nor mapped out teleologically by 'one size fits all' Washington-consensus cartography; in fact there is no 'route' at all (Burawoy 2002; Ledeneva 2004, Stenning 2005). Coping mechanisms such as informal work (Stenning 2005 and Williams & Round 2007), economies of favours (Pavlovskaya 2004; Kuehnast & Dudwick 2004; Polese 2008), "social acknowledgement" (Morris 2012, Morris 2011, 629), gift exchange (Mauss 2002, Polese 2015, Stan 2011), memory (Buyandelgeriyn 2008), and social / kinship networks (Grabher & Stark 1997; Lonkkila

---

1 First published as Abel Polese and Thom Davies (2015) "Informality and Survival in Ukraine's Nuclear Landscape: Living with the Risks of Chernobyl" *Journal of Eurasian Studies 6(1)*. Oxford: Elsevier. Reprinted with kind permission.

1997, 1999; Walker 2010) have not only helped navigate the post-Soviet 'every-day' (Bruns 2012; Morris 2012; Polese 2006; Round & Williams 2012; Urunboyev 2013; Sasunkievich 2014). They have also, and possibly more importantly, pointed to the existence of a persistent and complete system in which "informality is here to stay" (Morris and Polese 2014: 1).

Whilst initially relegated to particularistic and empirically-grounded case studies, unlikely to provide normative or universalistic value to further studies, the growing amount of research and their progressive theoretical engagements have been pointing to the social significance, persistence and size of informal activities (Morris and Polese 2014, Williams et al 2010, Round et al 2010). Indeed, such is the prevalence of these behaviors that one could argue that "'formality' could safely be concluded as an exception and 'informality' the rule" (Routh 2011, 212).

Studies on informality have rapidly grown out of their initial framework that saw an informal economy (Hart 1973) or resistance (Scott 1984) originating in the poor, the marginalised and the excluded (Gupta 1995). New directions in the study of informality have suggested that it is also a significant phenomenon in richer countries, including industrialised ones (Williams 2011) and that both winners and losers of transitions make extensive use of it (Giordano 2015, Morris and Polese 2015, Polese 2014), including in political spheres (Isaacs 2011, 2012, Kevilhan 2012, Levitsky 2011, Navarro 2007). In many respects, informal activities may be seen as complementary to formal processes or, in a market logic, as occupying the niche that remained vacant because of limited action of the formal sphere (Polese et al 2014).

2 Informality and (lack of) Welfare

There is a growing literature discussing social solidarity, social justice and other micro social phenomena that do not necessarily come from the state (Kuznetsova & Round 2014; Polese et al 2014). Post-Weberian conceptions of a state advocate several degrees of state intervention (Darden 2007): from little—a liberal logic, where the state does not interfere in market activities but creates the instruments for control of fair behaviour—to more proactive intervention, where the state is the warrant of most economic rights and obligations.

In Western Europe, as in other geographical regions, the "ethics of austerity", enhanced by the recent economic crisis (Windebank and Whitworth 2014), along with a wider desire to decrease public deficit, has encouraged a number of states to reduce the amount of money available for public services and enabled the private sector to penetrate previously state-monopolised aspects such as healthcare or education (Ó Beacháin et al 2012; Kovacs 2014; Rogers and Sheaff 2000; Tatar et al 2007). This process has been somehow less rapid in Central and Eastern Europe but only because it is building on a *de facto* process of privatisation (Harboe 2014; Polese 2006b) as opposed to a *de jure* one in more advanced economies. Traditionally, privatisation issues have been a major concern for economists or public policy specialists. Scholarship, however, has often neglected various grey situations that are, nonetheless, frequent in a number of regions, including the one we are studying here. If we see the economic and social life of a state shared between two, or in some cases three, main forces, as in figure 2, we can think of three situations that have been underrepresented in scholarship so far.

Figure 2 Complementarity of competencies of the private, public and non-profit sectors.

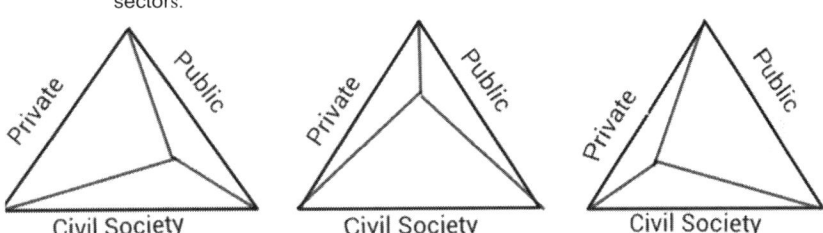

The first one is the transition between public and private services. If a state decides to privatise a service—fully or partially—then it is possible that at the end of the privatisation process, the new system will work even better than the preceding public one. However, there is generally an adaptation period during which time gaps in provision may appear, sometimes lasting long enough to be more than just 'transition'. For instance some competencies might remain "uncovered" because both state and private sectors claim it is the other side's responsibility. In a second case, one can find a gap between a service that has been promised and the way it is actually delivered. This could simply be due to bureaucratic issues, where a need is identified, money to address the need is allocated, but it takes a number of signatures and years, to unblock proper implementation. It could, however, also be due to the third situation, in which the state fails to address a given issue and simply leaves (or never enters) the game. This is the case when providing a service is too costly, or there is little interest or awareness of a given need to be addressed. The case study in this article is most closely related to the last two scenarios.

Table 1 Table showing the causes of welfare ineffectiveness and potential consequences of welfare failure.

Causes of ineffectiveness	Reasons	Possible consequences
Transition period	Adaptation period Holes in the system	Informal economic and social practices
Gap between service	Failure to identify a need Bureaucratic huddles in allocating money	Informal practices, there might be room for organised crime to take over some aspects
State "exits"	Service is too costly No awareness or pressure to address a social need	Organised crime, mafia structures replace the state; some informal economy develops

In all three situations, citizens might become or consider themselves 'abandoned' because of a limited, or complete, lack of welfare service. Privatisation is, in some cases, a solution, but it also raises questions. What would happen if the private sector provided a service at a price that was too high for a significant number of people? What happens if private sector actors do not see the advantage of occupying that niche, and leave a service tackling a particular social need unprovided?

In the recent past, situations where citizens expected or were promised A, but delivered B have resulted in a conflict that has been solved in different ways. Contestation and contentious politics is one of them, when citizens openly criticize and challenge the state, asking for a change from the status quo (Tarrow 2005; Della Porta 2009). Organised criminality and illegal flows are another well studied field, with some groups taking advantage of the void of power to create a system within the system with its own rules of engagement and different distributions of welfare and benefits (Bruns and 2012; O'Brien and Penna 2007; Pinotti 2011; van Schendel and Abrahams 2005). There are also cases where an initiative starts from citizens who organise in a less hierarchical structure than a mafia to provide a service, competing with the state in welfare distribution (such as Time Banks or other alternative currencies). Those actions can either be formally coordinated, such as when civil society organisations or informal groups start providing services, or uncoordinated, but still widely popular within a certain segment of a society (Koven and Michel 1990, Mollica 2014). We are clearly indebted to Scott's (1978, 1984) works on everyday forms of resistance when framing the approach of this article. Our question, however, starts from the possibility to apply this framework more broadly and see it not only as resistance or a survival strategy, but in a more structural way.

We start from the question of what happens when a state retires, or refrains, from (providing services to) a particular geographic area and what kind of mechanisms, practices and institutions are created to make up for this. We suggest that, in the absence of an entrepreneurial actor, be this the state or a private one, delivering a service that is needed by a given segment of a population might end up being provided informally. To do this, this article takes the region around Chernobyl in north-central Ukraine as a case study to document the way the absence of de facto welfare protection leads to the creation of local informal markets and economic activity. In the Chernobyl region the excluded and abandoned have created a set of informal mechanisms independent from the state. While Harboe (2013) has documented the life of *Invisible Citizens*, who avoid formal institutional relations with the state due to a general skepticism towards such establishments, we here deal with those that the state has decided to avoid a relationship with. Although the provision of a small state pension paid out each month, tiny food subsidies, or the permission to live in a given place might indicate that the state has 'not forgotten' about these people, the amount of benefits received and the way this compares to the rest of the country seem to point to the fact that state support is nominal than real, showing little or no difference to those who receive nothing from the state. The post-Chernobyl Ukrainian state offers only a 'Potemkin village' of welfare support—a complex web of de jure entitlements but a lived reality of de facto state abandonment.

The choice of this case study is connected to the possibility to position Chernobyl as an example of a 'state of exception' (Agamben 2005), where its affected population use informal economic activity and non-formal understandings of radiation risk as a way to enact agency and subvert their post-disaster status of 'bare life' (Agamben 1998). The state's failure to 'see' into the hidden spaces and processes of informal activity around the Exclusion Zone reveals the non-expert experience of having to cope in a landscape where radioactive danger is *invisible*. This radioactive landscape reverses the old adage '*what you can't see won't hurt you*', and blurs the boundary between 'contaminated and safe'; 'seen and unseen'; 'formal and informal'. While acknowledging that formal and informal activity can be viewed as a "multicoloured" (Smith & Stenning 2006) spectrum, we also conclude that informal activity can be a lens through which to view wider issues, such as how people use informality to renegotiate their vulnerable status of post-nuclear bare life. Informal activities around Chernobyl, which are often enacted through local knowledge and unofficial understandings of the nuclear landscape, cultivate mechanisms of informal welfare that replace or sit alongside the failed and retreating state welfare system.

This research is grounded in long-term ethnographic fieldwork between 2010–2013 around the Chernobyl border region, which is a few hours by bus (*marshrutka*) north of Kyiv. Food and goods such as scrap metal from within the Exclusion Zone and the wider region are often informally traded within local urban areas, including the capital, linking the Chernobyl landscape to the rest of Ukraine, involving formal business structures, through informal supply chains. Ethnographic methods were employed with over one hundred semi-structured and informal interviews with local residents, border guards, former liquidators, scrap collectors, gatekeepers, returnees, and local elites. Other key research tools included the extensive use of participant observation and a visual methodology involving participant photography, explored in a previous article (Davies 2013). Given the sensitivity of the material, the identities of all participants are concealed and any information that may be harmful to the research participants has been omitted.

3 Structure and agency in debates on informality

Since Hart's first mention of 'informal economies' in 1973, the debate on informality has been enriched by a wide number of empirical and theoretical studies exploring the nature and diversity of alternative, informal, or diverse economies (Gibson Graham 1996, Escobar 1995; Law and Urry 2004; Spinosa et al. 1997). It is possible to see the debate on informal economies, and the different positions resulting from it, as an extension of the structure-agency debate. Modernists and transitionalists, in particular, tend to consider the existence of informal economies and related phenomena (informal employment, work and undeclared activities) as mostly depending on structure. According to their position, informality results from temporary, or transitional, adjustments in the path to modernity that are bound to disappear after a country, or a sector, has been modernised (Boeke, 1942; Geertz, 1963; Lewis, 1959). Structural perspectives share, to a different extent, the belief that participation in informal activities is an imposition rather than a choice. They start from the idea that informal economic practices are more spread and important in economic systems where the state is unable to protect its citizens against social risks, pushing a number of them into informal employment, and unregistered economic activities (Davis, 2006; Gallin, 2001; Slavnic, 2010). In both cases the central idea is that it is mostly the marginalised who engage in informal transactions because of lack of alternative options (Amin et al. 2002; Castells & Portes 1989; Hudson 2005; Sassen 1997).

Those two positions put emphasis on structure, be these economic and institutional frameworks or structures created by the ensemble of economic and administrative actors that either decide on work conditions or their regulation. Exclusion is sometimes prompted, according to some critics of capitalism, by the lack of need to maintain a reserve army of labour or lack of desire to act as a welfare state for those who have been formally excluded by the economic life of the country (Amin et al. 2002; Hudson 2005). This leads scholars to consider that informal activity is largely involuntary with people just falling into it for the sake of survival (Amin et al. 2002; Castells & Portes

1989; Sassen 1997) meeting a desire by large actors to reduce costs and maximize profits (Bender 2004; Hapke 2004; Ross 2004) and thereby leaving 'everyday' people with no alternatives.

In contrast to the above approach, neoliberal, ultraliberal and some behaviouralists (Gaal and McKee 2004) argue that non-participation in and non-contribution to an economic system is a matter of choice. Rather than being initiated by an overarching system, lack of participation to the formal economic life of a system largely depends on the fact that people themselves choose not to be part of a system they do not trust, or that they believe is bringing them more damage than benefits. Reasons vary, from high taxation through corruption to lack of formal benefits of acknowledgement for micro economic actors (Harboe 2014, 2015; De Soto, 1989; 2001; London and Hart, 2004), but the general approach is that informality complements the formal economy when economic or administrative hurdles make it more convenient (Cross 2000; Gerxhani 2004; Perry & Maloney 2007) as a result of a micro cost-benefit analysis (e.g. De Soto 1989; Sauvy 1984, Minc 1982).

Recently, however, the above monetary centred vision has been challenged by a number of works coming from various disciplines. In particular, influences from feminism, new institutionalist economics, and critical empirically grounded studies on the meaning of money in socio-economic systems have informed a relatively new perspective considering monetary and financial transitions as socially embedded (Bourdieu 2001; Chakrabarty 2000; Davis 1992; Escobar 1995; Gibson-Graham 1996, 2006; Lee 2006; Leyshon et al. 2003; Zelizer 2005). Some scholars have insisted on the fact that these transactions are based on work or relations for a circle of friends, kin and acquaintances (Smith & Stenning 2006; Williams & Round 2008; Nelson & Smith 2009;). Other studies have focused on social relations and social/redistributive motives (Williams, 2004; Jensen and Slack 2009). This post-structural perspective has proven to be a good interdisciplinary synthesis (e.g. Maloney 2004; Gurtoo & Williams 2009) between scholars looking at the market, or the economic logic as prevailing over everything else (Egbert 2006) and those seeing the meaning of every transaction in a social and societal framework with no apparent economic logic (Gudman 2001).

Our article starts from this perspective and explores the meaning of transactions assuming a logic that transcends the self-interested, utility-maximising economic one. We do not deny here the economic gain informal transactions bring or that they are essential to the survival of most of the involved actors. We consider, however, that economic reasoning is embedded in a larger framework that prioritises a long-term logic, and subsequently long-term relationships, interactions and the embeddedness of economic and social life. We draw here from a growing body of literature in anthropology about favour exchanges in different regions of the world (Ledeneva 1998, 2006, Tlaiss and Kauser 2011; Yang 1994) but also the social and cultural significance of economic and social exchanges that Parry (1989) has pointed out both for unreciprocated gifts and even for the symbolic function of money that can be social or economic depending on culture (Parry and Block 1989; Polese 2015). We also build on works looking at informal transactions as building respectability, hierarchies and status (Pardo 1996) that confirm or subvert the social symbolic order of a community or even a society. As White has pointed out, there exists the possibility that social and economic relations become so embedded to be indiscernible so that "money makes us relatives" (1994).

These premises allow us to approach post-structuralist perspectives going beyond the survival logic that sometimes features in scholarly works. We look at the way social and economic functions of informal transactions engender a redistributive system that generates, allocates and allows the sharing of welfare and how this system is based on a balance between economic benefits and the construction of social relations and social facts.

4 Chernobyl

Whilst mostly explored by scholars from the hard or life sciences, Chernobyl has recently gained popularity in the social sciences, across fields such as human geography (Davies 2013; Rush-Cooper 2013), anthropology (Petryna 2002; 2011; Phillips 2005; 2012), sociology (Kuchinskaya 2011; 2012; 2014), history (Kalmbach 2013), studies of tourism (Goatcher & Brunsen 2011; Stone 2013; Yankovska & Hannam 2013), culture (Falkof 2013), and visual studies (Bürkner 2014). What these scholars share is the realization that the Chernobyl disaster has multiple interpretations and realities, with contested impacts that stretch both within and beyond post-socialist space. For some, the 1986 nuclear disaster has come to embody the demise of the Soviet era—both in the way the accident itself contributed to the sudden implosion of the internally vulnerable Soviet system (van der Veen 2013), but also in the way that the Exclusion Zone today has become a frozen microcosm of late-Soviet everyday life (Davies 2013). For countless people, Chernobyl remains an ongoing disaster. Its consequences extend beyond its unknowable death toll, and well past the confines of its official nuclear spaces, penetrating many social, psychological and economic facets of everyday life.

Adriana Petryna (2004, 263) describes how after Chernobyl, a new "informal economy of diagnoses and entitlement" emerged. In a world where radiation risk is invisible to the lay perspective, informal means of overcoming this technological blindness began to surface. Doctors were bribed not simply for preferential medical treatment, but to diagnose a more financially rewarding Chernobyl disability status. Hospitals and sites of health care are well-documented arenas of informal exchange (Polese 2006 and 2008; Mæstad & Mwisongo 2011, Morris & Polese 2014, Stepurko et al. 2013), but Chernobyl presented a situation where an individual's entire bio-political status could be won and lost at the turn of a brown envelope. The new forms of 'biocitizenship' (Petryna 2002) that emerged after Chernobyl, where a higher disability status equalled more social benefits, meant that an individual's biology became bio-capital to be informally traded within the State's healthcare system; "bare life" (Agamben 1998) could be informally renegotiated.

Here—like in other modern spaces of exception suggested by Giorgio Agamben (2005), such as Nazi concentration camps or Guantanamo Bay—certain people are excluded from the normal protections of the law, and allowed a "death without consequences" (Doty 2011, 610). We follow calls from human geographers to "bring Agamben out from the battlefield" (Laurie 2014) and can apply his framework to the nuclear landscape of Chernobyl. We find that in Chernobyl, a permanent state of emergency is enforced geographically through the construction (and performance) of nuclear 'Exclusion Zones', and through its governance from Ukraine's 'Ministry of

Emergencies', thus ensuring that the state of exception persists. As such, those living in Chernobyl-affected territories can be viewed as 'bare life' (Agamben 1998); their lives stripped of the protection of the law, and abandoned through insufficient welfare and compensation protection to an uncertain fate; their potentially damaged biologies are placed outside the responsibility of the state to face the hidden violence of abandonment. To live inside contaminated territory is therefore to live outside the de facto protection of the law.

5 Chernobyl Welfare

After Ukrainian independence in 1991, the baton of responsibility for Chernobyl passed from the USSR to Ukraine, making it one of the least welcome and most toxic inheritances of the Soviet collapse. At first, a newly independent Ukraine increased welfare payments and provisions as a method of publically and politically distancing itself from its former Soviet masters, but recent developments have seen a new approach to Chernobyl management. In 2010 the '*Ministry of Emergencies and Affairs of Population Protection from the Consequences of Chernobyl Catastrophe of Ukraine*' was supplanted by the much pithier '*State Emergency Service*'.[2] The dropping of reference to 'Chernobyl' was more than semantic efficiency, part of a wider move within Ukraine and beyond to rebrand the catastrophe from an ongoing process to a bounded and fixed event in late-Socialism. This move preceded the construction of the EU funded 'New Safe Confinement'; a huge structure that will envelop the infamous Sarcophagus of Lenin Reactor 4, and thereby attempt to physically *and* symbolically 'put a lid' on Chernobyl as an event.

Chernobyl welfare, too, has been constantly threatened with overhaul by successive Kyiv regimes, often met with protests from Liquidators and other Chernobyl victims (*Chernobiltsi*). With estimates of 5–8% of Ukraine's annual state budget being dedicated to post-Chernobyl management (Oughton et al 2009; Stone 2012; Danzer & Danzer 2014), it is no wonder that Kyiv has made moves towards reframing the disaster from an open-ended question to a geographic

---

2 This ministry was renamed again in 2012 to the similarly succinct 'Ministry of Emergencies of Ukraine', with reference to 'Chernobyl' being equally absent.

and temporally closed-off 'certainty' in late-Soviet history. This shift in Chernobyl management follows calls from the World Bank that describe Chernobyl welfare as a "dead weight" on Ukraine's floundering economy (Petryna 2011)—a political view that will doubtless increase following Ukraine's dire post-Euromaidan position and stringent IMF loan conditions (Davies 2014).

Unlike other spheres of state protection in post-Soviet space, the sprawling and underfunded Chernobyl welfare system is not something that the private sector is willing to enter. Referring back to figure 1, welfare has remained in a de jure sense entirely within the remit of the state, yet in a real sense informal activity has had to plug the gap that state welfare has left bare. As the state reduces the size of Chernobyl's welfare and benefit system, which already falls well short of protecting its exposed citizens, it will become even more necessary for informal mechanisms to step in where welfare fails, and circumvent the consequences of de facto state abandonment. As Chernobyl citizens face a "double exposure" from the combination of nuclear pollution and failed governance (Davies 2013, 116), they increasingly rely upon informal mechanisms to subvert their position as post-nuclear bare life.

Chernobyl is, in fact, no case study proper. It is a highly anomalous relationship between the population of an area and the welfare state. Nonetheless, despite its multiple forms of uniqueness, Chernobyl is still a representative element of more generalised state withdrawal.

6 Food and welfare

There are over 2.15 million people in Ukraine who live on territory officially designated as contaminated by Chernobyl (Ministry of Emergencies of Ukraine, 2011, 42)—around 4% of Ukraine's population (State Statistics Committee of Ukraine, 2004)[3]. Those who live on this Chernobyl-affected land are entitled to monthly compensation payments designed to help people buy clean food, and thus mitigate the low-level risk of consuming produce grown in polluted soil. However, the lived experience of this welfare system is quite different from its aim, as demonstrated in the following ethnographic vignette.

---

3   These statistics were produced before the 2014 annexation of Crimea and continuing crisis in East Ukraine.

For Bogdan—a former Liquidator—and his wife Klara, informal economic activity is vital because it supplements their small formal income and tiny welfare payments they receive as compensation for living with Chernobyl. In 2008 Bogdan was sacked from his job as a driver in Chernobyl after an argument with his boss about not being paid for half a month's work. His wife Klara, now the main breadwinner, works two jobs as a school dinner lady and a carer for the elderly, getting paid around $230 per month. Their combined formal income gives them just enough to get by. On top of this, explains Klara, "*the government give us 2 Hryvnia and 10 Kopeks a month to buy clean food*". Many research participants complained about the extremely low level of Chernobyl food compensation, which varies from 1.6 Hryvnia in places with lower levels of radiation, to Klara and Bogdan's case of 2.1 Hryvnia, for those who live with higher recorded radiation levels. At the time of writing, this is just 13 to 16 cents per month—a virtually useless amount in the Ukrainian context, where food prices are comparable to the UK (Round et al. 2010). As Klara rhetorically continued—"*What the hell can we get with that?*".

Although some welfare payments in Ukraine such as pensions or disability subsidies "are adjusted periodically according to changes in the national average wage and inflation" (SSPTW 2012, 307), this has not been the case with Chernobyl food benefits, which are—as a Ukrainian diplomat explained during an interview—"*fixed at the same rate since the early 1990s*". As such, this dismally low rate of compensation only serves to designate a territory as contaminated by nuclear pollution, yet does nothing to alleviate the problem. It reinforces the reality of contamination, reminding people each month when they collect their compensation, yet does nothing in the way of actually helping. This example of welfare failure in Ukraine can be seen as a form of "stealthy violence" (Gilbert & Ponder 2013), where individuals are exposed as bare life through inadequate compensation and de facto state-abandonment. Chernobyl governance produces lives that can end without consequence—not killed, but not protected from radiation either, effectively "kept alive through a state of injury" (Mbembé & Meintjes 2003). "*We couldn't even buy bread with that*" complained Bogdan, who echoes a sentiment held by many who live within this stigmatized "landscape of threat" (Parkhill et al. 2013, 1).

As in other post-socialist rural spaces, self-provisioning is an important survival strategy in the post-nuclear context of economic and environmental precarity. The irony of this broken Chernobyl welfare system is highlighted by the fact that most of the food that people eat in contaminated regions around Chernobyl is grown by themselves, in the very soil that the compensation is supposed to protect them from. In the face of a retreating state, many people in this nuclear landscape have developed other mechanisms of social protection that are independent from state welfare, involving informal activity, unofficial understandings of radiation risk, and social networks.

Standing in a small barn by his house, just a few kilometres from the Exclusion Zone fence, Bogdan explained how he intended to exchange surplus sacks of potatoes with members of his social network who lived nearby: "*I have no money to pay them, only potatoes. If I have the money to pay them then I do*". The potatoes were stored below the wooden outbuilding where he and Klara keep a few livestock: three pigs and a cow—their chickens roaming around the yard. The smallholding was typical of the parcels of land found in the Chernobyl border region, more "household plot" (Czegledy 2002, 203) than farm. Between formal employment and looking after their elderly relatives who lived nearby, there was little time for growing surplus cash crops. In the small cool cellar, above the mounds of potatoes grown earlier in the summer, an array of other self-cultivated or foraged foods stood high on shelves, pickled in large jars. Onions, tomatoes, mushrooms, beetroots, berries, gherkins and a variety of other fruit and vegetables sealed in glass. Though a banal and ordinary scene to anyone familiar with post-Soviet rural *and* urban life, it is one made unusual and distinct by the assertion that radiation's "consumption in food products— especially for those living near Chernobyl—is practically unavoidable" (Phillips 2005, 288). Yet this array of hard-earned produce in Bogdan's cellar was, for him at least, untarnished by the threat of radiation.

If the jars represented anything, it was not the invisible threat from contamination, but the months of toil it had taken to put the food there in the first place; domestic food production in Ukraine should not be over-romanticised (Polese 2009; Round et al 2010). Like other forms of informality, the self-cultivated and gathered food was an expression of agency—minor victories against the uncertainty of poverty, each jar an "economic cushion" (Czegledy 2002, 209) that exists beyond the formal economy and failed welfare system.

Wide-scale post-socialist marginalization has meant many Ukrainians "are compelled to worry more about putting food on the table than about the 'ecological state' (*ekolohichnyi stan*) of that food" (Phillips 2005, 288). As one elderly woman who lived near the edge of the Exclusion Zone explained, in the confusion and chaos after Chernobyl, she was told to avoid eating various foodstuffs such as berries and mushrooms, or to drink locally produced milk, but:

> "If you are not going to drink or eat everything that they say, then you won't even have the energy to move even your legs ... you'll have no power to even move your legs..."

In the wake of a de facto absence of formal welfare protection, many people continue to participate in risky and informal food practices, normalized and reinforced by local social networks. Bogdan took the potatoes to his friend who was sitting in a boat moored at the water's edge very near the border of the Exclusion Zone. Concealed from the road, between a smallholding and the tall reeds that are synonymous with the Pripyat Marches, around thirty men were busily folding fishing nets, repairing their boats, fixing out-board motors, and hauling-in the morning's catch. The number and size of the fish suggested this was not just evidence of "the growing commercialization of rural household production" (Pallot & Nefedova 2003, 47), but part of a wider industry of informal (and formal) activity that takes place in this nuclear border region. Dilapidated concrete signs nearby read *'Fishing is Strictly Forbidden'* as the river here runs past the "most contaminated water body in the zone of the Chernobyl accident" (Kryschev 1995, 217). The unfixed and ephemeral character of this watercourse that flows through the Exclusion Zone itself adds one more layer of liminality to an already fuzzy nuclear border. While it was not possible to trace the end destination of these prohibited fish via a 'follow the thing' (Cook 2004) approach, respondents suggested the fish were destined to be sold for money in cities such as Kyiv, as opposed to being solely exchanged within localised kin networks—the sheer amount of fish collected in large nets made this monetary outcome inevitable. Environmentally risky foodstuffs from restricted areas such as mushrooms, game, barriers and fish regularly enter the foodchain in Ukraine through various informal actions involving trespassing the official borders of the Exclusion Zone (Davies 2011).

Uncertainty about radiological health, as well as economic insecurity and a lack of adequate welfare support has produced informal understandings of radiation risk in communities that surround Chernobyl. These unofficial nuclear risk perceptions have become a shared welfare resource, allowing abandoned communities to act beyond the official nuclear limits and rules of the Exclusion Zone. The act of exchanging potatoes grown in soil around Chernobyl with illegally caught fish from within the Exclusion Zone, relies on collective risk consciousness that reinforces and reciprocates informal understandings of radiation, and ways of alleviating the lack of welfare provision. In this way, the excluded and abandoned population of Chernobyl have created new mechanisms for social security that are independent from the state's failure to provide 'clean food'—by communally and informally redefining what is considered 'clean'. New 'social facts' about radiation risk are demonstrated and reinforced through risky food practices and informal activity. This does not deny that dangerous food activities around Chernobyl are based partly on necessity (of having little practical alternative), but these behaviours are also normalised, reinforced and renegotiated by a local and embedded understandings of radiation risk that is fostered and reproduced informally through social networks.

For example, during a conversation about food, one mother who lives adjacent to the contaminated space of the Zone, compared her home-grown (and gathered) food to shop-bought produce:

> "Everything you buy is full of chemicals and genetically modified stuff. I know this is my food, so I know it is absolutely natural."

Like many in this region, this opinion that home-grown and gathered food is safe was held inharmoniously with a wider belief that Chernobyl radiation is deadly. To "know" the food, is to grow it yourself, and to toil your own soil ensures its safety. "*Why should we be afraid of growing our own?*" she continued, "*The soil is ours*". Others relied upon local informal knowledge, describing how they knew which fields they should avoid cultivating because the potatoes grew black—in their opinion—because of radiation.

These informal risk understandings occur in tandem with 'normal' informal economic activity that has been well documented elsewhere (Round et al 2010; Cassidy 2011; Williams et al 2013; Morris & Polese 2015), and add a new layer of resistance to state abandonment and the lived realities of bare life. The collective risk consciousness that is embedded in these practices and normalised in everyday informal activity around Chernobyl allows people to dwell in a landscape where the state has retreated from its welfare responsibilities.

7 Rejecting welfare and embracing place

One key welfare provision available for Chernobyl affected citizens is the option to be resettled in non-contaminated space. Beyond the 350,000 forcibly displaced people who were made to leave the 'Zone of Mandatory resettlement' (Ministry of Emergencies of Ukraine 2012), those who still live in areas of high contamination outside the Exclusion Zone in Ukraine have—at least in theory—the option of state-assisted voluntarily relocation. In reality, however, many people reject this welfare provision. This can be only partly explained by the long waiting lists involved in securing alternative housing, which are synonymous with welfare systems inherited from the USSR (Gentile & Sjöberg 2013). People also reject this relocation welfare because of a reliance on informality that connects people to place. We see the ability to perform informal activity, and the social networks that informality relies upon and reproduces, as key factors that dissuade people from leaving the spaces they inhabit, including Chernobyl's nuclear landscape. This is explored in the following ethnographic vignette, which continues from Bogdan's exchange at the river.

"All of the men you saw are criminals, you see—it is illegal to fish there. And they are dangerous..." said Bogdan that evening over a bowl of soup made from the traded fish "... but I am not afraid of them". Nor was he afraid of higher levels of radiation that could be found in the food. Bogdan is a well-connected man, his large social network vital to his household survival strategies; allowing him to weave in between the informal and formal. When asked if he was ever tempted to move away from this region to somewhere less contaminated he explained how it would be worse for his health to emigrate from the landscape he knows best:

> "most of the people who left here died very quickly, because they had not been accepted into their surroundings ... when they left separately, away from people they knew, they died from stress."

This is a widely held opinion expressed by those living in this region: that it is better to live with the invisible threat of radiation than to risk the tangible reality of severing social networks, and thus harming the ability to use informal methods of survival and reciprocity. This was *not* based on an opinion that Chernobyl radiation is risk free, indeed *every* respondent had personal experiences of bereavement and tragedy associated with the accident, but rather on an understanding that the alternative was much worse.

The significance placed on the agency of informal activity—even in this extreme environment—speaks to the importance of informality throughout Ukraine in general, and across many other spheres of post-Socialist space. Even on the edge of the Chernobyl Exclusion Zone, where radiological risk makes some informal activity dangerous, this ability to act informally is given a very high importance by local inhabitants. The capacity to use social networks, informal activity and local knowledge to survive outside the formal economy and beyond (or alongside) the welfare system is seen as more important than avoiding the risk of contamination. This has parallels with previous research in highly marginalized areas of the former Soviet Union such as Magadan in Russia's Far East. Here, Gulag survivors who faced extreme climatic and economic conditions refused to be relocated to more affluent areas due the risk of severing their social networks and informal survival tactics on which they so completely depended (Round 2006).

To an outsider, the nuclear borderland around Chernobyl is an anti-"therapeutic landscape" (Gesler & Kearns 2002, 132). However, to marginalised individuals who are able to negotiate everyday life through subverting the Zone's "border processes" (Newman 2006), as well as through social networks and informal economic activity, the risk from radiation is less of a threat than the reality of migrating elsewhere.

This reliance on a local knowledge of the landscape and on social networks creates an informal pull of place that goes beyond formal techno-scientific understandings of place and radiation risk. The informality of place attachment is a resource that creates spaces where the state can be supplanted by local knowledge. In this case, forms of state welfare (e.g. relocation) are actually *rejected* in order to ensure the continuation of informal activity and the fostering of social support. Here we can view informality as a logic that not only transcends the formal economic one, but also moves beyond formal understandings of health.

When analysing why individuals keep on living with environmentally dangerous environments such as Chernobyl, the ability to perform informal activities that subvert the official understandings of space and place should not be underestimated. A key example of such informal activity is the prosaic yet illegal, and potentially harmful act of gathering goods from *inside* the Exclusion Zone (Davies 2011). For instance the normalised and highly risky activity of collecting, consuming, and exchanging mushrooms and berries from inside the forbidden forests of the Zone. This is an extremely pervasive behaviour, despite these foodstuffs being some of the most harmful produce in a nuclear landscape, with recorded levels of human contamination increasing during foraging season (Botsch et al 2001).

Scrap metal collection from within the Exclusion Zone is also key among a spectrum of informal activities that takes place in this marginalised nuclear landscape. This prohibited activity of crossing the nuclear border to salvage (and sell) the abandoned detritus from the Zone, contributes to the informal renegotiation of Chernobyl citizens' status as post-nuclear bare life. It draws upon local place-knowledge and agency by subverting the official rules of this nuclear 'space of exception' (Agabmen 2005). The fence around the Chernobyl Exclusion Zone is the physical embodiment of a failed state-attempt to contain harmful radiation. Low-level radiation is not stopped by it, nor too are the informal ebbs and flows of people and goods from within the Zone—as indicated by the many person-sized holes that can be found all along the border between 'clean' and 'unclean' space. This informal behaviour is infused with dangers and risks beyond those associated with radiation however:

> "... the militia sometimes wait in the forest and then wait for you to cross the border, then they catch you. It depends on who caught you, you may be able to bribe."

Several participants described how they remove scrap metal from the Zone, taking it from the many deserted buildings on the other side of the fence. One participant described selling the metal: "*to different dealers. We take it to the factory where it is crushed, melted down, and mixed with other metals ...*". From here it is in the formal economic sphere and "*... it is impossible to find or trace it.*"—it becomes invisible. The ubiquitous yet unseen presence of informality also dwells within the 'floating mists' (Lefebvre 2000, 98; Round et al 2008, 172) of Chernobyl's spaces of exception, not threatening the marginalised but helping them negotiate everyday life in the context of de facto state-abandonment.

8 Conclusion

Despite Chernobyl being a relatively limited geographical area in Ukraine, we would suggest that it is possible to take the micro data used above to extrapolate some lessons that can be applied more widely within post-Soviet space and beyond. Starting from apparently pure monetary transactions that could be considered from a solely economic logic, this article has attempted to provide a more systemic explanation to the series of exchanges happening in the region. The transactions analysed, we suggest, can be considered as a whole, a system that is occupying a vacant welfare niche in an area where the state has unofficially decided not to assert its role.

For many marginalised individuals, despite a belief that Chernobyl has caused widespread sickness, the risk from invisible radiation is considered less of a health threat than the tangible reality of leaving behind social support networks after moving, and the ability to employ local informal economic tactics. From a state perspective, the marginal role the area plays in the economy and politics makes it unattractive or at least not worth efforts, compared to other regions.

By framing the Chernobyl landscape as a space of exception, this article shows that informal activity provides a key means of subverting the official rules of this space, and the lived realities of 'bare life' (Agamben 1998). These informal behaviours take place against a backdrop of de facto state abandonment that exposes Chernobyl's vulnerable citizens to the stealthy violence of harmful radiation and a retreating state.

This sense of abandonment is matched, however, by an intensification of social networks, unofficial risk understandings, and informal activities, making possible life with this nuclear landscape, that cannot possibly be considered 'illegal'. Illegal is a term one uses for an activity going against the state, or better the operating of a state. If the state retires from an area, or from providing a service, how can the coping mechanisms possibly be 'illegal'?

Cited works

Agamben G (1998) Homo Sacer: Sovereign Power and Bare Life. California: Stanford University Press.

Agamben G. (2005) State of Exception. London: The University of Chicago Press

Botsch W., Romantschuk L.D., Beltz D, Handl J., and Michel R. (2001) Investigation of the Radiation Exposure of Inhabitants of Contaminated Areas in northern Ukraine Centre for Radiation Protection and Radiocology

Brown L. (2011) World on the Edge: How to Prevent Environmental and Economic Collapse. W.W.Norton & Co Publishers: London.

Bruns B. & Migglebrink J. (2012) Subverting borders: Doing Research on Smuggling and Small Scale Trade. Germany: VS Verlag für Sozialwissenschafte.

Buraway M. (2002) Transition without Transformation: Russia's Involuntary Road to Capitalism pp. 290–310 in Nugent D. [ed] Locating Capitalism in Time and Space: Global Restructurings, Politics and Identity. Stanford University Press: London.

Bürkner D. (2014) The Chernobyl Landscape and the Aesthetics of Invisibility Photography and Culture 7(1): 21–39

Buyandelgeriyn M. (2008) Post-Post-Transition Theories: Walking on Multiple Paths. Annual Review of Anthropology 37: 235–250.

Caldwell M. (2007) Feeding the Body and Nourishing the Soul: Natural Food in Post-Socialist Russia. Food Culture and Society: An International Journal of Multidisciplinary Research 10(1): 43–71

Cassidy (2011) Performing the cross border economies of post-socialism. International Journal of Sociology and Social Policy 21(11): 612–618.

de Certeau (1984) The Practice of Everyday Life. London: University of California Press

Cook I. (2004) Follow the thing: Papya Antipode 36(4): 642–664.

Czegledy A. (2002) Urban Peasants in a Post-Socialist World: small-scale agriculturalists in Hungary, in Leonard P. and Kaneff D [eds], Post-Socialist Peasant? Rural and Urban Constructions of Identity in Eastern Europe, East-Asia and the Former Soviet Union. New York: Palgrave, 200–221.

Danzer A. and Danzer N. (2014) The Long-Run Consequences of Chernobyl: Evidence on Subjective Well-Being, Mental Health and Welfare CESifo Working Paper Series No. 4855 [accessed via http://papers.ssrn.com/sol3/papers.cfm?abstract_id=2463587 on 1/08/2014]

Davies T. (2011) Nuclear mushrooms: attitudes to risk and the state through food consumption in the Chernobyl border region, in Universitas 21 Graduate Research on Food Proceedings Nottingham University, Malaysia Campus June, 92–96.

Davies. T (2013) A Visual Geography of Chernobyl: Double Exposure International Labor and Working-Class History 84: 116–139.

Davies T. (2014) Ukraine's other crisis: Living in the shadow of Chernobyl—where victims receive just 9p a month and are left to fend for themselves Independent Newspaper 27/4/2014 [accessed via http://www.independent.co.uk/news/world/europe/ukraines-other-crisis-living-in-the-shadow-of-chernobyl--where-victims-receive-just-9p-a-month-and-are-left-to-fend-for-themselves-9293832.html on 1/8/2014].

Doty R. L. (2011) Bare life: border-crossing deaths and spaces of moral alibi Environment and Planning-Part D, 29(4), 599.

Escobar, A. (1995) Encountering development: The making and unmaking of the third world. New Jersey: Princeton University Press.

Falkof N. (2013) Heroes with a Half Life: Teenage Mutant Ninja Turtles and America's Repression of Radiophobia after Chernobyl Journal of Popular Culture 46(5): 931–949.

Foucault M. (1977) Discipline and Punish: the birth of the Prison. New York: Pantheon Books.

Gentile M. and Sjöberg O. (2013) Housing allocation under socialism: the Soviet case revisited. Post-Soviet Affairs 29(2): 173–195.

Gesler W. and Kearns R. (2002) Culture, Place and Health. London: Routledge.

Gibson-Graham J.K (2008) Diverse economies: performative practices for 'other worlds'. Progress in Human Geography 32(5): 1–20.

Giordano, C. (2015) The importance of personalized relationships in Post-Socialist rural Bulgaria: Informality of new capitalist entrepreneurs. InInformal Economies in Post-Socialist Spaces. London: Palgrave Macmillan, 175–192.

Goatcher J. and Brunsden V. (2011) Chernobyl and the sublime Tourist Tourist Studies 11(2): 115–137.

Grabher G. and Stark D. (1997) Restructuring Networks in Post-socialism legacies, linkages and localities. London: Clarendon Press.

Granovetter, Mark (1973) The Strength of Weak Ties. American Journal of Sociology 78(6): 1360–1380.

Granovetter, M. (1985), "Economic Action and Social Structure: the Problem of Embeddedness.", American Journal of Sociology, 91: 481–93.

Hart K. (1973) Informal Income Opportunities and Urban Employment in Ghana, Journal of Modern African Studies 11(1): 61–89.

IAEA (2011) Statement to International Conference on Chernobyl: Twenty-Five Years On—Safety for the Future, International Atomic Energy Agency: Kyiv.

Kalbach K. (2013) Radiation and borders: Chernobyl as a national and transnational site of memory Global Environment No. 11 130–159.

Koven, S. and S. Michel (1990) Womanly Duties: Maternalist Politics and the Origins of Welfare States in France, Germany, Great Britain, and the United States, 1880–1920, The American Historical Review 95(4): 1076–1108.

Kryshev I. (1995) Radioactive Contamination of aquatic ecosystems following the Chernobyl accident, Journal of Environmental Radioactivity 27(3): 207–219.

Kuchinskaya (2011) Articulating the signs of danger: Lay experiences of post-Chernobyl radiation risks and effects Public Understanding of Science 20(3): 405–421.

Kuchinskaya (2012) Twice invisible: Formal representations of radiation danger Social Studies of Science 43(1): 78–96.

Kuchinskaya (2014) The Politics of Invisibility: Public Knowledge about Radiation Health Effects after Chernobyl MIT Press.

Kuehnast K. and Dudwick N. (2004) Better a Hundred Friends than a Hundred Rubles? Social Networks in Transition—the Kyrgyz Republic. Washington DC: World Bank working paper.

Kuznetsova I. and Round J. (2014) Communities and social care in Russia: The role of Muslim welfare provision in everyday life in Russia's Tatarstan region. International Social Work 57(5): 486–496.

Law, J. and Urry, J. (2004) Enacting the social. Economy and Society 33, 390–410.

Ledneva A. (2004) Ambiguity of Social Networks in post-communist contexts. Working Paper No. 48. School of Slovanicand East European Studies, UCL.

Lefebvre H. (2000) Everyday Life in the Modern World. London: Athlone.

Lonkila A. (1997) Informal Exchange Relations in Post-Soviet Russia: A Comparative Perspective. Sociological Research Online 2(2)

Lonkila M. (1999) Social Networks in Post-Soviet Russia: continuity and change in the everyday life of St Petersburg teachers. Helsinki: Kikimora Publications.

Mæstad, O., and Mwisongo, A. (2011) Informal Payments and the Quality of Health Care: Mechanisms Revealed by Tanzanian Health Workers, Health policy 99(2): 107–115.

Mauss M. (2002) The Gift: the form and reason for exchange in archaic societies. London: Routledge.

Massey D. (1994) Space, Place, and Gender. Cambridge: Polity Press.

Mbembe, J. and Meintjes L. (2003) Necropolitics Public culture 1(5): 11–40.

Ministry of Emergencies of Ukraine (2011) Atlas: Ukraine Radioactive Contamination commissioned by Ministry of Ukraine of Emergencies for Ukraine. Intelligence Systems GEO, Kyiv.

Morris. J (2011) Socially Embedded Workers at the nexus of diverse work in Russia: an ethnography of blue-collar work informalization. International journal of sociology and social policy 11(3): 619–631.

Morris J. and Polese A. (201X) Informal Health and Education Sector Payments in Russian and Ukrainian Cities: Structuring Welfare from Below European Urban and Regional Studies (forthcoming).

Morris, J., & Polese, A. (2014) The informal post-socialist economy: Embedded practices and livelihoods. Routledge.

Morris, J., & Polese, A. (eds.) (2015) Informal Economies in Post-Socialist Spaces: Practices, Institutions and Networks. Palgrave Macmillan.

Newman D. (2006) The lines that continue to separate us: borders in our 'borderless' world, Progress in Human Geography 30(2): 143–161.

Ó Beacháin, D., V. Sheridan and S. Stan (eds) (2012) Life in Post-Communist Eastern Europe After EU Membership. Routledge Contemporary Russia and Eastern Europe.

Oughton D., Bay-Larsen I. and Voigt G. (2009) Social, ethical, environmental and economic aspects of remediation Radioactivity in the Environment 14: 427–451.

Pallot J. & Nefedova T. (2003) Geographical differentiation in household plot production in rural Russia. Eurasian Geography and Economics 44(1): 40–64.

Parkhill, K. A., Butler, C., & Pidgeon, N. F. (2014). Landscapes of threat? Exploring discourses of stigma around large energy developments. *Landscape Research 39*(5): 566–582.

Pavlovskaya M. (2004) Other Transitions: Multiple Economies of Moscow Households in the 1990s Annals of the Association of American Geographers 94: 329–351.

O'Brien, M & Penna, S (2007) Critical Criminology: Chaos or Continuity?, Criminal Justice Review 32(3): 246–255.

Petryna A. (2002) Life Exposed: Biological Citizens after Chernobyl. Oxford: Princeton University Press.

Petryna A. (2004) Biological citizenship: the science and politics of Chernobyl-exposed populations. Osiris 19(1): 250–265.

Petryna A. (2011) Chernobyl's survivors: Paralyzed by fatalism or overlooked by science? Bulletin of the Atomic Scientists 67(2): 30–37.

Phillips S. (2005) Half-Lives and healthy bodies: Discourses on "Contaminated" Food and Healing in Post-Chernobyl Ukraine pp. 286–298 in Watson J. & Caldwell M. [eds] The Cultural Politics of Food and Eating. Blackwell Publishing: Oxford.

Phillips S. (2012) Chernobyl Forever Samatosphere: Science Medicine and Anthropology [accessed via http://somatosphere.net/test/2011/04/chernobyl-forever.html on 29/07/2014]

Pinotti, P. (2012) The Economic Costs of Organized Crime: Evidence from Southern Italy, Working Papers 054,

Polese A. (2006) Border Crossing as a Daily Strategy of Post Soviet Survival: the Odessa-Chisinau Elektrichka, Eastern European Anthropology Review 24(1): 28–37.

Polese, A. (2006b). De jure oder de facto? Die Gesundheits- und Bildungssektoren in der Ukraine. Ukraine Analysen 16: 2–4.

Polese A. (2008) 'If I receive it, it is a gift; if I demand it, then it is a bribe': On the Local Meaning of Economic Transactions in Post-Soviet Ukraine, Anthropology in Action 15(3): 47–60.

Polese A. (2011) Who has the right to forbid and who to trade? Making sense of Illegality on the Polish-Ukrainian border.in Bruns B. & Migglebrink J [eds] Subverting borders: Doing Research on Smuggling and Small Scale Trade. Germany: VS Verlag für Sozialwissenschaften, 21–38.

Polese, A. (2014). Drinking with vova: a ukrainian entrepreneur between informality and illegality. In J. Morris, & A. Polese (Eds.), The informal post-socialist economy: Embedded practices and livelihoods. London and New York: Routledge.

Polese, A., Morris, J., Kovacs, B., & Harboe, I. (2014) 'Welfare states' and social policies in Eastern Europe and the former USSR: where informality fits in? Journal of Contemporary European Studies, 22(2): 184–198.

Rogers A and R. Sheaff (2000) Formal and informal systems of primary healthcare in an integrated system: evidence from the United Kingdom. Healthc Papers 2000 1(2):47–58.

Round J. (2006) Marginalized for a lifetime: The everyday experiences of gulag survivors in post-Soviet Magadan Geografiska Annaler: Series B, Human Geography 88(1):15–34.

Round J. and Williams C. (2012) Coping with the social costs of 'transition': everyday life in post-Soviet Russia and Ukraine in White S. and Moore C. [Eds] Post-Soviet Politics. Sage Publications, London.

Round J., Williams C. C. and Rodgers P. (2008). Everyday tactics and spaces of power: the role of informal economies in post-Soviet Ukraine. Social & Cultural Geography 9(2): 171–185.

Round J. Williams C. C and Rodgers P (2010) The role of domestic food production in everyday life in post-Soviet Ukraine. Annals of the Association of American Geographers 100(5): 1197–1211.

Routh S. (2011) Building Informal Workers Agenda: imagining 'Informal Employment' in Conceptual Resolution of 'Informality. Global Labour Journal 2(3): 208–227.

Rush-Cooper N. (2013) Exposures: Exploring selves and landscapes in the Chernobyl Exclusion Zone PhD dissertation, Durham University

Sik E. (1994) From the multicolored to the black-and-white economy: the Hungarian second economy and the transformation, International Journal of Urban and Regional Research 18(1): 46–70.

Smith A. and Stenning A. (2006) Beyond household economies: articulations and spaces of economic practice in postsocialism Progress in Human Geography 30(2): 190–213.

Sontag S. (1977) On Photography. Penguin: London.

Spinosa, C., Flores, F. and Dreyfus, H. (1997) Disclosing new worlds: entrepreneurship, democratic action and the cultivation of solidarity. Cambridge, MA: MIT Press.

SSPTW Europe (2012) Ukraine: Old Age, Disability, and Survivors in Social Security Programs throughout the world, Europe pp. 206–311 [accessed via http://www.ssa.gov/policy/docs/progdesc/ssptw/2012-2013/europe/ukraine.pdf on 28/07/2014]

Staddon C. (2009) Toward a critical political ecology of human-forest intereactions: collecting herbs and mushrooms in a Bulgarian locality, Transactions of the Institute of British Geographers 34(1): 161–176.

State Statistics Committee of Ukraine (2004) Statistical Yearbook of Ukraine 2003, Kiev: Ukraine.

Stenning A. (2005) Post-socialism and the changing geographies of the everyday in Poland. Transactions of the institute of British Geographers 30(1): 113–127.

Stone R. (2013) Dark Tourism, Heterotopias and Post-Apocalyptic Places: The Case of Chernobyl, in White L. & Frew E [eds] Dark Tourism and Place Identity Melbourne: Routledge, 79–93.

Stryamets N., Elbakidze M., and Angelstam P (2012) Role of non-wood forest products for local livelihood in countries with transition and market economies: case studies in Ukraine and Sweden. Scandinavian Journal of Forest Research 27(1): 74–87.

Tatar, M, Ozgen, H. S. Bayram, P. Belli and P. Berman (2007) Informal Payments in The Health Sector: A Case Study from Turkey, 26(4): 1029–1039.

Hayfaa T., S. Kauser, (2011) The importance of in the career success of Middle Eastern managers, Journal of European Industrial Training 35(5): 467–486.

Van der Veen M. (2013) After Fukushima: Revisiting Chernobyl and the Collapse of the Soviet Union Rethinking Marxism: A Journal of Economics, Culture & Society 25(1): 121–129.

Walker C. (2010) Space, kinship networks and youth transition in Provincial Russia: negotiating urban–rural and inter-regional migration. Europe-Asia Studies 62(4): 647–669.

Willams C. and Round J. (2007) Re-thinking the nature of the informal economy: some lessons from Ukraine. International Journal of Urban and Regional Research 31(2): 425–441.

Williams C., Nadin S., Rodgers P. Round J. and Windebank J. (2011) Mapping the Social Organization of Labour in Moscow: Beyond the Formal/informal Labour Dualism Sociological Research Online 16(1)

Yablokov A, Nesterenko V. and Nesterenko A. (2009) Chernobyl: Consequences of the Catastrophe for People and the Environment New York: Backwell Publishers.

Yang, Mei-hui (1994) Gifts, Favors, and Banquets: The Art of Social Relationships in China.

Yankovska, G., and Hannam, K. (2014) Dark and toxic tourism in the Chernobyl exclusion zone. Current Issues in Tourism 17(10): 929–939.

Yasmin-Pasternak S..(2009) A means of survival, a marker of feasts: mushrooms in the Russian Far East. Ethnology 47(2): 95–107.

The guest at the dining table: economic transitions and informal renegotiations of hospitality[1]

Nashe delo predlozhit, vashe delo otkazatsya (our task is to propose, yours to refuse)

Stumari ghvitsaa (a guest comes from God)

Ne stesnyaysya, a to ostaneshsya golodny (do not be shy or you'll stay hungry)

What is the relationship between hospitality and informality? I have been reflecting on whether it would be worth to use this study in a book on informality. The same question can be asked for the next chapter, on bazaars. However, I see these two chapters as an exercise broadening the scope of works on informality and describing the competition between formal and informal mechanisms. This chapter illustrates the changes in hospitality rituals and how traditional references are renegotiated once people start to have more money than time.

Dmitrievski, Odessa oblast', Saint Dmitri's day. A team of around 15 academics is invited to join a dining company outside the main church, where the locals have covered two 15-meter long tables with all the food one could imagine. A few steps away, on an improvised cooking-fire, cooking pots of one meter in diameter are used to prepare soup, meat and any other kind of food. On the tables all sorts of wines are offered; the wine is produced locally and stored in mineral water bottles.

The feast of Saint Dimitri is the apogee of food consumption in the village and will feed the locals for several days after its end. However, after the meal, some local women ask those who came from far away to take with them one or two bottles of wine and possibly some food. "There [in the city] everything is chemical," they say. "Take our food, it is homemade and genuine, good for your health."

---

1   First published as Abel Polese (2009) " The Guest at the Dining Table: Economic Transition and the Reshaping of Hospitality, Reflections from Batumi and Odessa " *Anthropology of East Europe Review* 27 (1): 65–77. St. Bloomington: Indiana University. Reprint with kind permission.

The city-countryside contrast invoked above and the association of the city with artificial food, and the countryside with "genuine food" seems to suggest that changes in practices of food and alcohol consumption mirror a strong social and economical change in Eastern Europe. I propose to explore these changes through the lens of hospitality, defined here as a positive attitude towards strangers that generates relationships of dependence and potential reciprocity between the guest and the host. Following the approach that objects are not what they are but what they come to be (Thompson 1991), I intend to explore the changing role food and drinks have in different situations and the different value they are given according to the spatial context.

Looking at the social and cultural practices related to food consumption, and comparing them in different contexts, I suggest that it is possible to gain insight into other social practices such as the relationship with the other, with time and with local social habits. The kind of food offered, the way hosts are invited to the dining table, the amount of time spent in the kitchen, and the relationship with homemade food—all these variables permit us to feel a transition in Eastern Europe that, from public spaces, spreads to private ones and affect lifestyles and styles of consumerism (see Mesnil and Michailescu 1998 and Polese 2008). These transitions are increasingly visible when comparing urban and rural contexts.

From 2003 to 2008 I had the chance to experience different kinds of hospitality in a number of post-socialist regions, from Chisinau to Ulan-Ude, in both urban and rural settings, and compare my information with colleagues' and informants' opinions. This gave me a basis for comparison and prompted my further interest when, during my stay in Odessa, I happened to experience several different kinds of hospitality behaviour. I was based in Odessa for almost two years between 2003 and 2006 and as I began to identify some patterns of hospitality in the city, I started collecting ethnographic material. Most of it was through participant observation and informal interviews, sometimes during a dinner or just as a reflection with some informants. During my stay I had the chance to exchange opinions with other colleagues working in the region (and I am grateful to Deema Kaneff and Tanya Richardson) and on several occasions I visited the provinces, spending time in small towns. This gave me enough insight to start thinking comparatively about the differences in hospitality and the influence of urban culture on hospitality practices. In the summer of 2005 I had the chance to do some fieldwork in Georgia related to a project on hospitality on the Black Sea, and I became increasingly fascinated with the way hospitality was lived in that country. In particular I concentrated on the coastal region and visited Poti and Batumi, as urban centres, stopping in several small settlements between the two cities.

Once based in Batumi, I felt an atmosphere similar to the one I was used to in Odessa. The city, capital of the Ajara autonomous republic, is a major Georgian port where a number of ships stop regularly. Thanks to their strategic location, both Odessa and Batumi cities enjoy an economic welfare that is not found elsewhere nearby, but they are still in regions that are less developed than the rest of the country. They have a high level of migration, and constant populations exchanges from the countryside to the rich urban areas, which makes the urban-rural contrast easier to notice.

Starting from the fact that food and drinks seem to have a different meaning in different contexts and they can be used to build up alliance and trust networks, I would suggest that a fast economic transition is urging a number of people to renegotiate the complex rituals linked with hospitality. More specifically, I find that people are proposing a re-elaborated version of local cultures in which traditional rituals become simplified. This, in turn, sheds some light on the ways in which, in urban cultures, hospitality practices developed over time get renegotiated, in terms of quality of food, quantity of time spent in cooking, and the perception of who is a stranger. Ultimately this may lead to the homemade food vs. supermarket food "dilemma." The relationship between homemade and store-bought is ambiguous: on the one hand, homemade food represents genuineness, time and devotion invested into a social relationship; however supermarket food, in some manifestations, as symbol of modernity, can also be well valued in an elaborate code that mixes homemade and processed food.

The case studies presented here are intended to show that hospitality rituals, although surviving marketization and modernization, have gone through a simplification process. This process of simplification is visible to different extents in urban and rural settings, but also in the two different regions analysed. While necessary to the perpetuation of social life and the creation of personal networks, these rituals have been brought into question and challenged by the economic transition. This, in turn, has led to the simplification of some aspects of the rituals, even as attempts are made to keep their core substance unaltered. In this respect food and drinks, the way they are lived and their consumption, is strongly dependent on the economic settings. If we drew a continuum we could see at one extreme the situation in which ample time is available, and thus the cost of labour is very low, and it is possible to make the investments necessary to get fresh food (grow poultry, go fishing, prepare the food at home, produce homemade wine). On the other extreme of the continuum, the economic opportunity of an hour of labour is so high that one prefers to work the maximum amount of time and buy all the food in a supermarket. An intermediate situation may be having time to do shopping in a bazaar, or visiting friends and relatives in rural areas to get homemade food to be prepared at home. Those behaviours are indicative of an economics that is explorable through food and drinks, for people, no matter how busy they are, tend at least to preserve the basic meaning of such rituals and their socio-economic functions.

1 What's So Special about Eating? What All that Food Means

To understand the current meaning of food and drinks in Batumi and Odessa one needs to explore the social relationship with food and drinks over the past years. While during the Soviet period access to basic products was not a major problem, finding some specialised products was a matter of skills and risk. Contributing to this was a situation where the production of luxury goods was extremely specialised. In Riga it was possible to buy the most famous chocolate of the USSR. People traveling to and from Kiev had a chance to buy a Kiev cake, in Odessa visitors would try so secure a bottle of champagne of *Frantsuskii bulvar*, and in Moldova a bottle of *belyi aist* cognac (brandy) or homemade wine. Visiting the south of Ukraine it was possible to buy fresh fruits in spring or summer, in the Caucasus a visitor would buy dried fruits, and in the Far East it was possible to buy "red fish" (trout or salmon dried and salted) or *seledka* (pickled herring).

Such specialised goods were imbued with two kinds of prestige: one was given by the brand, well known throughout the country, and the other from the alleged quality of the product that was genuine and thus appreciated. Although their meaning was different, homemade and shop goods could both to some extent be used for a token of thanks or informal payment, for instance when thanking someone for a service. Little distinction was made between homemade and purchased goods as "substitutes" for money (and perhaps for one another), a situation that changed with the introduction of free market economies (see below). Because of the high amount of forced savings in the Soviet Union, investing one's time in the production of goods revealed itself to be a good strategy. Apart from cash, one could start up a series of exchanges and barter with neighbours and friends that allowed people to acquire desirable things that were not necessarily on the market.

This also encouraged some leisure time practical activities. After the working day one could devote time to a social life and to "hobbies" like alcohol production so that in some cases goods as a commodity might replace money. Producing alcohol, collecting mushrooms or repairing clothes could be bartered with other services or goods, while developing networks of trust among different segments of the population. In addition, since time represented a widely available commodity, it was possible to prepare and exchange homemade food and goods, a practice that sometimes proved advantageous to buying them.

Odessa and Batumi were in a unique position. On the one hand their climate allowed people to take advantage of natural resources: both regions produce good vineyards and the soil is adequate to grow vegetables and fruits, at least some months of the year. They were, and are, also relatively close to other countries like Moldova or Armenia, which facilitates exchanges of different products. Finally, they were two important ports and most shipments to Moscow passed through one of those two cities (where, incidentally, a decent amount of goods disappeared on the way).

An initial change was introduced by the opening up of the countries in the early 1990s, for products became available on the market after an initial transition period, and choice widened rapidly, including Western foods. The symbolic meaning of these Western foods was such that they were sometimes bought for their origins rather than their quality (which was indeed dubious, according to Jennifer Patico (2002)). However, according to several informants, a number of local brands remained competitive with Western food. Going on a business trip to Odessa it was almost a moral obligation to come back with a bottle of *Shampanskoe* (champagne) from *Frantsuzski bulvar*, the name of the street where the factory is located. From Chisinau everybody was expected to bring back a bottle of *Cricova*, and in Georgia wine was one of the national attractions, with bottles of *Saperavi* highly requested. While those goods were available in a limited quantity, there were a number of things that could be bought more easily from the locals themselves, like homemade wine, *nalivka* or *nastoika* (herbal and berry alcoholic drinks).

As a result, during Soviet times daily consumption and social relations tended to be based primarily on homemade alcohol and food. Marketization, introduced recently, has divided the population into at least two categories: those who have enough money to buy in a supermarket (where less time is spent) and those who have enough time to buy at the bazaar (where goods are cheaper) Time is not a commodity that everybody has, homemade food and supermarket food are no longer perfect substitutes for one another as they were in the past. Homemade food is cheaper and allegedly more genuine, but it costs more time, whether in terms of time taken to prepare it or to visit the person who prepared it instead of going to the supermarket. Supermarket food is likely to be more expensive or, at the very least, less "genuine" because it is not homemade, but it saves you much time. Since in urban areas wages have risen much faster than in the countryside, those whose urban dwellers whose earnings are rapidly growing prefer to have less time but more money at their disposal, which enables them to simply buy what they exchanged or bartered before. With leisure time one can buy extra working hours and thus extra earnings, and alcohol or food can be quickly bought in a supermarket.

Market laws therefore influence hospitality and food consumption, and the way food in hospitality rituals is used nowadays mirrors local customs while also unveiling the symbolic meaning of things used to construct alliances. In particular the growing gap between city and countryside can induce us to reflect on the compromises that urban constraints pose, which prompt people to renegotiate in order to accommodate tradition and conciliate it with a working life.

In the next sections, I explore two main themes in two regions, Odessa and Batumi: 1) the rituals associated to hospitality; and 2) the ways different people can be perceived as strangers and potential guests. In these two regions I have experienced hospitality and gathered information on hospitality related attitudes, both in the countryside and urban context, to "taste" the way economic development, marketization and urbanization have reshaped cultural practices and alliance building in post-Soviet territories.

2 What is Hospitality?

Whilst is it accepted that hospitality rituals exist and are widely performed around the globe, the motivations for extending hospitality and engaging in hospitality practices at all seem only partially explored. Starting from a question a colleague asked some years ago, posed as the "Enigma of the gift" (Gerard 1998) I would introduce the "enigma of hospitality": why does a person decide, apparently spontaneously, to offer hospitality to a stranger? How is this person going to choose the object of his or her hospitality? And finally, how is this person going to select the kind of hospitality to be offered?

Hospitality, just like gift exchange, may be regarded, from a Maussian perspective, as a social fact (1924) in which, although the formal obligations and forms of engaging in giving and taking rituals with foreigners can change across cultures, its substance seems quite stable. A gift, for Mauss, is a fundamental structure of the relationship between people in a society, which always retains an element of its giver and involves three obligations: the obligation to give, to receive, and to reciprocate. Whilst giving and receiving are quite straightforward as concepts, some questions may arise about reciprocating.

There is a tendency in anthropology to consider host-guest exchanges as binding and leading to a continuation of the relationship by causing new obligations (Lashley 2000), performing moral authority (Selwyn 2000) or confirming control of the other (Erb 2000). It has also been suggested that the host may expect to become a guest in the future and thus does what others should do with him like in the article *la table sens dessus dessous*' [a very broad translation would be: discovering what is really under the host's table] in which Mesnil and Mihailescu (1998) suggest that some attitudes to strangers might reflect the host's perceptions of the expectations he would have were he to became a guest (though they will be, most likely, deceived).

I would suggest that hospitality, and its rituals, aliment the already intense flow of informal economies and exchanges, though not necessarily in a direct way. In a long term perspective, in which the guest and the host are likely to engage in a lasting relationship, hospitality's rationale may lay behind the fact that such a relationship is supposed to strengthen social ties and boost trust networks among individuals (Heatherington 2001; Herzfeld 1998; Yang 1994). This can go further and generate a kind of favour exchange relationship destined to last (Ledeneva 1998; Lonkila 1997) or a more disengaged one in which commodities, money and favours are a way to pay back a "favour" (Patico 2002; Polese 2008b). However, there might be cases in which reciprocity may not apply, or might not even be expected, as when a host coming from far away is received and honoured and no continuation of the relationship is expected. What would push someone to give with no gain expected?

If we go beyond a materialistic conception of reciprocity, there are a number of ways hospitality can be reciprocated. It would become otherwise impossible to explain why some hosts may be ready to indebt themselves to provide their guests with the best of the best, be this a chicken or some sugar in places where this is a luxury (Cole 2006). In addition one might need to explain the aggressive manner in which hospitality can be manifested, becoming "hellspitality" ("you looked at it, it means you want to eat it!") and obliging the guest to roll away, rather than walk away, from the dinner table (Zanca 2003). What is the gain of forcing guests to accept more food than they can swallow?

If we recall the idea of the "Indian gift" by Parry (1986) hospitality can be considered something that enriches the host morally, before his neighbours, his guest, or God, for the fact of having acted generously. Hospitality can thus be seen as cathartic or as a moral obligation of the host, who is supposed to share with the one who has less (and the guest, once outside his home, definitely has less). Only by taking complete care of the guest may the host present himself as respectable and respectful and fulfil his moral obligations. In addition, if a person is perceived as a prestigious guest in a particular setting, hosting this person will become a source of prestige for the household that hosted him or her, so that receiving guests might increase the respectability and reputation of the house and thus of its occupants (Cole 2006, Visser 1991, Zanca 2003). A guest also brings news and stories from the outside world, which is a way to break up the local routine, and is thus appreciated (Cole 2006). It may ultimately transform unknown people into friends (Selwyn 2000). All this suggests that reciprocity may be achieved in several different ways and that the border between social relationships and money (or commodity) motivated exchanges is more blurred than is generally acknowledged (Patico 2002, Polese 2008b, Raheja 1988, Williams 2005).

In my study on hospitality to strangers on the Black Sea I have suggested some reasons why one might want to be generous to strangers (Polese 2006: 115); the next sections add to this by providing further evidence on practices and expectations of hospitality. While a religious component is certainly present, I had the impression that hospitality was more socially than a religiously motivated, being prompted by the following factors:

1) Curiosity: this may also mean that the obligation to reciprocate is respected—the guest can offer some information, anecdotes and stories to the host.
2) Human fellow-feelings: the basic principle that, if someone is in trouble, that person should be helped.
3) Limits of social welfare: in areas where the state is absent or too busy to take care of its citizens, citizens tend to interact more and create informal structures to make up for failure of formal ones. This applies also to the stranger, once he or she enters the circle.
4) The idea that hospitality is honourable behaviour: this will boost the respectfulness of the host, both in his or her own eyes and in the eyes of others.

5) The perception that a stranger's visit is a gift that produces trust and reciprocity: like in the 'Indian gift' (Parry 1996), the fact that the stranger accepts the host's gifts creates a relationship of trust and (potential) reciprocity

In such a context food (and drinks) comes to assume a symbolic meaning of primary importance, as anthropologists from Van Gennep ([1909] 2004) on have acknowledged (see also Van Gennep et al. 1984). Food becomes thus not the aim but the means to construct alliances and create dependence relationships (Menner, Murcott, and Van Otterloo 1992). The typology of food offered, the way it is prepared and presented, and the time devoted to the guest all become indicators of the perception of the guest, his or her potential prestige, and the gains the guest is expected to bring to the household or at least to the host.

The next sections will explore how social and cultural practices are negotiated and adapted to specific contexts, as well as the ways in which economic development and marketization impact such practices. In line with this, time devoted to the guest depends on the prestige a guest will bring and consequently the food offered will be chosen accordingly. In addition, the opening up of these formerly Soviet countries (Ukraine and Georgia) means that a much wider range and variety of food and drinks are available, so that imported and domestic foods today are systematically combined in various contexts so to provide the perfect combination for a given situation. Even though the substance of hospitality rituals has been altered, it becomes all the more important to preserve them, since they function as a starting point for further economic exchanges. To explore these nuances, I offer stories of my own personal experiences as the beneficiary of hospitality rituals, as well as the hospitality stories told me by friends, colleagues, and others.

3 Who is a Guest? Who is a Stranger?

There are places where hospitality enwraps you from the very moment you cross the border of a country, like I experienced in Batumi, where people seem ready to share with the guest whatever they have. As one informant (a French traveler) reported:

> I stopped being a vegetarian when travelling in the former USSR. You know, a Westerner, easy to spot, hiking around in the mountains is pretty much an attraction. You are walking in the mountains and they see a foreigner...they look nearby and they see mutton...so on their right they have a foreigner and on their left mutton...the natural consequence is a mutton barbecue. And you cannot refuse that meat 'because you are a vegetarian' (personal communication, translated by the author from French)

I once was invited for a dinner in Batumi and, after a number of courses (I do not dare to count them!), while collapsing on my chair, incredibly the man of the house started looking around, asking what else he could offer. Such an engaged hospitality is time consuming and thus not possible (or not worth it) to offer to every person you come across. What to do if you do not have enough time? The words of an Ukrainian friend provide some clues:

> We went to use an international telephone and the lady asked where we were from. Once our status of 'guest of the country' was acknowledged, she wanted to act as host but could not close the shop and spend time with us. Her choice was to propose to us to come later in the day and she would make us try a real homemade *khachapuri* [Georgian oven baked bread with cheese inside](personal communication, translated by the author from Russian).

Walking in the centre of Odessa or Batumi it is not likely (though not excludable) that you will be invited into someone's house; such a scenario is, however, easily possible in the province (countryside). A Ukrainian colleague found a very singular way to provide a group of conference speakers (of which I was one) with accommodations in Odessa *oblast'*. We arrived in a small town and went straight to the Old Believers' Church, whose priest had been previously informed of the imminent arrival of around 20 people. After a few minutes I heard a loud voice from outside: 'Pilgrims have arrived!' and the local community of Old Believers come around to pick up two or more 'pilgrims' who would be their guest for two nights.

Hospitality may be considered a full time job by the host. However, under certain conditions this changes and may even be rather reversed, so that the best hospitality is considered to be the most unobtrusive one. In this scenario, the best thing to do when you have guests is to leave them alone as much as they want, not invade their personal space, and act upon the guest's request, not on one's (the host's) own initiative. The same is expected from guests, who should not be a burden to the daily life of their host.

Time that the host will devote to the guest is one of the main differences between urban and rural settings. In places where time is a cheap commodity, it will be relatively easy to dedicate more time to your guest; this can be performed by a few members of the family, with the working ones joining the company only in the evening. However in an urban context, which usually requires all members of the family to work, this will be lived differently. The host might apologize, or perceive this as natural, but will not be able to spend all his or her time with the guest.

Where hospitality is a 'full time job', if the host is not able to provide the guest with 'minimal standards' or if his house is not 'honourable', he might then refrain from inviting a guest. Hospitality in this case is not perceived as a commodity (I give you my house) but as a service (I give you my house and put myself at your disposal), so that an 'empty' house (emptied from the host) is no commodity to be offered to strangers, as a fellow Georgian reported.

> In Georgia the house is holy. If your enemy comes into your house you have to treat him like your guest, not your enemy. They may become again your enemy [hopefully not] once they leave your household (personal communication, translated by the author from Russian).

Engaging in a host-guest relationship ultimately depends on two things: the person's desire to be perceived as a guest, and the perception that locals have of that person. This will eventually determine the number of material contact points the potential guest and host will have. Locking oneself up in a hotel room certainly invites less hospitality that walking freely around, especially outside the city centre. Likewise, even in the most hospitable cultures, you are more likely to be perceived as a tourist than as a guest if you hang around in some specifically designated 'tourist areas'. Hospitality, once you are perceived as a guest, will concretise as an attitude that people would not direct towards locals. For example, people can smile at you for no reason, or show some interest and stop to talk to you.

Anton Krotov is not an anthropologist but one of the most hardcore hitchhikers in the world. His reflections on travelling are extremely useful to understanding how to enter a host-guest relationship. Born in Moscow, he should have passed one million kilometres hitchhiked at the time of writing, spending half the year on expeditions to Asia or Africa and the rest of the time writing books. Krotov writes books on how to get free rides not only by car, but also by train, ship, regular buses and even airplanes; he also suggests the easiest way to sleep or eat on a the minimal budget (his principle is 'spend on the road as much money you would spend at home'). His main advice to get a free ride is to "introduce yourself as different, as not from the reality of your potential 'host' (driver). Win his interest somehow, with a story, an anecdote, a veiled request for help. Everybody is good in his heart, you just have to find the way to this person and this person will help you."

I consider this one of the main points underneath any host-guest relationship. Your host must become interested in you as a person, in your specific situation, and then will be willing to offer a gift of hospitality. Hospitality is not necessarily in the form of a dinner or a home stay. Hospitality is everywhere: it can be a smile, information, a small gift or hidden help that you will never discover. Once host and guest are interested, and ready, to engage in a relationship of reciprocity, a material point of contact has to be created; then one can begin the negotiations on which will depend the nature and the result of an exchange and its urgency, depending on how long the guest will stay, and how easy it will be for the guest and host to meet again. (However, in places where time is an expensive commodity, contact points with the locals or with neighbours tend to be reduced.) As a general rule, the smaller and the more relaxed the place, the more the potential contact points increase. But in some places it might be much easier than elsewhere, as two Russian informants reported:

> Hitchhiking on the side of the road in Georgia you will most likely strike the attention of a local driver who will take you home, feed you, and then put you on the next coach to your destination, and there will be no way to refuse his hospitality without offending him (personal communication, translated from Russian by the author).

We were once hitchhiking from Batumi to Tbilisi. The police stopped us and asked what we were doing. We explained our aim and itinerary and they listened carefully. Then they stopped a car and told the driver (who seemed afraid of the 'police control'), that we were guests of their country and he had to take care of us and bring us to his final destination. They even said, "We are taking down your license plate number, because we want to be sure that everything will be okay with them" (personal communication).

Hospitality in Batumi, as in a number of other countries, may look almost aggressive. It is quite likely that the visitor can be "hijacked" from his destination and will have to change his plans. Once a truck driver who was to take me for 20 km offered to bring me with him to the border with Ossetia, a 12 hour drive; another time when travelling in the province I had to insist to be left at my destination and not be "kidnapped" to Batumi. In Odessa and surrounding areas this never happened: people will be much more reserved and, although you will enjoy genuine generosity once you pass their doorstep, this will be not as easy as in Ajara. It seems, thus, that a stranger and the company of a stranger, has a different value in the two regions.

4 Step I: Entertaining the Host's Belly

Once perceived as a potential guest, one is likely be invited to visit a household. The kind of attention the guest will receive and the kind of rituals in which he or she will be engaged are strongly dependent on the cultural context. In the city, where ancestral practices are often modified, coming for dinner means one arrives when the dinner is ready. In contrast, in the countryside one is more likely to be present during part of the food preparation process. If in the countryside homemade food is the rule, the city will be much more variable and time will be a more precious a commodity, whether in terms of time devoted to cooking, to entertaining, or simply spending time together.

The man of the house will be expected to entertain 'his' guests with tea and conversation. The classic Soviet tea is black, and the custom has remained, although green tea is now available. A *zavarka,* in both Odessa and Batumi, will be prepared by pouring boiling water into a teapot well filled with tea to brew (tea can be in packets or loose); the brew is then poured into big cups or mugs and warm water is added. This gives each person the possibility to decide how strong to take his or her tea. Boiling water will be prepared and poured from a kettle or a samovar into the cups, which are brought from the kitchen or taken out of a glass shelf. A more modern alternative is a mug with a packet of tea and boiling water for each person.

The host (family) is meanwhile supposed to entertain their guests and cook at the same time. Gender specialization will help out in this. The man (or men) of the house will spend time with the guest and make sure the guest does not feel lonely, whereas the women will have a double role of cooking and entertaining. A modern substitute for the host is a television, which sometimes seems to be perceived as part of the family. The guest will be placed in front of a screen with a remote control and told to "relax". This will allow the host to keep the situation under control while doing other things and periodically entering the room to check that everything is okay.

It is not unlikely that more than one generation of women lives in the house and their roles are distinct. The owner of the house must take care of the whole preparation process whereas the other generations are supposed to help out. Female hosts younger than the 'main host' are supposed to prove their ability to be good wives and thus will help in the preparation, whereas females of the older generations have to make sure that everything is done properly.

The guest is hungry. This is a primary assumption and the guest has to eat as much as needed to placate his ravenous hunger. If visiting more than one household, the guest will be pulled into a spiral of endless eating with no possibility to refuse. The only exceptions are national feasts where it is understood that the guest might be visiting several households and will have to eat in each of them. Still, the host has to make sure the guest does not leave his household 'hungry'.

Eating has two main symbolic meanings. The first one is mutual recognition as host and guest. By offering food the host is making clear that the guest is welcome and is building a relationship of trust. The second symbolic meaning has to do with duty. By feeding the guest the host is also fulfilling his duties; he is creating dependence and gratitude and is proposing himself as a honourable person. It is of no matter that this dependence might never be of use in his life; it is important to know that it exists.

Provisioning before the guest comes is a must, as long as it is possible. If not, the dinner has to look special somehow:

> Two of us were picked up from the street and invited into a house in Batumi. This was a last minute invitation so that purchases for the dinner were already done. The man of the house asked his sons to go for some beer to distinguish the current dinner from the one they would have had without us (personal communication, translated from Russian by the author).

Hospitality rituals come to be renegotiated once lack of time becomes evident. Not only is time short in the city, but also the renegotiation of gender roles means that some women now spend less time in the kitchen. Once when a woman in Odessa invited me to her home for dinner, she produced some *farshirovanaya ryba* (stuffed fish), joking that she had just prepared it and put into a supermarket box. This is a long and complicated dish to prepare and she was trying to explain in a polite way that her working life allowed no time for preparing such a dinner.

5 Food without Borders: The Dinner

As noted above, the main assumption nearly everywhere is that the guest is starving and has to be fed. This can play out in a more or less aggressive way but it will happen and the guest will be invited (or ordered) to eat beyond his or her capacities. The number of dishes in a meal varies and it is incremented according to the guest, his or her importance and the occasion. It might also depend on the family economic possibilities but there is the possibility that the family will indebt itself to provide the best food, a scenario more likely to take place in rural areas.

The first distinction that applies is the 'home-supermarket' distinction. It is considered much more 'honourable' to feed the host with homemade food. The more the process is retrievable to the house the better: a cake has to be home baked, it will be all the more valued if eggs are from the house and vegetables from the garden, or even if the chicken is from the courtyard (or some neighbours have them). In that case the host might insist even more strongly that the guest eat heartily, since the quality of the food is guaranteed: the host 'knows the chicken that lay those eggs,' or know that 'they grow those vegetables with no chemical fertilisers'.

A second distinction (mentioned above), the city-countryside juxtaposition, might also morph into a distinction made between 'developed countries' versus 'less developed but more natural ones,' or simply a local versus non-local distinction. The guest will be advised to eat more because 'it is all ours', meaning that hosts are consciously offering products that are natural and prepared in a natural way, in contrast to those from the city.

In cities, distinctions are made between bazaars (open-air or covered markets) and supermarkets as sources for food. Shopping at the bazaar is more time consuming and has uncertainty, food can be extremely fresh and made with love but also almost rotten. Western style supermarkets are perceived as generally safer and less time consuming, so in the city there might be a tendency to provision there. A general rule might be the following: as long as one has time and is able to tell good meat or vegetables from bad ones, the bazaar is preferred.

Dishes themselves are hierarchized. There should be a main dish, and a number of side dishes from which one is supposed to start. Usually the main dish will consist of meat or fish, but not both. In addition the classic barbecue (*shashlik*) is made of meat, despite the fact that both Batumi and Odessa are on the sea. The main host will then guide the guests by indicating the order and hierarchy of dishes to be consumed, but meat will be approached after a number of entrees, like salad, *khachapuri* (bread) and other vegetables. Once the dinner is over the tea ritual will start again but with less fear that the guests will eat too much so that more sweets may be served along.

6 Discovering your Limits: Drinking

As a general rule, eating and drinking are complementary ways to construct alliances, brotherhoods and trust relationships. Getting drunk with someone means coming to trust this person, to trust that even in weaker conditions this person will not abuse you, and you are mutually responsible for one another's safety. There is no rule on when to start drinking, even though one might prefer to drink at the end of the day, after all duties are over. There are numerous exceptions to this rule and the Russian saying 'drink in the morning and you will have the whole day free' warns the anthropologist that he or she is just as likely to be encouraged to begin drinking at 10am as at 10 pm. However, 'heavy' drinking usually is reserved for the evening, at least in the city.

In the Georgian countryside I was told by one villager, "I have friends who like to fight, and spend time fighting with one another, other friends like to smoke...but I just like getting drunk." Subsequently he sent a younger brother to buy some transparent alcohol (whose origins I dared not ask), bread, tomatoes and cucumbers so we could spend the rest of the afternoon toasting together. This scene seems rather absent in the city, where the guest will be invited to drink mainly as a social occasion or to construct an alliance, during or after dinner, rather than as an alternative way of spending time.

On a train to Odessa I was approached by a soldier: "Excuse me...I do not want to bother you...would you mind drinking with me? My mother gave me a good bottle of cognac but I feel silly drinking alone." That was perhaps my longest night on a train and an anecdote to be told in future evenings.

There is a Russian saying, 'no matter how much vodka you buy, you will have to run to the shop twice anyway.' This seems to be incredibly true although in the countryside alcohol is stored in bigger quantities and one just has to run 'twice' to another room. The availability of products has prompted an elaboration of tastes and several kinds of alcohol may be at the disposal of the guest, who can choose between wine, vodka and cognac, and *shampanskoe, nalivka* or even beer may be an option.

Toasting is a complicated ritual and the length of toasts seems correlated with the quantity of alcohol already swallowed. But in my experience post-Soviet countries are unique for the fantasy and diversity people have for toasting, wishing all kinds of good to everybody, touching every aspect of people's life, from health to love to friendship. In Ajara I almost passed as impolite several times because toasts are long: the host might start telling a long story or making a long wish, stop, reflect for a while...and start again so that it was not clear to me when one should drink. In Odessa toasts might also be elaborate (with the third toast normally to love) but will rarely compare to Georgian ones in length.

If your glass is full you are supposed to drink, and refilling comes just before the toast. At any given moment, somebody will feel the urgent need to give a toast; people will hurriedly scan all the glasses on the table to spot those that need a refill. Sometimes this will mean that they will have to ask the toast-person to hold his toast for a few more seconds to allow time to refill.

Incidentally, drinking rarely comes alone. The Russian expression *zakuska* means something you can 'bite' (zakusivat') while drinking. It is habit in Odessa and Batumi to immediately fill your stomach with something to limit the effects of the alcohol. The classic *zakuska* will be salted cucumber or tomato but anything will do, from bread to fruit juices (though I once was told of persons who used vodka as *zakuska* for vodka), the important thing is to stuff something down your stomach to better withstand alcohol's short and long term effects.

7   Final Reflections on Hospitality, Food and Guests

Following what I have called the "ethylical transition in Eastern Europe" (Polese 2008), a hospitality transition is happening in Eastern Europe, prompting the host to adopt a more disengaged and time saving approach. Rituals are being renegotiated and cut shorter, while their modality and meaning seem to remain similar. Hospitality rituals thus become affected by a number of factors, including perceptions of neighbours and neighbourhood, conception and perception of time and space, and perception of oneself and the other in socio-economic relationships. In this context, the narrowing of distances has further altered the perception of guests and their importance in many in people's mind. The dichotomy 'homemade food vs. factory food' has acquired new significance and the social meaning of a purchased good lies in conferring social status to the giver and the taker, a distinction that is less visible with homemade alcohol or food. The compromise that the city seems to have found depends on time availability and use of time.

Recalling the most famous quote 'time is money' we can propose that the time devoted to a guest is a loss in economic opportunity, and thus the host might be less reticent to spend more time for the guest, once time becomes precious a commodity. Time is needed to cook homemade food, prepare homemade alcohol, entertain the guest and follow all the traditional rituals that were elaborated in a moment when time was abundant for ordinary people.

Hospitality rituals become then renegotiated, but their complexity remains. In some contexts the guest will be devoted all possible attention, but in other contexts where time is short the host will have to elaborate a new strategy: showing respect and devotion to the guest without taking too much time from income-related activities. The process of food preparation will be one of the first to be sacrificed, with less complex dishes and more supermarket ingredients. Drinking rituals might be reduced or circumscribed to the dinner, when food will help to limit effects of alcohol better than *zakuski*. Finally, the perception of a stranger and the decision of whom is granted status as a guest will also be affected, and the number of times one becomes able to engage in such rituals will decrease. However the friendships, the genuineness and the good moments—these, at least, seem to remain.

Cited works

Cole, S. (2006) Hospitality and Tourism in Ngadha: An Ethnographic Exploration in Lashley, Conrad, Paul Lynch, Alison Morrison Hospitality: A Social Lens, London: Elsevier.

Du Boulay, J. (1991) Strangers and gifts: Hostility and hospitality in rural Greece. Journal of Mediterranean Studies 1(1): 37–53.

Erb M. (2000) Understanding Tourists, interpretations from Indonesia, Annals of Tourism Research 27(3) 709–736.

Gerard, M. (1998) Essai sur le don. Humanités Modernes 113: 67–72.

Harrison, G. (1999) Corruption, development theory and the boundaries of social change', Contemporary Politics 5 no. 3: 207–220.

Heatherington, T. (2001). In the Rustic Kitchen: Real Talk and Reciprocity. Ethnology 40 (4): 329–345.

Herzfeld, M. (1988) The Poetics of Manhood: Contest and Identity in a Cretan Mountain Village. Princeton: Princeton University Press.

Lashley C. (2000) Towards a Theoretical Understanding, in C Lashley and E Morrison (eds.) In Search of Hospitality: Theoretical Prospects and Debates Oxford: Butterworth Heinemann.

Ledeneva, A. (1998) Russia's economy of favours: 'Blat', networking and informal exchange. Cambridge: Cambridge University Press.

Lonkila, M. (1997) Informal exchange relations in post-soviet Russia: a comparative perspective. Sociological Research Online 2 (3) www.socresonline.org.uk/socresonline/2/2/9.html (last accessed 5 March 2007)

Malinowsli, B. (1922) The Argonauts of the Western Pacific. London: Routledge and Kregan Paul.

Mauss, M. ([1924], 1990) The Gift: Forms and functions of exchange in archaic societies. London: Routledge.

Mennel S, A. Murcott and A. Van Otterloo (1992) The Sociology of Food: Eating diet and Culture. London: Sage.

Mesnil M. and V. Mihailescu (1998) La table sens dessus dessous. MAUSS Recherches 12: 185–194.

Parry, J. and M. Bloch (eds.) (1989) Money and the Morality of Exchange, Cambridge: Cambridge University Press.

Parry, J. (1986) The gift, the Indian gift and the 'Indian gift'. Man 21: 453–473.

Patico, J. (2002) Chocolate and cognac: Gifts and the recognition of social worlds in post-soviet Russia. Ethnos 67(3): 345–368.

Pelkmans, M. (2006) Defending the border: identity, religion, and modernity in the Republic of Georgia. Cornell University Press.

Polese, A. (2008) Du samogon a la vodka de supermarche. Regards sur est 49.

Polese, A. (2008) 'If I receive it, it is a gift; if I demand it, then it is a bribe': On the Local Meaning of Economic Transactions in Post-Soviet Ukraine. Anthropology in Action, 15(3), 47–60.

Polese, A. (2006) The good Samaritan. In Man of the global south: a reader ed. Adam Jones, 113–118. London: Zed Books

Raheja, G. (1988) The Poison of the Gift. Chicago: University of Chicago Press.

Selwyn T. (2000) An Anthropology of Hospitality. In Lashley C (2000) Towards a Theoretical Understanding. In C Lashley and E Morrison (eds.) In Search of Hospitality: Theoretical Prospects and Debates Oxford: Butterworth Heinemann.

Thomas, N. (1991) Entangled Objects: Exchange, Material Culture, and Colonialism in the Pacific. Cambridge, Mass.: Harvard University Press.

Van Gennep, A. ([1909] 2004) The Rites of Passage. London: Routledge.

Van Gennep, A., Pelizzo, A., and Marić, S. (1984) Coutumes et croyances populaires en France. Paris: Le chemin vert.

Visser M. (1991) The Rituals of Dinner. London: Penguin.

Watson, J. and M. Caldwell (eds) (2004) The Cultural Politics of Food and Eating, London: Blackwell.

Werner, C. (2002) Gifts, Bribes and Development in Post-Soviet Kazakhstan' in Jeffrey H. Cohen and Norbert Dannhaeuser (eds.) Economic Development: an Anthropological Approach (Walnut Creek, Lanham, New York, Oxford: Altamira Press), 183–208.

Weiner, A. (1992) Inalienable Possessions: The Paradox of Keeping While Giving. Berkley and Oxford: University of California Press.

Williams, C. (2005) A Commodified World? Mapping the limits of capitalism, Zed, London.

Yang, M. (1994) Gifts, favours and banquets: the Art of social relationships in China. Ithaca and London: Cornell University Press.

Zanca, R. (2003) "Take! Take! Take!" Host-Guest Relations and All that Food: Uzbek Hospitality Past and Present. Anthropology of East Europe Review, 21(1), 8–16.

Why bazaars are not wiped out by supermarkets: reflections on a possible bazaar economy[1]

With Aleksandr Prigarin

1 Introduction: the role of bazaars in Odessa

Since Polanyi's forecast of his "great transformation", a growing number of scholars have considered informal economic practices, and in general the informal sector, as deficiencies of economic systems that would otherwise tend towards complete formalisation. Although challenged by evidence (ILO 2002, OECD 2002) the predominant assumption, since then, has remained that the economic situation of a country affects the volume and role of informality. In contrast, a small emergent stream of literature has begun to suggest alternative accounts and reasons that prompt actors to engage with informal economic practices (Escobar 1995, Gibson-Graham 1996, Nelson and Smith 2009, Williams 2004).

Starting from this standpoint, this essay draws from, and contributes to, this direction in emergent literature by analysing the role and function of the bazaar (or bazaars) in the post-socialist world and in particular in Odessa, a major Ukrainian port on the Black Sea. It is suggested that their survival, despite quick marketisation and mushrooming of Western-style supermarkets, is based on factors that economic analyses can only partially grasp. In contrast, we concentrate on the symbolic meaning of the bazaar, as institution, to suggest that some of its features can only be appreciated when looking at it through the lenses of diverse or informal economies. We see them as institutions with a strong capacity to evolve and adapt throughout time

---

[1] First published as Abel Polese and Aleksandr Prigarin (2013) "On the Persistence of Bazaars in the newly Capitalist World: Reflections from Odessa" *Anthropology of East Europe Review* 32 (2): 110–136. St. Bloomington: Indiana University. Reprint with kind permission.

and compete with more economically-effective competitors like supermarkets.

Our aim is to show that the survival of the bazaar, and the niche it has been earning in post-1991 Odessa, is not only due to its low prices but also other factors. We refer here to the bazaar's capacity to evolve and adapt, providing not only always different demand-driven goods but being able to respond to cultural and spiritual needs (by giving a sense of continuity to tradition and culture) as well as offering socialisation and networking opportunities. To illustrate this feature we concentrate our analysis on the social and cultural settings in which the bazaar has been located, fulfilling spiritual and social needs of the city as well as giving a sense of cultural continuity that Odessans are proud of.

Originally a place where meat, vegetables and subsistence goods were sold, bazaars, in Odessa, have evolved to places where virtually everything can be found, be this food, clothes, furniture, legal or illegal goods. Our case studies are drawn from what we deem the two most representative bazaars in Odessa. 7-oj Km ("7th kilometer"), located seven kilometers outside the city, has been growing exponentially since 1989, when it was moved out of the city centre. It now occupies an area of 170 acres (for comparison, the largest shopping mall in the US is 96 hectares (Myers 2006)) and has earned a reputation for extremely cheap goods but also for all sorts of illegal trade. In contrast, Privoz, located in the city centre, has seen a gradual formalisation of its activities and its offspring "New Privoz" is an elegant mall, built as an extension of the historical bazaar Privoz, with some of the newest and most fashionable shops that can be found in the city.

Methodologically, we draw from several different sources: one is a survey of historical documents and secondary sources on the city, complemented by informal interviews with two generations of Odessans identified during several long term research stays in 2005/2006 and 2012/2013 and by 4 focus groups conducted in 2012/2013 with shoppers. Finally, participant observation by the authors has served to complete the picture. One of the authors (Polese) has been spending two years in the city to complete his PhD project and devoted a substantial amount of time to the study of bazaars in Ukraine; the other (Prigarin) is a resident of the city with extensive research experience in, and long term commitment to, ethnographical studies of the region.

Sources have been anonymised and fictive names used in order to protect our informants.

2 On the persistence of informal economic practices in the (post-Soviet) world

The word transition, or transitional, has often been employed, in post-socialist studies among others, to point at phenomena that could be considered transitory or "moving towards" something that would be then stable or more "normal". Notwithstanding this, more than twenty years after the beginning of this transition, it is still unclear a) how long this transition will last, and b) how long a transition ought to last before one can acknowledge that it might not be a transition but simply a different system, with its values, dynamics and actors.

Scholars from various disciplines have engaged with work aimed at understanding the post-socialist transformation and economic practices (formal and informal) have been studied from political, economic, anthropological and sociological standpoints. A distinctive position is held by those scholars seeing informality as transitory and condemned to disappear as soon as the country in question can set up the right structures, institutions and policies that will facilitate formalisation of the social and economic life. Within this position, two extremes visions exist. On the one hand we have the classic attempts to fight corruption, a phenomenon that has fed an increasing "anti-corruption industry" (Sampson 2004, 2010); on the other one we have those defined as ultra-liberal (Rose-Ackerman 2010) who see corruption, and in general informal exchanges, as making up for market inefficiency or excessive red tape. Anthropologists who have partially tapped from the ultra-liberal argument have suggested that informality springs out of a tension between the state and the citizen (Humphrey and Mandel 2002, Lomnitz 1988) whilst economists, especially from New Institutional Economics, have sometimes seen the solidarity networks generated by informality in an economic-functionalist perspective (Ergbert 2005).

A second view holds that informal economic practices are generated by the incapacity of certain actors to enter the formal sector (de Soto 1989, 2002). Also in this case, two sub-directions are visible. Some scholars maintain that those excluded from the formal sector would happily participate in the formal economic life of a society but current conditions make this difficult (Cross 2001, de Soto 1989, Perry and Maloney 2007). Others argue that even those remaining in the informal sector are all the same capable to participate to the economic and political life of their society, although in different ways (Scott 1985, Gupta 1995) and that the formal and the informal are both important because they complement one another (Harth 2005).

The above-mentioned positions imply that costs and benefits of an attitude, a behaviour, or an action are not only fully measurable but also measurable economically or monetarily. The gains of staying informal or going formal seem to depend mostly on prospective economic benefits. Whilst agreeing that there is a correlation between the economic behaviour of a state and the amount of its shadow or informal activities (Bovi 2003), a growing body of literature by scholars in anthropology, human geography and public economics has been suggesting that informal, diverse, or shadow economies are not necessarily the result of an economic choice and that, to understand the phenomenon, one might want to go beyond the capitalist framework many works have been injected with (Gibson-Graham 1996). Retrieving the distinction between the community and the market realms that persists in every economy (Gudeman 2001, 2008) anthropologists have shown that gains in economic exchanges are not necessarily material (Parry 1986, Parry and Bloch 1989, Pardo 1996) and that there is a market for "spiritual needs". The value of informality, in this perspective, is not measurable in material terms, a thing that questions more materialistic approaches in the study of post-socialism (Gugushvili 2011, Keller and Robert 2011). The difficulty of clearly distinguishing between the market and the community (Rasanayagam 2003, 2011), the society (Hann and Harth 2005) or political processes (Isaacs 2010, 2011, Polese 2010) has pointed at a gap in theory that has encompassed several disciplines to the debate on the nature of diverse or informal economies (Community Economies Collective 2001; Morris 2011, 2013; Morris and Polese 2013; Samers 2005; Stenning, Smith, Rochovská and Swiatek 2010; Williams and Windebank 1998).

This paper furthers a concern of postfeminist geographies about the monolithical notion of capitalism and its role as sole possible economic system to be applied to the modern world (Gibson Graham

1996, Gillian 1993, McDowell 1993, Moss 2007). We endorse the idea that exchanges in a capitalist world may not always be money-motivated (Pardo 1996, Williams 2005) and that the (fungible) social capital (Bourdieu 1980) some transactions generate may make up for the lack of economic capital accumulated (Zanca 2003)˙. Other scholars have demonstrated the multi-faceted functions of the bazaars (Cieleska 2013, Humphrey and Skvirskaja 2010, Ozcan 2010, Polese 2006) and in particular their capacity to foster informal exchanges.

What is interesting in the case of Odessa, and the "dichotomy supermarket—bazaar" (Polese 2009), is the competition between tradition and modernity, sterilised and home-made products. In spite of supermarkets mushrooming, the bazaar has been evolving to occupy a niche in the economic and social life of Odessans and this is not necessarily, or not only, depending on the low-price of the products; in contrast, in some cases prices might be higher (or higher is the likelihood to be ripped off), conditions might be worse (no trolleys, cold in winter). Bazaars, in this respect, incarnate a desire to concentrate on values other than monetary ones and that the main reasons why the bazaar has survived in Odessa are twofold. First, the new demand in consumption has prompted a transformation of bazaars from a place where things happen to a cultural and economic space where traditions are preserved, social relationship enhanced and transactions, not necessarily money-oriented, are carried out. Second, originally a place where meat, vegetables and subsistence goods were sold, bazaar, in Odessa have evolved into places where virtually everything can be found, be this food, clothes, furniture, legal or illegal goods.

The transformation of the city has caused bazaars to evolve from place into space over the years. We draw here from the definition of place as a locale, that is a setting and scale for people's daily actions and interactions (Castree 2009), which has also been the starting point of Tanya Richardson's works on the city of Odessa (Richardson 2008, 2009). However this definition has geographical limits, not only given the role of place-based agency, but also in that it varies from place to place (Derek 1982, Pred 1986). Such limits have been acknowledged to suggest that the global, the international and people's place-based agency are interrelated in an approach that shifts attention from an overemphasized historical dimension of phenomena to a more conscious awareness of how deeply dynamics of power, especially those created in capitalism, are inscribed in spatial relations (Giddens 1984; Smith 1984; Soja 1989).

Space, in this case, is conceived as folded into social relations through practical activities (Harvey 1996), paving the way to an idea of space as undergoing continual construction as a result of the agency of things encountering each other in more or less organised circulations (Thrift 2009). By so doing so space is no longer viewed as a fixed and absolute container where things are passively embedded, but as a co-production of those proceedings, as a process in process (Thrift 2009). Agency and reproduction of space, in this respect, become key issues that other authors studying the city have explored (Richardson 2008; Sapritsky 2011, 2012) and which we'll take as a starting point to show a unique degree of entanglement between the bazaar and the city, with the former following the evolution of the latter and its necessities from a topographic and product-wise perspective so as to incarnate the city's desires and (evolution of) consuming habits.

3 The origins of bazaars in Odessa

The two most prevalent characteristics of Odessa in local historical literature are possibly multi-ethnicity and trade (Bukh 1876, 1909; Skal'kovskii 1839), both of which have been entangled in a mutually-dependent relationship: multiculturality, it was often reported, impacted the development of (international) trade which, in turn, had an impact on the diversity of the city (Odessa 1895).

Once hosting a Greek colony on the Black Sea, the region of Odessa was occupied by a number of populations during the Middle Ages. The Crimean Khanate, the Grand Duchy of Lithuania and the Golden Horde, among others, were all trying to secure this piece of land. Conquered by the Ottoman Empire after 1529 it became part of the Yedisan region and in the 18th century the Ottomans rebuilt a fortress on the remains of an ancient city known as Hacibey (Hadjibey, named after Haci and Giray; nowadays Hacibey is a port in the outskirts of town) and then named the place "Yeni Dunya" (New World). The region passed to the Russian Empire as a result of the Russo-Turkish wars (1787–1792) to become known under the name of *Novorossiya* (New Russia). From 1794 the name of Odessa appears in historical registers thanks to the desire of Ekaterina (Catherine) the Great to build a bastion of defence against future invasions, and the city developed extremely rapidly (Sapozhnikov 1999). Herlihy (1977, 1989) compares the city to Chicago, in terms of growth in the 19th century, but taking advantage of the fact that no fire destroyed it.

As reported by Herlihy, according to the 1897 All Russian Census in terms of religious affiliation only 56% of the population was Orthodox Christians or Old Believers. A good many were Jews, about 32%, so people from other religious groups, mostly Muslims, would have to be in the mix of the rest of the 12%. From 1795 to 1814 the population of Odessa reached 20,000 people, having increased 15 times since its foundation. This was due to a desire to populate the city as quick as possible, to make it a solid defence against Ottoman attacks, so that the authorities welcomed whoever wanted to settle into the city. Odessa became, since its inception, a shelter for people wanted by the police elsewhere in the world. Local authorities, however, were ready to turn a blind eye on the past of new settlers, and even offer land to them, as long as they contributed to the growth of the city.

Despite politically leaving the Muslim world, the city's cultural foundations draw, at least partially, on institutions and practices that perpetuate its Muslim traditions. This is visible in gathering places, with big bazaars in the city being as old as the city itself, but also in consumerism habits with a factory of *rahat lukum* and other similar sweets well spread in the city, and the fact that mutton is more popular than pork meat, which is otherwise widely consumed in the rest of the country. Because of its Ottoman legacy the bazaar was first developed as wide open with few kiosks or shops. This is probably due to the Ottoman classification, according to which a bazaar is a large square with traders coming in the morning and leaving in the evening, whereas a *çarşı* is more similar to the set of covered shops and roads that elsewhere may be called *souq* (See Gharipour 2012). This conception of the market would eventually allow bazaars to migrate more easily than *souq*, a phenomenon that happened several times throughout the history of the city.

4 The morphology and function of bazaars of Odessa

Figure 1 Odessa, plan of the city with location of city bazaars, 1855 (private collection)

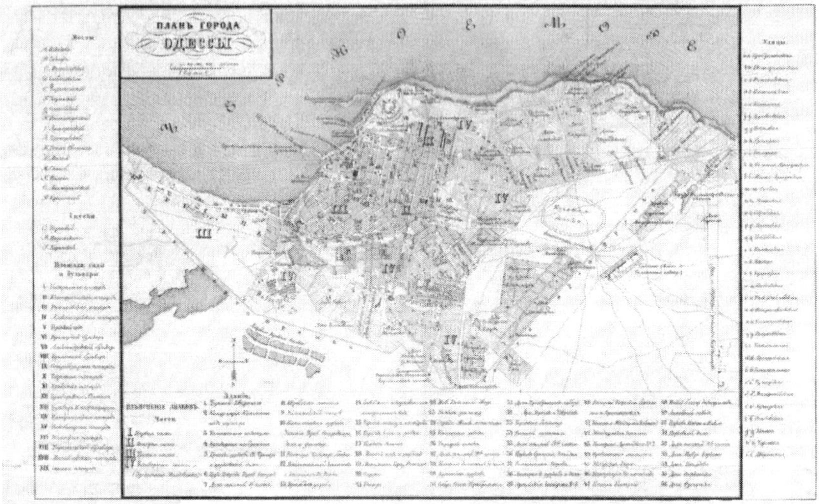

Odessa and its bazaars became entangled from the very inception of the city. Most of the buildings in the centre have only two or three levels and a big courtyard inside, where Odessans gather at special occasions like holidays or feasts. This is also visible given that its centre is composed of all parallel and perpendicular streets, for its construction was started all at once.

The necessity to build shopping places was clear from the outset, when Ekaterina the Great showed a genuine interest in developing the settlement and making it grow to the size of the big city it would become. City and trade became entangled from the very beginning. As early as 1795 one could observe the setting of the *volnyj rynok* (Free Market), conceived for the sale of living goods (*zhiznennykh pripasov*):

> it was then renamed "Old bazaar" and then "Tolkuchij" (from the verb tolkat' = to push) market. In 1799 sellers Afanas'ev and Samarin, among others, were allowed to chop and sell meat on the stone benches in a separate area beyond the volnyj rynok in the direction of the steppe. A few years later in ulitsa Rybnaya (Fish street) and Sadovaya (Garden street) stands for the selling of fish and fruits were built. In 1810 the construction of the Greek Bazaar (between the Greek place and Libknekhta street) was completed. In 1830 the Old Bazaar was equipped with a commercial centre composed of four pavilions with a main corpus in the middle,

built by the Italian architect Torricelli. This structure would survive two wars and will stop being used only in 1958 (Gubar 1999).

The Old Bazaar would be a reference for all Odessans and a starting point for subsequent modifications of the city. However, it would soon be joined by other market places. The first step was the installation at its side, near *Krasnyj pereulok* (Red Lane), of some "red lines" for selling manufactured goods. In 1827 on Privoz (from the verb privozit'— to bring) square a huge market place was built. It would be modified several times, burnt once, and its construction would be completed only in 1913, with the addition of four two-story fruit passages but its importance would remain untouched (Gubar 1999). The construction of trading places continued and in 1842 the *Palais Royal*, a gallery of 44 stands, was built by the Italian architect Torricelli, who also added some trading rows on the territory of the Old Bazaar closer to *prospekt Mira* (Boulevard of Peace). In 1903 the New Bazaar was finally completed. Despite its name, it is one of the oldest places in the city and was built just outside the centre, in 1812, to lighten the burden of the other bazaars that were growing out of control. In the 1840s some two-story buildings with an open gallery were added, and in 1896 a corpus with high trade halls and glass roof that would be then into a space to use for meetings, concerts and circus.

Figure 2   View on the "New Bazaar", early XX century postcard (private collection)

The size of the city, and its importance as a port on the Black Sea, attracted an increasing number of buyers, a phenomenon that prompted selling points to multiply in the city. As a result, a system of "communicating bazaars" connected the historical centre – *Aleksandrovskij bulvar*- with the port, the Greek square with Privoz, passing through the "red rows" and the Old Bazaar, that extended from *Uspenskaya* to *Bolshaya Arnautskaya*.

Privoz was not used as a real bazaar until the second half of the 19th century. It first was a place used to load and unload wheeled vehicles brin*ging (priv*ozit' in Russian) goods, taking advantage of its location and size, that allowed easy circulation of goods and cars. This was until at least 1865 (Gubar 1999). The area between the Old Bazaar and Privoz kept on gaining importance, and some other sub-bazaars were established. For example, there was a German one for sausages, sour cream, butter, cottage cheese and eggs. Besides, some stands for row meat sided vegetable ones where country products like flour, cereals and frying oil were sold. In between those one could also buy herbs and fruits, and a short distance away the fish stands were installed. On the right hand side from meat and fish vendors offered slaughtered poultry and, not too far away, live birds (Gubar 1999).

All these trends contrasted with the rather chaotic morphology of Privoz. All products were sold close to each other, remaining coloured and diverse like no other bazaar. This non-structure was maintained until it became the main bazaar of the city in 1958, the year when the Old Bazaar was abandoned. At this point the necessity arose for more control and the first step was building up a proper place for the sale of meat in the place of the original slaughter. However, because the place had to be covered to keep higher hygienic standards, the issue of lighting arose. Following a strategy already consolidated with other places like the New Market, a Basilica-like architecture was used. Such a structure allowed sunlight to illuminate its interior while keeping most of the market covered and would also be used for the construction of further sections, such as the dairy one.

Figure 3   Trading in Privoz, end of XIX century (private collection).

Figure 4   Overview of Privoz, end XIX century (private collection).

Figure 5   Overview of Privoz, end XIX century (private collection).

Figure 6   Overview of Privoz, end XIX century (private collection).

Figure 7 Starobazarnaya ploshchad' (Old bazaar square), beginning of XX century (private collection).

The last main modification of the Soviet times happened in the seventies, when four buildings for the trade of fish were inserted between the main corpus and the railway station. In the eighties the entire Privoz street, on the west side of the market, stopped working and, after disassembling the whole block between ulitsa Preobrazhenskaya (former Sovetskaya armiya) and Panteleimonovskaya (former Novorybnaya), the regional bus station occupied its place.

A main feature of the bazaars in Odessa is their oscillation between legality, extra-legality and illegality. The control imposed, or attempted, on the flow of goods in the USSR paved the way to a growing informal sector where alcohol, clothes, goods and many other things were exchanged (not necessarily for money; exchange of favours or long-term relationships, like *blat*, were also common). The place with the highest availability of uncontrolled goods and exchanges was the bazaar. In Soviet times Privoz was well known as the place where everything could be found. After 1989 this role was gradually taken up by Sedmoy kilometre (7th kilometre), which is now the quintessence of "total sale" where everything can be bought. Odessa's location, in this respect, facilitated such developments since the high maritime traffic allowed for bringing in virtually everything. In addition, its location close to Transdnistria allows for further variety of goods to be brought in, given the peculiar political status of the region (Ó Beacháin 2012, 2013).

This earned Odessa a reputation as a place where "alternative" products could be found. Among the "miracles" practised at the everyday level in local bazaars it would be possible to witness: the production of several kinds of gems, sold as true ones; second-hand (used and dried) black tea; and fake amber accessories and watches. But the most interesting stratagems were perhaps the selling of low cost goods on which the profit would be limited, but still considered worth it. Fakes included: coffee, butter, sunflower oil and a range of products that urged the city administration to create a special commission, headed by chemistry experts, to investigate the various "ripping offs" organized in the city. The popularity and function of the bazaars prompted the creation of other selling places that happened to be called bazaars and were placed in populated areas. Since the city's earliest expansion, several bazaar-like places where built in different areas of the city. *Cheryomushki* and *Malinovskij* are in the southern *Malinovskij rayon* (area), the *Severnyj* (northern) in *Suvorovskij rayon*, *Yuzhnyj* (southern) and *Kievskij* are in the *Kievskij rayon*. The Greek bazaar has resisted until nowadays but is now replaced by a modern variant of the bazaar, the *Afiny (Athens)* shopping-mall, a four-story building with a food court and Western imported goods.

5 Post-1991 bazaars and their challenges

Ukrainian Independence, achieved in 1991, was accompanied by a "thirst for modernity" that was associated with goods from the capitalist world. Many still remember the endless queues outside the first McDonalds and the neologisms "Euroremont" and "Eurostandards" became widely used to refer to goods imported (or copied) from Western Europe. This prompted a demand for Western goods that, regardless of their quality, were considered better than the local offerings. Jennifer Patico described this phenomenon as "consuming the West but becoming third world" (2003), referring to the fact that Western companies offered low quality goods that were in high demand for their symbolic, rather than real, value. New restaurants were striving to offer "European cuisine" (without specifying whether it was French, German or Bulgarian cuisine—it was all Europe for them); shops were selling "furniture from Europe" ("Europe" is normally associated with Western Europe and such branding was a marketing strategy for goods from Romania or Bulgaria); plastic bags also came to represent a new world and their use grew beyond real needs (an informant went to buy a pack of chewing gum in a supermarket and was asked "do you need a plastic bag"?). Contemporary literature also reflected this thirst for modernity (for one thing, think of Pelevin's, Generatsiya P [Pepsi]).

All this modernity was not available for everyone to the same degree. A division, depending on the cost of labour of different strata of the population, emerged. Homemade food is cheaper and still considered more genuine, but it costs more time, whether in terms of time taken to prepare it or to visit the person who prepared it instead of going to the supermarket. Supermarket food is likely to be more expensive or, at the very least, less "genuine" because it is not homemade, but it saves you much time. Since in urban areas wages have risen much faster than in the countryside, those urban dwellers whose earnings are rapidly growing prefer to have less time but more money at their disposal, which enables them to simply buy what they exchanged or bartered before. With leisure time one can buy extra working hours and thus extra earnings, and alcohol or food can be quickly bought in a supermarket (Polese 2006, 2009).

These changes had very contrasting effects on the bazaar as institution. On the one hand supermarkets and Western food become the new fetishes; on the other hand, however, the importance of bazaars increased because they became the place where demand and supply of homemade goods meet. Only in bazaars could garden-originated products be sold, often with little control from the authorities. This went as far as to reinvent some bazaars as mostly places where beyond-state-control transactions were happening. Institutions such as the Stadium in Warsaw, 7-oj Km in Odessa and many more became the only way people could survive the turbulent 1990s (Cielewska 2013; Polese 2006, 2012; Sasunkevich 2013). Nowadays bazaars seem to incarnate not only the illegal aspects of the economy but also the informal ones, with a desire of socialisation and the necessity to keep long term relationships or personal contacts, as an informant recalled:

The bazaar for me is the place where you can interact with the sellers. Not only can you try things before buying them, not only it is possible to find fresh and tasty goods, it is also the place where socialisation is important. You know the same people and they know you, your taste, they might even keep things for you instead of selling them to other people. These small things make a real difference to me. It's true that supermarkets are more comfortable, there are carts and everything is there, but perhaps we should think of a way to merge the good of bazaars and supermarkets (Mariya, 24).

Bazaars, in the collective imaginary, are often associated with genuineness, freshness and quality that you cannot find elsewhere. One should not forget that a substantial amount of products sold in Odessa bazaars come directly from gardens and small lots of land where there is a direct relationship between the farmer (or simply the owner) and thier vegetables, meat or eggs. Other informants reported:

True, in a supermarket you can always be sure of the quality, everything is wrapped, boxed and possibly more hygienic. Even service is better since in a supermarket it is unlikely that they will "tell you off (*poslat' tebya*)" if they get tired with your requests. However, the bazaar is the place where meat and dairy products are always fresh and I prefer to buy them there. It is like you could feel they are coming from someone's place (*domashniye*) and they do not compare to anything else (Oksana, 27).

In a supermarket you can exchange things after you purchased them if you are not satisfied, but in a bazaar you can try before you buy them, vegetables are fresh and genuine and prices are lower (Anton, 35).

This is not to say that bazaars are suitable only for goods. The case of 7-oj Km, where virtually everything but food is sold, shows that bazaars can evolve around different products. Many informants pointed to the bazaar as a place where cheaper clothes, furniture, equipment and make-up could be easily found and where it would be cheaper to buy them than in a shop. The real competitor of the bazaar, at least for such things, is internet shops, some informants reported. However, they require the capacity to pay online with a credit card, something that not everyone is able or willing to do in Odessa at the moment. As a result, the bazaar is the place where you can touch (*shchupat'*) the things you want to try and check their quality before buying them, be this meat, clothes or vegetables.

Consumers' habits may be influenced by scale economies. Big supermarkets and international retail chains are able to offer food at prices lower than in the bazaar. Meat is chopped, cheese is packed, time is saved. In addition, packaged foods last longer in your fridge and you do not need to shop every day. Those who have more money than time may just opt out from popular culture patterns and save time by buying in supermarkets. Supermarkets may also win some customers due to a generational gap. Going to the bazaar means having to negotiate the price of most goods, keep relations and invest some time in keeping up with the price of products, with the risk of being ripped off, if one is not knowledgeable enough about local prices. In a supermarket prices are fixed and there is less need to make efforts to learn the prices.

If the bazaar is connected to traditions and history, those who are more for modernity might tend to prefer the shops, or the capitalist version of the bazaar, the hypermarket. This is also connected to another phenomenon, that is the change in demand for goods, especially food. In recent years there has been an increasing tendency to purchase Western food and drinks. Where possible, French cheese, American soda drinks or Italian wine—promptly joined by local variants—have entered the range of possible items to accompany a dinner. Likewise American style pizza has come to challenge traditionally oven baked foods for the simple fact of representing modernity and prosperity. Finally, with the adoption of demanding hygienic standards sellers get under pressure and scale economies might work better in keeping the price low.

A final issue is the change in the demand. The peak of the change in the demand is perhaps represented by the increasing demand for electronic and high technology goods that might not fit a bazaar. The issue is that they now normally come with post-purchase assistance. Buying high-tech means not only to buy hardware but also software and assistance, with the assurance/insurance that should something happen, the retailer or the producer would take care of it. That part of the risk in the purchase of an expensive good remains with the seller, a guarantee that shopkeepers might not always be able to offer, or that it would be more time consuming than in a bigger shop, where the broken or defective good might simply be exchanged straight away. In spite of all this, bazaars in Odessa continue to prosper and are even expanding, as the next section will show.

6 The transformation of bazaars

Marketisation has prompted the bazaars to change their structure and functioning; it has changed their role and the way people live them. Bazaars have remained a core component of the city's life but have evolved towards different models. A common feature is the widening of the availability of goods and non-edible goods have increased exponentially, just as their availability on the market has increased. This section takes the case studies of two bazaars that can be considered the most representative for Odessa. Privoz has moved in this direction: it used to be the largest food bazaar in the city where everything was findable informally; it was a matter of asking the right people (urban legends insisted that the person wishing to purchase a bomb could easily do it in Privoz). While remaining a food market, Privoz has been elected a symbol of the city and has undergone a modernisation process that no other bazaar has lived through. Being in the very centre of the city, and a two-minute walk from the central station, a park and an *akvaterrarium*, urban planning has wanted it to be clean and modern. The informal role of Privoz has been taken up by 7-oj Km, an expanding market seven kilometers from the city centre that has grown to 170 hectares as result of a growing demand and its capacity to repair virtually anything. 7-oj Km may be seen as a city inside the city, with selling and buying of anything (legal and illegal, with papers or without) mostly beyond the control of the city administration, let alone the Ukrainian authorities.

Privoz

Privoz is a bazaar that has been of strategic importance to the city since its inception and where legend has it that you can find anything, from pomegranates to bombs. As a journalist reported:

> I headed over to Privoz market, which is sort of like a cross between a department store on the one hand and a recycling center on the other. There's caviar, shoes, accessories, food, perfume, toiletries, things like that. And then there are the guys selling things like rusty old tools laid out on moth-eaten blankets. Or the old school five and a quarter inch floppy disk drives. There's even somebody selling wheels, just wheels, including a matching set of three that were obviously taken from a perambulator at some point (Nyad and Manasek 2002).

In the post-USSR chaos, thanks to its tradition of black market, Privoz remained a main reference for Odessans and a number of other people. Strategically located on the Black Sea and close to the Moldovan border, the tradition of smuggling in Odessa is such that virtually anything could be found in Privoz, given that the right connection is made and the right amount of money is paid.

Some people still remember the notorious *odesskij vorovannyj chaj* (Odessa stolen tea). The standard tea in Soviet times was a black variety produced in Georgia (*gruzinskij chaj*) and used by millions of people. Taking advantage of the increased exchanges with the rest of the world it was possible to find a mix of black teas with a taste different from the classical Georgian one that some Odessans with some degree of wit and honesty made up a brand named "Odessa stolen tea."

While the transition was bringing huge gains for a number of people in the city, a number of Odessans, and Ukrainians in general, were undergoing harsh hardship. For those people Privoz was a way to survive. Immediately after the end of the USSR, in a moment when finding goods became very hard, Privoz was the place to go in cases of necessity. This is not to say that all the shadow trade had to pass through the bazaar but that Privoz became a space with its own laws where there were chances to buy, sell or barter.

In a moment when the cost of labour was extremely low, all those who used to produce something at home could use their skills to barter it on the black market. A growing number of families would go to the market and look for goods, sell goods or look for mediators who would take their goods. The market became close to an immense shadow stock exchange, where everything could have a value and be tradable with other goods.

The market is nowadays one of the main references for the city economy and the city administration, aware of it, decided to change its face and regulate it more. Wishing to offer better hygienic standards, but also to keep control on the trade of the bazaar, a restructuring of the market was initiated and several store buildings were built. These make up the New Privoz, which retains nothing but the name from the old and legendary market. A Western style supermarket and shops now dominate the eastern façade of this four-story (soon to be five) shopping mall, built beside (or better, inside) the old Privoz bazaar, where traditional marble tables for other living goods still remain in use.

The new morphology of the bazaar is now a mix of tradition and modernity, of different selling and living styles. On the one hand we still have traditional bread brought on old trolleys, whereas on the other side big trucks offer large quantities of factory produced goods. Modern shops, boutiques with appealing names such "Golden Cherry", "Alex Horse", or "Venetsiya (Venice)" sell gifts, sunglasses, fashion clothes, jewelry, and even erotic toys. Around the mall, a number of Western-style fast food joints have opened. A few meters further homemade street food and "*stolovyje*" (traditional Soviet canteens) serve the intrepid, or simply tradition oriented, hungry customers. The new morphology of Privoz places the old and the new together, accommodating several categories of consumers who, for economic or other reasons, prefer either section of the market.

Figure 8   Old selling banks in Privoz. In background "New Privoz" constructions (by Aleksandr Prigarin 2011).

This contrast is now also visible on the Web. New Privoz has a dynamic website, http://www.newprivoz.com/, with a picture of the glass facade building dominating the main page. Here all shops are listed, news is announced and directions to the market show the best way to get there. The self-proclaimed official webpage of the "old" Privoz is a basic and old page with most links not working but promising work opportunities to those who want to provide the retailers with food (the page states "Exclusively comfortable cooperation" or "Extremely Favourable cooperation" as the English version reads. Also included are a short history of the market and a section on health, where a rehabilitation clinic is advertised (http://www.odessaprivoz.narod.ru/index.html).

The importance of Privoz, and bazaars in general, is visible from the fact that price indexes are still calculated on the price for meat, milk, and potatoes in the different bazaars (*Novyj, Yuzhnyj*) of the city. Most of the shadow trade has moved to 7-oj km which, given its location, is more difficult to keep under control.

Sedmoj Kilometer

Whilst Privoz seems to move towards a legal framework, the necessity to boost informal transactions has been satisfied by another open air market, described as:

> "...part third world bazaar, part post-Soviet Wal-Mart, a place of unadulterated and largely unregulated capitalism where certain questions — about salaries, rents, taxes or last names — are generally met with suspicion." (Myers 2006)

Figure 9 Overview of selling stands, rykok Avangard (7Km) (by Aleksandr Prigarin 2010).

Sedmoj Kilometer was once established as a local market situated in the centre of the city. Eventually it was moved out to the *Moldavanka*, one of the oldest parts of Odessa and later, when its size was growing beyond control, it was relocated once more, this time to the outskirts of the city. This allowed for expansion enabling the trading of a higher quantity of goods but also made it easier to escape strict state control. The 1989 date of birth of the market given by the Guardian (2012) seems, in this case, to refer to the time when the market was moved outside the centre.

After 1960 *Sedmoj Kilometer* became practically illegal but it remained active and functioned as the biggest smuggling market of the USSR (Nikolskij 2006). Given its location as a border city (less than 50 km from the Moldovan border) Moldovans have a long history of trading with Odessa in order to obtain what was lacking in the rest of the region and what Odessa sailors and traders were able to ship into their city through their networks. Odessa's markets were, and are, the place where any item (from Japanese cars to Italian mopeds) can be found for sale if you are willing to pay.

In recent times, two phenomena have increased the variety of goods purchasable in Odessa: the opening up of Ukraine to foreign imports, which started with *perestroika* and the overproduction in some neighbouring countries, especially Turkey, of what could easily be shipped across the Black sea.

Located seven kilometers from the centre of Odessa, on the Odessa–Ovidiopol highway, the market spreads over 70 hectares and opens every day but Friday. 7-oj Km now has around 16,000 traders and a central staff of 1,200, mostly security guards and janitors, making it the region's largest employer. An estimated 150,000 shoppers come each day, traveling in hundreds of buses from as far as Russia more than 500 kilometers away in search of the bargains that the evident avoidance of customs and taxes make possible (Nikolski 2005). "Over the 15 years of its operation, it has been called different things," the Ukrainian newsweekly, *Zerkalo Nedeli*, wrote in 2004, "but in fact it is a state within a state, with its own laws and rules. It has become a sinecure for the rich and a trade heaven for the poor." (Myers 2006).

It is open 24 hours a day; during the daytime normal goods are traded while at night time the typology of goods traded is unknown to most. Low cost goods are received mainly from Turkey and China but also from Russia, Poland and, at least officially from places such as Italy or Slovakia. The rental of a container to store goods can cost from $1,500 USD upwards (prices for cars, apartments and other goods are unofficially quoted in USD in Ukraine). As a result, although numerous people go to the markets simply to shop, there are others who live on the daily export and smuggling of goods. Some of the workers from neighbour factories are paid in goods rather than money and come to the market to get some cash or products in exchange for what they have to sell (Myers 2006). For instance those working in factories producing fluffy animals are paid in animals and come to sell them

The increasing number of migrants attracted by the city has expanded its surface and the scope of its activities, with unofficial exchange offices, containers and any sort of goods now shared between CIS citizens and new migrants, particularly from China and

Vietnam. The size and importance of the market is also visible through its websites. The official site of the market administration (www.7km.net) has information about the market, how to get there, and the kinds of goods and shops one can find there. A second website, most likely set up by some sellers, is an electronic bazaar (http://7bazar.com.ua) where it is possible to find wholesale and retail goods. There is a section about the sellers, which are listed by name (no surname is given) with the number of the container and a mobile phone contact. Being so far from the city centre, and having people literally living there, not only is the bazaar equipped with restaurants and toilet facilities far beyond those one would expect in a bazaar, but even a big first aid point and a fire station have become needed features.

The flow of informal transactions that happen in the light of day make one only imagine what happens during the night. Growing Chinese and Vietnamese communities are increasing their trade with the city and the place seems to gather people from the whole of Africa, Asia and Europe, who tend to avoid the city centre so as not to be bothered by the authorities (Humphrey and Skvirskaja 2010). A number of them are not fully regular with documents so that, from time to time, policemen might catch a whole bus of Asian-looking persons and detain them until they pay a "release fee".

7 The future of bazaars in Odessa

Despite the challenge of external influences and western style supermarkets that are threatening practices long-ago consolidated, the bazaar has responded to a change of environment by surviving as a two-fold institution. On the one hand it represents values such as genuineness, tradition, and socialisation, which are not necessarily present in modern supermarkets. On the other hand, it responds to a demand for cheap, illegal, or extra-legal goods that may be seen as arising from the incapacity of the state to carry out reforms (Polese 2010).

By giving more importance to traditions, kinship and social networks, people acknowledge the importance of social capital in a country. Most of what escapes state control, be this smuggling or fiscal evasion, socialisation, or networking needs, passes through the bazaar.

This is all the more important in a country that has not secured even development for the whole population and where, aside from a very rich economic class (the so called "New Russians") a great portion of the population struggles to get to the end of the month. For a number of people the bazaar is the place to exchange time with money, spend more time but pay less, or invest time in long term relationships that will bring some benefits in the future. This will be used to create the connections and ties that may secure cheaper goods, help to find a job, some extra income, or simply meeting the need for socialisation people have.

It is hard to predict who will win the bazaar-supermarket competition. What may be said, however, is that the bazaar, as institution and as space, will continue to play a central role in the life of Odessans for some time.

Cited works

Bourdieu P. (1986) The forms of capital, in Handbook of Theory and Research for the Sociology of Education. John G. Richardson ed, 241–258. New York: Greenwood Press.

Bovi, M. (2003) The Nature of the Underground Economy-Some Evidence from OECD Countries'", Journal for Institutional Innovation, Development & Transition 7: 60–70.

Bukh L. (1909) Iz zapisok turista. Odessa kak torgovyj tsentr, Russkie vedomosti no. 160.

Bukh L. (1876) Odessa – tsentr torgovli Yuga Rossii, Odesskij vestnik no 169.

Castree N. (2009) Place: Connections and Boundaries in an Interdepent World in Key Concepts in Geography. Nicholas Clifford, Sarah Holloway, Stephen Rice and Gill Valentine ed 153–172. London: Sage.

Cieślewska, A. (2013) From shuttle trader to businesswomen. The Informal Post-Socialist Economy: Embedded Practices and Livelihoods, 121–133.

The Community Economies Collective (2001) Imagining and enacting non-capitalist futures, Socialist Review 28(3): 93–135.

Cross, J. (2000) Street Vendors, Modernity and Postmodernity: Conflict and Compromise in the Global Economy, International Journal of Sociology and Social Policy 20(1): 29–51.

Derek, G. (1982) Regional transformation and industrial revolution: A Geography of the Yorkshire Wollen Industry. University of Minnesota Press.

De Soto, H. (2002) The Mystery of Capital: Why Capitalism Triumphs in the West and Fails Everywhere Else. New York: Basic Books.

De Soto H. (1989) The Other Path: the Economic Answer to Terrorism. New York: Basic Books.

Ergbert, H. (2005) Cross-border Small-scale Trading in South-Eastern Europe: Do Embeddedness and Social Capital Explain Enough? International Journal of Urban and Regional Research 30(2): 346–61.

Escobar, A. (1995) Encountering Development: The Making and Unmaking of the Thirld World. Princeton, NJ: Princeton University Press.

Gerligi, P. (1999) Odesa, istoriya mista 1794–1914, Kyiv.

Giddens A. (1984). The Constitution of Society. Cambridge: Polity Press.

Gharipour, M. (2012) Bazaar in the Islamic City, Cairo: American University of Cairo Press.

Gillian, R. (1993) Feminism and Geography: The Limits of Geographical Knowledge. University of Minnesota Press.

Gibson-Graham K. J. (1996) The End of Capitalism (As We Know It): A Feminist Critique of Political Economy. Oxford and Cambridge: Blackwell Publishers.

Gubar, O., (no date). Istoriya rynka Privoz, available at http://live.od.ua/history/10/ (last accessed 3 April 2010).

Gubar, O. (1999) Ob istorii samogo znamenitogo rynka Odessy, Vikna Odessa available at http://viknaodessa.od.ua/?Gubar_06 (last retrieved 3 April 2010).

Gudeman, S. (2001) The Anthropology of Economy: Community, Market, and Culture. Oxford: Blackwell.

Gugushvili, A. (2011) Material Deprivation, Social Class and Life Course in the Balkans, Eastern Europe and Central Asia. Studies of Transition States and Societies 3(1): 39–54.

Gupta, A. (1995) Blurred Boundaries: The Discourse of Corruption, the Culture of Politics, and the Imagined State, American Ethnologist 22(2): 375–402.

Hann, C. and K. Harth (2005) Market and Society: The Great Transformation Today, Cambridge: Cambridge University Press.

Harth, K. (2005) Formal bureaucracy and the emergent forms of the informal economy, Research Paper, UNU-WIDER, United Nations University (UNU) 2005/11, available at: http://hdl.handle.net/10419/63313 (last accessed 12 March 2013)

Harvey D. (1996) Justice, Nature and the Geography of Difference. Oxford: Basil Blackwell.

Herlihy P. (1986) Odessa: A History. Cambridge MA: Harvard University Press.

Herlihy, P. (1977) The Ethnic Composition of the City of Odessa in the Nineteenth Century, Ukrainian Studies I, 533–578.

Herlihy P. and O. Gubar. (no date) The Persuasive Power of the Odessa Myth. Ukrainian Research Institute, Harvard University, available online at www.2odessa.com/wiki/index.php?title=The_Persuasive_Power_of_the_Odessa_Myth (last accessed 6 March 2009)

Humphrey, C. and R. Mandel (2002) Markets and Moralities: Ethnographies of Postsocialism. New York: Berg and NYU Press.

Humphrey, C. and V. Skvirskaja (2009) Trading places: Post-socialist container markets and the city FOCAAL 55: 61–73.

Keller, T. and P. Róbert (2011) Structural Components of Lifestyle and Beyond: The Case of Hungary. Studies of Transition States and Societies 3(1): 55–75.

ILO (2002) Decent Work and the Informal Economy. Geneva: International Labor Office.

Isaacs, R. (2011) Party System Formation in Kazakhstan: Between Formal and Informal Politics. London: Routledge.

Isaacs, R. (2010) Informal politics and the uncertain context of transition: revisiting early stage non-democratic development in Kazakhstan, Democratization 17(1): 1–25.

Lomnitz, L. (1988) Informal Exchange Networks in Formal Systems: A Theoretical Model, American Anthropologist 90(1): 42–55.

McDowell, L. (1993) Space, Place and Gender Relations, Progress in Human Geography 17(2): 157–179.

Morris, J. and A. Polese (2013) The Informal Post-Socialist Economy. London and New York: Routledge.

Morris, J., & Polese, A. (2014). Informal health and education sector payments in Russian and Ukrainian cities: Structuring welfare from below. European Urban and Regional Studies, 0969776414522081.

Morris, J. (2013) Beyond coping? Alternatives to consumption within a social network of Russian Workers, Ethnography 14(1): 85–103.

Morris, J. (2012) Unruly Entrepreneurs: Russian Worker Responses to Insecure Formal Employment, Global Labour Journal 3(2): 217–236. Online. Available: <http://digitalcommons.mcmaster.ca/globallabour/vol3/iss2/2> (accessed 31 March 2015).

Moss, P. (2007) Feminisms in Geography: Rethinking Space, Place, and Knowledges. Rowman & Littlefield Publishers.

Myers S. (2006) Ukrainian 'mall' not for the dainty, The New York Times, 18 May.

Myers, S. (2006) Seventh-Kilometer Market Journal; From Soviet-Era Flea Market to a Giant Makeshift Mall, The New York Times 19 May.

Nelson, M. and J. Smith (2009) Informal Work in Small Town America, in Marcelli, E. and C. Williams, Work in the Informal Economy. London: Routledge.

Nikolskij K. (2005) 7-oj vykhodit iz teni, Korrespondent, 4 June.

Nyad, D. and J. Manasek (2002) "Attempts to recreate a movie scene in Odessa" Savvy Traveler, 21 September.

Odessa 1794–1894, Publishing House of the City's Society [Izdatelstvo gorodskogo obshchestva upravleniya k stoletiyu goroda].

Ó Beacháin, D. (2012) The Dynamics of Electoral Politics in Abkhazia, Communist and PostCommunist Studies 27(1–2): 165–174.

Ó Beacháin, D. (2013) The Role of the EU and the OSCE in Promoting Security and Cooperationin the South Caucasus and Moldova, in Ayca Ergun and Hamlet Isaxanli (eds) Security and Cross-Border Cooperation in the EU, Black Sea Region and the Southern Caucasus. NATO Science for Peace and SecuritySeries, IOS Press, 42–57.

Odessa's 7km bazaar has its own language of globalisation, The Guardian 31 July 2012.

OECD (2002) Measuring the Non-Observed Economy: A Handbook. Paris: OECD Publication Service.

Ozcan, G. (2010) Djamila's Journey from Kolkhoz to Bazaar: Female Entrepreneurs in Kyrgyzstan, in Entreprising Women in Transition Economies. F. Welter, D. Smallbone and N. Isakova (eds.). Fulham: Ashgate.

Pardo, I. (1996) Managing Existences in Naples: Morality, Action and Structure, Cambridge: Cambridge University Press.

Parry, J. (1986) The Gift, the Indian Gift and the "Indian Gift", Man 21: 453–473.

Parry, J. and M. Bloch (eds) (1989) Money and the Morality of Exchange, Cambridge: Cambridge University Press.

Patico, J. (2003) Consuming the West but Becoming Thrid World: Food Imports and the Experience of Russianness, The Anthropology of Eastern Europe Review 21(1): 31–36.

Perry G. and W. Maloney (2007) Overview: Informality—Exit and Exclusion. Perry G, E. Maloney, W. Arias, O. Fajnzylber, P. Mason and Saavedra Chanduvi eds. Informality: Exit and Exclusion. Washington: World Bank.

Polanyi, K. (1957) The Great Transformation. Boston, Massachusetts: the Beacon Press.

Polese, A. (2012) Who has the right to forbid and who to trade? Making sense of illegality on the Polish-Ukrainian border, in Subverting Borders: Doing Research on Smuggling and Small-Scale Trade, Bettina Bruns and Judith Miggelbring (eds.) Leipzig: VS Verlag.

Polese, A. (2010) At the origins of informal economies: some evidence from Ukraine, Working Paper, University of Jena.

Polese, A. (2010) The formal and the informal: Exploring 'Ukrainian' Education in Ukraine, Scenes from Odessa, Comparative Education 46(1): 45–62.

Polese A. (2009) The guest at the dining table: economic transition and the reshaping of hospitality, reflections from Batumi and Odessa, Anthropology of Eastern Europe Review 27(1): 65–77.

Polese A. (2008) Du samogon à la vodka de supermarché: Petit voyage dans la transition ethylique en Europe orientale Regards à est 46 http://www.re gard-est.com/home/breve_contenu.php?id=861 (last accessed 3 April 2010).

Polese, A. (2006) Border Crossing as a Daily Strategy of Post Soviet Survival: the Odessa-Chisinau Elektrichka, The Anthropology of Eastern Europe Review 24(1): 28–37.

Portes, A. (1998) Social Capital: Its Origins and Applications in Modern Sociology, Annual Review of Sociology 24: 1–24.

Portes, A. (2000) The Two Meanings of Social Capital, Sociological Forum 15(1): 1–12.

Pred, A. (1986) Place, Practice and Structure: social and spatial transformation in southern Sweden. Cambridge: Polity Press.

Rasanayagam, J. (2011) Informal Economy, Informal State: the Case of Uzbekistan. International Journal of Sociology and Social Policy, 31(11/12): 681–696.

Rasanayagam, J. (2003) Market, State and Community in Uzbekistan: Reworking the Concept of the Informal Economy: Max Planck Institute for Social Anthropology Working Paper No. 59.

Richardson, T. (2009) The Place(s) of Moldovanka in the Making of Odessa, The Anthropology of East Europe Review. 30(1): 72–89.

Richardson, T. (2008) Kaleidoscopic Odessa: History and Place in Contemporary Ukraine. Toronto: University of Toronto Press.

Rose-Ackerman, S. (2010) Corruption: Greed, Culture and the State, the Yale Law Journal, 120 Yale L.J. Online 125, http://yalelawjournal.org/2010/11/10/rose-ackerman.html.

Samers, M. (2005) The Myopia of "Diverse Economies", or a Critique of the Informal Economy, Antipode 37: 875–886.

Sampson, S. (2010) Diagnostics: Indicators and Transparency in the Anti-Corruption Industry. Transparenz: Multidisziplinäre Durchsichten durch Phänomene und Theorien des Undurchsichtigen, Wiesbaden, VS Verlag für Sozialwissenschaften, 97–111.

Sampson, S. (2004) Too Much Civil Society? Donor-Driven Human Rights NGOs in the Balkans. Dhundale, L. Andersen, E. Eds pp 197–220. Revisiting the Role of Civil Society in the Promotion of Human Rights, Copenhagen: Danish Institute for Human Rights.

Sapozhnikov I. V. (1999) Materialy z istorychnoi geografii del'ty Dunayu, Chasopys Zaporiz'nogo naukovogo tovarystva im. Ya Nobitskogo "Pivdenna Ukraina" 4: 272–274.

Sapritsky, M. (2011) Transformation of Jewish Identities and Community Building in Post-Soviet Odessa, Ukraine. PhD dissertation, London School of Economics and Political Sciences.

Sapritsky, M. (2012) Negotiating Cosmopolitanism: Migration, Religious Education and Shifting Jewish Orientations in post-Soviet Odessa, in Caroline Humphrey and Vera Skvirskaja eds., Explorations of the Post-Cosmopolitan City, New York: Berghahn Books.

Sasunkevich, O. (2014) Business as casual: shuttle trade on the Belarus-Lithuania border. The informal post-socialist economy: embedded practices and livelihoods. London: Routledge, 135–151.

Scott, J. (1985) Weapons of the Weak: Everyday Forms of Peasant Resistance, New Haven and London: Yale University Press.

Skal'kovskii A. (1839) Istoriko-statisticheskij opyt o torgovykh i promyshlennykh silakh Odessy, Trudy Odesskogo statisticheskogo komiteta.

Smith N. (1984) Uneven Development: Nature, Capital, and the Production of Space. Oxford: Blackwell.

Soja E. (1989) Postmodern Geographies: The Reassertion of Space in Critical Social Theory. London and New York: Verso.

Stenning, A., Smith, A., Rochovská, A. and Swiatek, D. (2010) Domesticating Neo-Liberalism: Spaces of Economic Practice and Social Reproduction in Post-Socialist Cities, Malden MA and Oxford: Wiley-Blackwell.

Thrift, N. (2009) Space: The Fundamental Stuff of Geography, in Key Concepts in Geography ed Gill Valentine, Sarah Holloway and and Nicholas Clifford. London: Sage.

Ukrainskij "moll" ne dlya priveredlivykh" Korrespondent, 19 may 2006.

Williams C. (2005). A Commodified World? mapping the limits of capitalism. London: Zed Publishers.

Williams, C. and J. Windebank (1998) Informal Employment in the Advanced Economies: Implications for Work and Welfare. London: Routledge.

Zanca, R. (2003). "Take! Take! Take!" Host-Guest Relations and All that Food: Uzbek Hospitality Past and Present. Anthropology of East Europe Review, 21(1), 8–16.

New directions in informality studies? policy making and implementation

The focus of this chapter slightly deviates from the path that has been developed in the first four to add a non-economic dimension to the study of informality. Apart from Keith Hart (1973), most approaches on informality have emphasised its economic component (Benjamin et al 2014; La Porta and Shleifer 2014). This is certainly a legitimate claim, given that two-thirds of the world are engaged in informal labour (Bacchetta et al. 2009; ILO 2012, Jütting and de Laiglesia 2009). However, the aspect of informality dealt with by this chapter is a non-economic (or non-necessarily economic) one, which has recently come to the attention of a variety of disciplines. It is difficult, however, to expand the boundaries of research on informality in a way that looks consistent without ceding to the temptation of declaring that informality is everywhere. In some respects, Misztal's (2000) attempts to conceptualise informality fall into this trap. Although she has the merits of turning the attention to a phenomenon that was under-studied at that time, her suggestion that informality permeates most aspects of post-communist life makes it impossible to define a clear object in the study of informality. Since then, research on informality has expanded not reaching its boundaries yet but engaging with a variety of disciplines, from urban studies to management, international relations and political sciences, in addition to the already established economic anthropology and sociology.

This chapter is a further attempt to stretch the boundaries of research on informality by looking at the way it can be used to renegotiate policy making. I refer, in particular, to the aspect of policy making that is likely to generate tensions between the state and its citizens when the state demands what the citizens are not ready to do. This is often the case and the very meaning of reforms, or policy making, which suggests a change in behaviour or attitude of the citizens. However, there is a limit in what can be demanded. Imposing fines to those not buckling their seatbelts when driving can be met with some resistance but is ultimately acceptable. In contrast, attempts to change the religion or language in a particular part of the country might generate a higher amount of discontent among the population.

When this happens, that is when the gap between what the state and the citizens broadens, informal practices are likely to emerge, leading to several possible outcomes. To begin with, a new informal practice is used to complement a formal rule or to react to the new instructions that cannot be complied with immediately by the totality of the population. The informal practice can either remain marginal and tacitly accepted, or disappear, so that the state does not feel the need to intervene. When, in 2008, the city of Hanoi introduced the obligation of wearing a helmet for all motorbike passengers not all of the population abided, not least because of the extra costs this would entail. A task force of street policemen who were ready to literally jump onto drivers wearing no helmets was a strong incentive to comply. However, they could not possibly cover the entirety of the city so it became known that if they avoided riding on the main roads, they would not have to adhere to the lawon. As a result, the great majority of the people riding on some of the major roads now wear helmets but this is not the case on the minor roads. The practice has remained limited to some areas and in numbers so that the authorities are tolerating it for the moment. A new informal practice can also, however, grow in popularity when a state decides to intervene, leading to four possible outcomes:

1) repression: a good combination of positive and negative incentives to phase the practice out
2) institutionalisation: the state realises that the practice is actually helpful and "buys" it, that is it formalises and integrates it into exiting formal mechanisms and practices
3) contentious politics: repression attempts to prompt citizens to organise themselves in movements to assert their rights with regards to the area regulated by the practice and challenge the state. An extreme case is that a group or a region rejects the role of the state and creates another state-like entity that claims to rule formally on a given territory (insurgency)

4) status quo maintained: failed repression is matched by an understanding of the fact that it is too difficult, or costly, to eradicate a practice. This is possibly matched by the understanding that the practice is marginal and can be tolerated. As a result, the practice remains in use.

This chapter deals with a case that, at the moment, can be seen the closetr to number four (in the example above) and is informed by a microstudy on the reaction of a local population to language policies in Ukraine. The idea is that, after independence, attempts to redefine a national identity have been largely centred around the use of the Ukrainian language and its expansion to most spheres of public life. As a result, Ukrainian has been considered, already for some time in state discourses, not only as the state but also as the "the native language" (ridna mova, as defined in school textbooks) of the Ukrainians. The Russian language, as a result, has been largely phased out, at least officially, from the public life. This attitude is not new but rather the way language policies have worked in most of Europe when constructing identities. Szporluk has documented the diffusion of the Polish language and identity on the Polish border areas (1990), Chanet has illustrated the processes, and mechanisms, that have made French accepted as the national language also in regions where it was a minority language (1995). What is special about the Ukrainian case is the relatively high speed at which the language has been expected to replace Russian and other minority languages. The question I asked myself when I started this research, which was part of my PhD project, was: what would be the attitude (of the people, institutions, other actors) towards the request to switch from Russian to Ukrainian in a city where Russian is largely accepted as the lingua franca and is used as the main means of communication. Located in the south of the country, Odessa seemed the ideal choice given that, by force of its history, it is impossible to classify it as a "Russian" or "Ukrainian" city. The city, and even more the oblast', hosts a high variety of ethnicities and multilingualism is well spread. The case study that is considered here is the evolution of linguistic tendencies in the city of Odessa, which is located in a region (oblast') populated by villages that were founded by Bulgarians, Gagauzians, Germans, Greeks, Moldovans ad, Ukrainians to mention the main ones. Ukrainian is spoken in some areas, and to some limited extent in the city, but most respondents would confirm that in Odessa, Russian is the language most people use for communication. Odessans would claim to have an identity that is neither Russian or Ukrainian: it is Odessan, as Tanya Richardson illustrated (2008). However, the request to switch from Russian into Ukrainian almost overnight, as the section below will show, might have generated tensions between the citizens and the state.

Surprisingly enough, these tensions never evolved into direct confrontation. Odessa seemed to quickly and peacefully adapt to a new language and the state did not have to intervene to assert its decisions with regards to identity marker or the use and status of the Ukrainian language. This, in my view, was based on an informal compromise between the two parts. Odessans would strive to create a facade of Ukrainian-ness and officially use the language when asked to. A number of Russian schools (where Russian was the medium of education) quickly became Ukrainian, that is their official mean of instruction. However, little control would be enforced by the state to check whether, behind this façade, people would actually use Ukrainian (beyond the official letters sent to Kiev and the fact that the schools and other state institutions translated their curricula into Ukrainian).

The empirical part of this chapter outlines the informal mechanisms used to mediate between the position of the state (Ukrainian is your native language) and the citizens (Russian is our language of convenience). A substantial amount of literature on informality focusses on its negative and disruptive aspects (London and Hart, 2004; Nwabuzor, 2005) or its role in limiting the hindrances of excessive red tape (Gallin 2001; Slavnic 2010). In contrast to the above mentioned tendencies, this chapter is intended to show some possible constructive aspects of informality and, in particular, suggest that it can be used to mitigate frictions between policy choices and a target population that cannot live with these choices. By so doing, presence of informal practices, and the extent to which they are present, can be regarded as a feedback mechanism showing the degree of satisfaction of the population targeted by a given policy measure. As Scott (1998) has shown, policies are conceived to harmonise various aspects of life and often adopt a one-size-fit-all approach. It is unlikely, however, that policies that are conceived to bring benefits through change among a variety of actors will perfectly meet the needs of, or benefit, all the segments of a given population. Some projects, as Scott showed, fail by their very virtue of attempting to harmonise and uniform a far too diversified population. Like cartilage between bones, informality may be seen as the way to smoothly connect two actors and actions of governance that do not perfectly suit one another for their shape and size. A low level of informality may be seen as an indicator of relative success of a policy measure or of a package of reforms. In contrast, a high level of informality may be showing that something is wrong with the way a policy is implemented and prompt some corrective action. The informal mechanisms identified may be fought, and sometimes defeated, but could also be institutionalised. Once a tendency is identified and deemed to have a positive effect, it is possible that a government may want, instead of fighting it, to endorse and formalise it because it sees the benefits out-weighting the costs of keeping a given mechanism alive.

1 Methodological considerations

A major question in this research is on the reliability of what could be called visible or tangible data. I refer here to what Hobsbawm and Rude wrote already in 1969 to suggest that scholars often fall into the mistake, widely spread among politicians, of downplaying events that do not hit the headlines. The boundary between invisibility and inexistence is more fluid than one may think. If there are no reporters to write on them or, worse, if a given phenomenon does not seem to rise interest, it may be ignored or downplayed to the point that, when noticed, it seems as if it has popped out of nowhere. The wave of violence against women in India had its peak at the end of 2012 and the beginning of 2013 with cases being reported almost daily. The international public opinion was apparently shocked by what seemed to be a dramatic increase in gender crimes. However, are we sure that this is due to the increase of crime rate? Two alternative explanations are also possible. One is that a growing number of people are now willing to overcome the stigma of being a victim of violence and have started raising their voices. The other is that journalists and other key people have started to pay more attention to it.

As another example, think of the number of people who reported sexual assault during new year's eve between 2015 and 2016. The media initially reported it as something that happened in Cologne and, only after this it had become an international case, victims from a number of other countries spoke out and it became an international case. What would have happened if the story had not been reported in Cologne? We cannot be certain of the outcome but there is a chance that many victims would simply have remained silent thinking of their case being an isolated one. By the same token, can we be sure that this did not happen already in 2013 or 2014? Perhaps at a lower scale and was considered just an episode not worth reporting.

When dealing with Eastern Europe, Pichler and Wallace (2005) have used the term informal social capital to suggest that, despite not being officially registered as their Western European counterparts, a number of organisations and movements had been active in the region for many years. By resting on their definition, we were able to challenge the claims that civil society in the region had remained largely inactive and that the emergence of civic movements apparently overnight was nothing but the visible aspect of a phenomenon that had been developing for years before (O'Beachain and Polese 2010, 2010b, Polese 2009). Under-reporting is not the only risk when dealing with tangible and intangible phenomena. Numbers are also subject to manipulation and can be used to demonstrate both something and its opposite (Fioramonti 2014). The Italian criminal statistics were largely affected by a decision to classify non violent larceft of personal property such as wallets or mobile phones as lost. This meant that the police would ask you to tick the box "lost item" on the claim you fill, if this was taken from you with no violence (i.e. you were not attacked). Official crime statistics on petty larceny decreased, but in reality it remained the same.

In her seminal work "Faces of the State" (2002) Navarro-Yael started from the question, who is participating in the "production of the political" in a state or a community? Are small and atomised groups, that have apparently no connection with government structures, really able to make their voice heard in political processes? Anthropologists have shown that those excluded from political processes might try to participate informally through a series of means (Gupta 1995, Scott

1985) not necessarily organised or coordinated. However, it is also important to ask where is the boundary between atomised and coordinated actions. After all the indignados movement in Spain was something almost invisible, or at least not so relevant politically, until it became highly visible. What had changed in the process? In a recent paper, we have suggested that informal practices, social movements and insurgency are all but different expressions of a same phenomenon in different contexts and responding to different stimulations (Polese and Kevlihan 2015). People, and everyday actions, have the power of reshaping policies not only by massively protesting but also by performing a same action in an unorganised and apparently casual way, a thing we have been demonstrating also in the sphere of economic policies (Morris and Polese 2014, 2015).

By putting the Odessa case to the centre of this chapter's inquiry, I am trying to explore in what ways tensions between the state and its citizens can be negotiated, or mitigated. It is important to note that I do not claim total accuracy of figures and it is possible that different studies provide variations in the figures I am using. However, I am not interested here in assessing how many people speak what but only to justify my assumption that Russian is the "language of convenience" (Arel 1996) in Odessa. By virtue of this, I suggest to look at the empirical material through the prism of the Russian-Ukrainian language dynamics and the competition from both a formal and informal perspective. It is also worth noticing that the scope of this chapter is far from political. There has been a tendency, in Ukrainian debates but also more generally in regional ones, to classify scholars, positions and views in a bipolar way, either criticising Ukraine or Russia. It is well beyond the scope of this paper to give any assessments on the current events in the region. I happened to be in Odessa at a given moment of its history and I happened to observe some dynamics that might be replicated in a number of other multi-lingual settings. During class observations it was already clear that age may matter and younger pupils were sometimes more at ease with Ukrainian than older ones. It is possible that new generations are gradually using Ukrainian more often and it is far from my goal to give an assessment of today's effects of the Ukrainian language policies. The question that was important at that time, and to this day, is about the underlying mechanisms and dynamics of language use and choice. In other words: what are the resulting synergies and dynamics from a situation where a substantial amount of people are asked to use publicly (when working, studying or when expressing opinions) a language that they have tended not to use before, that some of them do not know as their native tongue and that some know relatively poorly?

To answer this question, I set out to observe the interaction between teachers and pupils in Odessa. I chose five Ukrainian schools, meaning that Ukrainian was the mean of instruction, and one Russian one, where most subjects were in Russian except for Ukraine related subjects. To have some variation in the sample I selected three elite schools, which are the best reputed and with a specialisation in one optional subject and three compulsory ones. My assumption was that the elite schools would adapt to state instructions at a higher speed and set a certain benchmark for the other schools for at least two reasons. One is that, they received more support from the state to further develop some aspect of secondary education (language, mathematics or physics) and should display more compliance. The other is that, by proclaiming themselves as the schools preparing the elite of the country they had an interest in following the establishment and emphasise the "Ukrainian" aspects of school education of education. Observation was carried out during several months of fieldwork for an overall stay of 20 months in Odessa, which allowed me to conduct some participant observation and 49 interviews with two generations of Odessans. Even if these results are not presented here, it is important to highlight the fact that the school observation was framed in a larger research thus allowing me to triangulate results, double check phenomena to avoid falling victim of local idiosyncrasies and be able to put things in perspective.

2 The context: evolution of language statuses in Ukraine

The nationalist mobilisation so well illustrated by Beissinger (2002), and that will have a crucial role in the end of the USSR, prompted a fast spread of civic pro-Ukrainian movements. Expression of Ukrainian feelings happened through a number of channels. First, with ecology

LIMITS OF A POST-SOVIET STATE 227

declared an official value of the USSR, it was possible to use the Chernobyl events to prompt a reflection on the state of the USSR. Second, taking advantage of the perestroika movement, nationalistic feelings were expressed through the creation of organisations with an officially cultural scope. In 1987 a dissident and member of Helsinki Union, Viacheslav Chornovil announced the birth of the Creative Intelligentsia Association in a letter to General Secretary Gorbachev. The Culturological club, the committee in defence of the Catholic Church, the ecological association "Zeleny svit" (green world) and the youth organisation "Tovarystvo lev" followed, with the latter launching the first youth magazine in Ukraine (Polese 2008). In 1989 the Ukrainian Soviet adopted, as in other USSR republics, a law equalling both Russian and Ukrainian as state languages. These events were followed by political ferments bringing to the registration of the movement Rukh and its victory (in L'viv, Ternopil and Ivano Frankivsk) at the semi-free elections of 1990. Students and miners joined together in protest, also in 1990, which completed a picture of a country that shows a firm desire to abandon the USSR and, at least formally, some of its values. The Communist Party leader Leonid Kravchuk senses the moment and starts building a nationalist rhetoric that will bring the country out of the USSR after a referendum where 90,5 % of the eligible voters cast their ballot in favour of Ukrainian independence.

The state and nation building measures that followed reflect, to a fair extent, these tendencies. Newly elected President Kravchuk introduced the Ukrainian language encouraging it into political discourse. The construction of an official narrative on Ukrainian identity preoccupied Kravchuk as much as the following President Leonid Kuchma who, in spite of being native a Russian speaker was unable to reverse the trend. He accepted the statement that a Ukraine with no language needed no president (Kuzio 1997) as a tacit message that his support largely depended on his capacity to put forward a Ukrainian narrative.

This was possibly helped by the growing support for nationalistic narratives in the country. The "Rukh" (National Movement for the Support of Perestroika), was created in 1989 in Kiev and hosted major opposition figures (such as the Viacheslav Chornovil who came second at the 1991 presidential election with 23.27%, against Kravchuk with

61.59%) in addition to quickly becoming second most important party in the country. At the 1994 parliamentary elections Rukh came in second with 5.15% of the votes against the communist party who received 12.72%. In the 1998 elections, Rukh gained 9.40% against the communist party at 24.65% before reorganising into many different movements because of internal disagreements but also the mysterious death of their leader Vyacheslav Chornovil. Still, the nationalist parties scored more than 30% at the 2002 elections (even if the result was unable to create a majority) and consolidated through the 2004 presidential elections. These political preferences resulted also in an assertive role of nationalistic forces putting pressure on the adoption, and re-discovery, of Ukrainian symbols, taking a distance from Russia and the USSR past and a more comprehensive set of measures promoting an official narrative on Ukrainian identity that would increase the pressure on its citizens to adopt a Ukrainian identity, or at least a number of its markers such as the new flag (blue and yellow) the trident. The project for a new currency foresaw the use of the historical Ukrainian currency hryvnia, firstly introduced in Ukraine in 1918 (when it was printed in Berlin), that was reintroduced as the national currency in 1996. Commemoration stamps bore representation of the Cossacks, who are considered the ancestors of the Ukrainian nation, and Mikhailo Khrushevski, president of the first Ukrainian Republic. Independence day (from the Soviet Union) was set the 24th of August, and Europe Day the 3rd of May (adopted more recently, in 2003) but the victory of the Soviet Union in WWII is still celebrated (9 May) as well as the liberation of Kiev from the Nazi troops (7 November). The lyrics of the national anthem were taken from a Ukrainian national poem from the XIX century and particular attention was paid to the construction of new monuments, like Prince Yaroslav the Mudry in Kiev.

National symbols were legitimized by the 1996 Constitution that would not allow dual citizenship (Ukrainians should only be Ukrainian). In contrast to what happened in the Baltics (Barrington 1995), the constitution made it nevertheless accessible to all those living in Ukraine in 1991 and those born in Ukraine with no other citizenship (like being stateless and/or those who give up their parents' citizenship). Although allowing the development of Russian, Ukraine was directed towards a single state language: Ukrainian.

Schools were progressively affected by this trend. The language law of 1989 introduced a whole series of provisions intending to curb Russification and make Ukrainian the dominant language in all spheres of public life (Janmaat 2000:59). Teaching was set in Ukrainian, with the possibility to have other languages of instruction, and the State Program on the Development of the Ukrainian Language of February 1991 laid down a detailed timetable to adjust to Ukrainian. Southern and eastern regions were allowed more time to do this (ten years) but the program, aiming at prompting groups of Russian speaking Ukrainians in the east and south to send their children to Ukrainian schools, suggested that the children were to receive instruction in the 'national language' of their parents. In this respect, it envisaged that all Russian schools previously Ukrainian were to open only Ukrainian first grade from the following year. Janmaat speculates that Russian language schools might then be too far to send one's children and preference would be given to geographic proximity rather than Russian language (Janmaat 2000:63).

While only 51 percent of pre-schools were in Ukrainian in 1991, the figure rose to 76 percent in 2000. Primary and secondary schools in Ukrainian were 49 percent in 1991–92 but became 70 percent in 2000/2001 (Russian ones were 29 percent) with figures higher than 50 percent all over the country. The exceptions were Odessa (47 percent), Zaporizhzhia (45 percent), Luhansk (17 percent), Donetsk (14 percent) and the Republic of Crimea (0,8 percent) (UCEPS 2002). As a result, it is estimated that by 2002, 74 percent of Ukrainian students, and 25 percent of Russian ones, studied in Ukrainian (Kuts 2004: 182). In addition, new types of schools (lyceum, gymnasium or college after which no exam was requested to enter a university) could only have Ukrainian as the language of instruction and the priority in receiving textbooks would be given to Ukrainian schools.

Printing of Ukrainian textbooks was not always on schedule and a number of schools, officially teaching in Ukrainian, were still using Russian language textbooks. However, one of the most visible results was that, already from 1997 the Russian language and literature had disappeared from curricula for the state sponsored Ukrainian schools and teaching in Russian had been largely phased out. In addition, new subjects had been introduced such as "ridna mova" (a course about

Ukrainians "native language") where ridna comes from the verb to be born (*naroditi*) and indicates something coming from the past, almost innate to people, which the Ukrainian language is not necessarily for everyone.

3 Domesticating Ukrainian identities

With Ukrainians growing from 72.7 to 77.8 percent in Ukraine, and Russians decreasing from 22.1 to 17.3 percent in Ukraine (comparing the 1989 and 2001 censuses) it could be argued that identity policies had some effects on the ethno-linguistic composition of the country. Surveys showed an irregular pattern in the language habits of Ukraine (Russian was at its peak in 2001, with 38.1 percent and decreased through 2005 to 34.1 percent). Opponents of this argument have suggested that classification of people as Ukrainians (and Ukrainian speakers) was sometimes forced or assumed against all odds (Stebelsky 2009). In either case, there was no open confrontation against Ukrainisation policies in the country and economic opportunities might have had a role in this. Knowing that their children would have more job opportunities being bilingual would encourage Russian families to support Ukrainian education.

"My mother is Russian, my father is Ukrainian, I am Odessan", says a popular quote. By virtue of this, I would like to avoid the binarisation, and politicisation of relations between Russian and Ukrainian speakers to just say: Odessa hosts a significant amount of people who might not think of themselves as Ukrainians immediately or might not adopt all of the markers proposed by the state. This is not to say, however, that they reject some of the identity markers. They just renegotiate them or live them in a different way.

Schools were an interesting point of observation since, in the majority of the cases I have observed, Ukrainian was neither the teachers' nor the pupils' first language. Still, rarely, if ever, Ukrainisation of schools was opposed or contested. There seemed to be a clear understanding that Ukrainian is the *derzhavna mova* (state language) and, in some cases, it was referred also as the *ridna mova* (native language) thus accepting the wording and narrative suggested at the national level. Acceptance of the discourse does not automatically mean interiorisation and blind faith in all its aspects. My respondents in schools seemed to have found a compromise between what, and how, they were expected to perform when dealing with pupils that only spoke Russian at home.

This pressure also translated into a fast side-switching attitude when discussing language education in their school. When respondents felt empathy towards the language directions they would openly complain or at least mention the inconsistency of using Ukrainian for subjects traditionally using Russian language sources. For one thing, most of the material for Odessa's history or even Russian literature were sometimes expected to be translated. However, when teased out to declare that they still stuck to Russian, most teachers would step back and declare that, after all, most people now use Ukrainian. They would also mention that 'not everybody understands (that) Ukrainian (is the state language) and that this has to be respected. Children are more open, but if you use both languages when teaching, it is better.'

From the teachers' side, there seem to exist two channels of communication in the previous situation. On the one hand, when they acted as civil servants and represent the state, they tended to use Ukrainian, the language of state. When talking as a person to other people they seem willing to remind the students and other teachers that they all are from the same milieu, culture, city and that they share the same fate. In this case, there are some educational messages transmitted not through words but attitude. Children are educated not only through notions but also educated on how to choose the right language for the right context. They learn that the *derzhava mova* has to be used in occasions where the state is present. I never had the impression that teachers were convinced that people had to speak Ukrainian in Odessa. Ukrainian was conceived as an asset, a sort of respect for the state that is hosting us. However, people were not going to change their life habits to comply one hundred percent with state requirements.

Teachers are captured between two positions. On the one hand, they are civil servants representing the state, and its official position. On the other hand, they are also people with their preferences, native language and ideas. Their position does not always overlap with the state's and they teach pupils whose first language is not necessarily Ukrainian. The result is that they do not teach a language but an attitude. They show that in Odessa, Ukraine, two languages are important and the choice of the language depends on the context they are in. Russian might be important when talking to peers but Ukrainian, and attitude towards it, is a crucial element in identity performance (Polese and Wylegala 2008, 2008b).

During in-class observations, a recurrent pattern one can observe is that the first contact with the pupils, once the teacher greats them in Ukrainian then switches to Russian for technical information that is not part of the programme (asking someone to stay silent, to bring some material). Once the class officially begins the teacher can switch to Ukrainian and keep talking in Ukrainian until someone becomes noisy, or someone seems not to be understanding. Russian will then be used to establish a more direct, and fast, channel of communication and to remind them that the teachers is "one of them". One informant once admitted that this was no one's native language but they all tried their best (to comply with state instructions).

It was often the case that some pupils would not understand new (Ukrainian) words during a class so that the teacher would get back to the explanation and repeat most of it in Russian, explaining the meaning of the new word or terms. This is a very important mediation task that teachers perform since they boost language skills of the pupils without creating a hostile environment (which would be the case, for instance, if they insisted to use only Ukrainian without any Russian explanation). In many respects they create the impression of a fully Ukrainian environment while keeping the situation comfortable for the students, who should progressively get them used to a relatively Ukrainian speaking milieu.

The complexity of the environment is also visible when observing pupils' reactions. Their capacity, and possibility, to use Ukrainian depends in large part on how the information is interiorised. It was often the case that by trusting their own intuition when guessing an answer, they would prefer using Russian. In contrast, an answer that they remember from a Ukrainian textbook would come out in Ukrainian. The role of the teacher would be to allow both languages, while translating Russian answers into Ukrainian to keep the official version. In this respect teachers create a symbolic space and show the pupils what should be done, as opposed to the reality of what is happening in the class.

Another important point is the creation of the impression that, in a(ny) particular moment, the use of Russian is an exception allowed only once because of dealing with a specific case. Teachers seem to suggest that they are using Russian (only this time) but in all other situations they would be using Ukrainian. Herzfeld wrote that "if people declare that something does not exist, then it does not" (Herzfeld 2005, ix). By massively denying the role of Russian in their daily and professional life, teachers seems to give the impression of satisfactorily complying with the requirements from Kiev.

An opportunity to go beyond the language façade was provided in observations during language classes. While learning French and having to translate words, sentences and even texts into a language they understood, pupils could pass on the obligation to use Ukrainian. Teachers showed awareness of the impossibility of the exercise and emphasis was put on the foreign language, so that asserting Ukrainian became less of a priority. Pupils would mostly translate from French into Russian and vice versa so that they could concentrate on the foreign language learning.

Integration, or even replacement, of information provided in official books is also very common and there are many reasons to do that. In addition from the books being old, out-of-date or simply lacking, teachers are endorsed with the task of delivering a version of history and other subjects that is quite different from what they have studied (Richardson 2008, Rodgers 2007) or they might be asked to teach something new that was not part of their formation so far and do not want to run the course on unknown textbooks.

These patterns were not circumscribed to class dynamics, even in a professional environment I noticed that it was common to start a conversation with a colleague, or simply greet them, in Ukrainian and to then switch into Russian (once sure that the interlocutor also prefers Russian or is at least fine with using Russian). Meetings with parents, just like many other official events (court hearings, negotiations with civil servants) allow the use of either languages, as long as the person chairing is committed to use some Ukrainian and thus build the necessary façade of Ukrainian-ness.

Numbers and official documents seem to show, in Odessa as in the rest of the country, that Ukrainian is widely spoken and used. A deeper look into the linguistic dynamics will expose an informal mechanism that mediates between how things should be and how they are. Odessans are able to limit the use of Ukrainian in their daily life but display it in a way that does not challenge state instructions. This is not very far from what happens in other contexts such as Kazakhstan, where the Kazakh language broadcasting quotas are mostly filled during night hours or where a classical music concert is introduced in Kazakh so that 2 hours of music count as Kazakh broadcasting (OBeachain and Kevlihan 2013). A similar situation is findable in political institutions such as the Odessa city administration where an informant reported:

> In my office, we all speak Russian and communicate in writing in Russian. However, sometimes we need to send some communication out and, when this happens, you would see people around panicking. For instance, when an official fax needs to be sent to Kiev we would start looking for the only one or two Ukrainian speakers in the office, asking them to translate them. In Kiev they would receive an official fax in the state language, thus crediting us for working in the state language. Nobody would question our language use in most other moments of our work.

One of my informants reported using Ukrainian in state offices, despite not being his native language, because the use of Ukrainian was often associated with a higher status in the city. To enter a public office and speak Ukrainian you must be someone important, he used to joke, and so he would use it to gain status in front of a civil servant. In many respects this is a move to put your interlocutor in a difficult position. As a civil servant they knew they should be using Ukrainian and so you tease their official and professional side out of them when using the state language.

In this respect, knowledge of Ukrainian is often considered as a business card, something you show when you have to introduce yourself (Sovik 2006). In practice, things are a bit different. Even if not legally mandatory, it is difficult to imagine an office job where knowledge of Russian is not needed.

4 Concluding remarks

This chapter has suggested some possible new directions in the study of informality. It started from the point that significance of informality goes well beyond its economic or monetary value, as suggested also in the introduction. Informal practices can be seen embedded in economic relations but this is not the end of the story. With informality occupying the space between two formal rules, informal practices can be seen as a way to renegotiate formal rules when they do not fully fit a given context or situation.

I cannot claim to be the first one to investigate non-economic aspects of informality. The value of this chapter, however, lies in its suggestion to look for a pattern and look at informality from a more holistic perspective. The case study engaged with language policies in Ukraine and, in particular, the way language patterns and perception are renegotiated informally if they do not sufficiently match people's expectations in a given context. The mechanism I identify involves unrealistic expectations by state institutions, assuming that Ukrainian can be the language of official communication in a very short spell, and the incapacity of the citizens to comply with such a proposal. In this context, instructions are renegotiated at several levels and even those in charge of implementing them might turn out to be unable to comply with them. The result is a substantial gap between what the state imagines doing and what in reality happens that I suggest patterns that go well beyond my case study. In the early moments of my research on identity in Odessa I was preoccupied with understanding language dynamics, who spoke what and how language attitudes could develop. While being interesting, I think the most important results from the study are those that can be extended to other spheres of life and that starts from the question: what happens when what the state and its citizens want does not overlap?

(good) Policy making is the art of identifying the incentives that prompt people to change. However, there is no guarantee that the first attempt will be successful and, even so, it might take a good deal of time before a sufficient number of people change their attitude and we can state that the policy was successful. What happens in all the other cases is that informality plays a key role in making a transition smoother, bend some rules to make them more acceptable or even make up for bad policy making.

I cannot claim to exhaust the whole range of possibilities and options but this chapter was an attempt to go beyond the usual informality economic framework to look for a pattern and points that are common to all, or at least most, the situations we can observe once informality comes to play a significant role. As in many cases in academia, there are perhaps more questions than answers prompted by this work and my hope is that a growing number of scholars can and will get interested in informality so to contribute to its study from a variety of perspectives, which is what is needed to make a contribution more significant.

Cited works

Arel, D. (1995) Language Politics in Independent Ukraine: Towards One or Two State Languages? Nationalities Papers 3, 597–622.

Bacchetta, M. E. Ernst and J.P. Bustamante (2009) Globalization and informal jobs in developing countries Geneva, ILO–WTO.

Barrington, L. (1995) The domestic and international consequences of citizenship in the Soviet successor states. Europe-Asia Studies 47(5): 731–763.

Beissinger, M. R. (2002) Nationalist mobilization and the collapse of the Soviet State. Cambridge University Press.

Benjamin, N., K. Beegle, F. Recanatini, M. Santini, (2014) Informal Economy and the World Bank The World Bank Policy Research Working Paper 6888.

Chanet, J. F. (1996) L'École républicaine et les petites patries. Paris: Aubier.

Fioramonti, L. (2014) How numbers rule the world: the use and abuse of statistics in global politics. Zed Books.

Gallin, D. (2001) Propositions on trade unions and informal employment in times of globalisation. Antipode 33(3), 531–549.

Gupta, A. (1995) Blurred Boundaries, American Ethnologist 22(2): 375–402.

Hart, K. (1973) Informal Income Opportunities and Urban Employment in Ghana, Journal of Modern African Studies 11(1): 61–89.

Herzfeld, M. (2005) Cultural Intimacy, New York: Routledge.

Hobsbawm, E., and Rudé, G. ([1968] 2014) Captain Swing. Verso Books.

ILO (1972) Employment, Incomes and Equality: A Strategy for Increasing Productive Employment in Kenya. Geneva: ILO.

Janmaat, J. (2000) Nation Building in Post-Soviet Ukraine. Educational Policy and the Response of the Russian Speaking Population. Utrecht, Amsterdam: Royal Dutch Geographical Society.

Jütting, J.P. and Laiglesia, J.R. (2009) Employment, poverty reduction and development: what's new? in Jütting, J.P. and Laiglesia, J.R. (eds.), Is Informal Normal? Towards more and better jobs in developing countries, OECD, Paris, 112–139.

Kuts O. (2004) Movna polityka v derzhatvochyskykh protsessakh Ukrainy, Kharkiv: Kharkiv National University Press.

Kuzio, T. (1997). Ukraine under Kuchma: political reform, economic transformation and security policy in independent Ukraine. St. Martin's Press.

La Porta, R. and A. Shleifer (2014) Informality and Development Journal of Economic Perspectives 28(3): 109–126

London, T. and S. L. Hart (2004) Reinventing Strategies for Emerging Markets: Beyond the Transnational Model, Journal of International Business Studies, 35: 350–370.

Misztal, B.A. (2000) Informality: Social Theory and Contemporary Practice. Routledge, London.

Morris J. and Polese, A. (eds.) (2015) Informal Economies in Post-Socialist Spaces: Practices, Institutions and Networks. London: Palgrave

Morris, J. and Polese, A. (eds.) (2014) The Informal Post-Socialist Economy: Embedded Practices and Livelihoods. London and New York: Routledge.

Navaro-Yashin, Y. (2002) Faces of the state: Secularism and public life in Turkey. Princeton University Press.

Nwabuzor, A. (2005) Corruption and Development: New Initiatives in Economic Openness and Strengthened Rule of Law, Journal of Business Ethics, 59: 121–138.

Ó Beacháin, D., and R. Kevlihan (2013) Threading a needle: Kazakhstan between civic and ethnonationalist state-building. Nations and Nationalism 19(2): 337–356.

Ó Beacháin D. and Polese A. (eds.) (2010) The Colour Revolutions in the Former Soviet Union: Successes and Failures, London and New York: Routledge.

Ó Beacháin, D. and A. Polese (2010b) 'Rocking the Vote': New Forms of Youth Organization in Post-Communist Spaces, Journal of Youth Studies 10(2): 1–16.

Pichler, F., & Wallace, C. (2007) Patterns of formal and informal social capital in Europe. European Sociological Review, 23(4): 423–435.

Polese, A., & Kevlihan, R. (2015) Locating insurgency, informality and social movements on a spectrum: is there a theory linking them all. In 9th Pan-European Conference on International Relations, Giardini Naxos, Sicily, Italy, September 23–26.

Polese, A. (2009) Ukraine 2004: Informal Networks, Transformation of Social Capital and Coloured Revolutions, Journal of Communist Studies and Transition Politics 25(2–3): 255–277.

Polese, A. (2009b) Une version alternative de la «révolution orange»: transformations identitaires et 'nation building spontané', Socio-logos 4.

Polese, A. (2008) Ukraine 1991–2006: Where are all the Communists Gone? in Uwe Backes and Patrick Moreau (eds.) Communist Parties in Eastern Europe after 1989. V&R: Gottingen.

Polese, A. and A. Wylegala (2008) Odessa and Lvov or Odesa and Lviv: How Important is a Letter? Reflections on the ‚Other' in Two Ukrainian Cities. Nationalities Papers 36(5): 787–814.

Polese, A. and A. Wylegala (2008b) Sprache und Identitat: Reflexionen aus Odessa und Lwiw, Ukraine Analyse 49: 13–17.

Richardson, T. (2008) Kaleidoscopic Odessa: History and Place in Contemporary Ukraine. Toronto: University of Toronto Press.

Rodgers, P. (2007) Compliance or Contradiction'? Teaching 'History' in the 'New' Ukraine. A View from Ukraine's Eastern Borderlands. Europe-Asia Studies 59(3): 503–519

Scott, J. (1985) Weapons of the Weak: Everyday Forms of Peasant Resistance, New Haven and London: Yale University Press.

Slavnic, Z. (2010). Political economy of informalization. European Societies,12(1): 3–23.

Søvik, M. (2006) Languages in a Ukrainian-Russian borderland: talking about history and identity, in Madeleine Hurd (ed) Border Crossing. Stockolm: Gondolin, 195–224.

Stebelsky, I. (2009). Ethnic self-identification in Ukraine, 1989–2001: why more Ukrainians and fewer Russians? Canadian Slavonic Papers, 51(1): 77–100.

Szporluk, R. (1990) Poland and the Rise of Theory and Practice of Modern Nationality 1770–1870. Dialectics and Humanism 17(2): 43–64

UCEPS (Ukrainian Center for Economic and Political Studies). (2002) The System of Education in Ukraine: Perspects and Development. National Security and Defence 4, 5–8. www.uceps.org/eng/show/582

By way of conclusion: on current and further directions in informality research

The problem with research on informality is that informality is not a marginal phenomenon. It is everywhere but, given its, mostly, intangible and dynamic form (you cannot see it, you can only estimate it – in some cases and with a possible high margin of error) it does not find a place in the agenda of politicians, who are under pressure to show concrete results. In this respect corruption or fiscal fraud are easily perceived as bad behaviour and curbing corruption or ensuring fiscal compliance are easier to "sell" to the electorate as good results. In contrast, the meaning, or meanings, of informality encompass too many different things and only when it is associated to something concrete can it be used as evidence for policy making or evaluation. A promise to "reduce informality" would inevitably lead to the question "what does informality mean" and result into a too complex an explanation for a political campaign targeting thousands of people. This is also linked to the fact that, apart from ultra-normative positions seeing informality as solely negative and thus too eradicate, informality may be, as many other things, actually both positive and negative depending on the context, the results and the intentions.

There is no objectively acceptable position on informality but there is, in spite of what it is usually claimed in the social sciences, a "wrong" position on informality. I am referring to the claim that informality can be wiped out of a society, of an institution or of a given context. At least if we use the definition given at the beginning of this book, informality being the space between two formal rules, this space can be filled in many different manners and by many different behaviours. The space changes as rules change. What was legal becomes illegal and then legal again, depending on state necessities one can perceive as being objective, but it depends, ultimately, on the number of human beings with their taste, their beliefs and their dogmas. Once a state outlaws a behaviour or an item, they will create incentives to abide the law but there is no guarantee that their citizens will ultimately follow the rules. Think of the policies from various governments on alcohol and drugs and how they have been known to be inconsistent. Throughout the centuries, the legality of products have often been reversed from being restricted to allowed so much that the logic is not always easy to follow. For one thing, cannabis has been banned for years before becoming a source of tax revenue in various US states. Alcohol was prohibited in the US during 1920–1933 and a number of other practices were formally forbidden in the former USSR even if they were informally accepted.

There is a state, suggesting – or better instructing on – how people should behave and then there are its citizens. Even though it would be nice to think of a situation where the state rules and the people take instructions and follow them, it is rarely so. There is, in fact, in many situations, a gap between what the state wants and what the people want. For one thing, the sum of individual goods (what a citizen thinks is better for him or her) does not necessarily, if ever, bring to the good of the collectivity but possibly to the opposite. Damage for a collectivity, or a society in the case of a state, comes from selfish individuals imposing their will on a number of aspects in society's life in a short-term and self-centred perspective.

This is possibly the logic behind the desire of a state, or other forms of human institutions, to "educate", or indoctrinate, people. It is possible to show them the big picture so to realise that, while little gain for them means a large loss for society, sometimes giving up some relatively small privileges might ultimately benefit the whole community. This is possibly the ultimate role of a state and of rules and laws regulating a society. When we were taught in school, or by our parents, not to litter we accepted being uncomfortable (keeping something we do not want any longer in our hand or pocket) for the benefit of the collectivity (to have a cleaner street, town, city). The same happened when we were taught not to steal: we gave up the potential of increasing our satisfaction (get something for free) in exchange for other benefits (a society where it is less likely that they steel our own property). In both cases, we were given a positive and negative incentive and many, though not all, of us thought it was a fair deal.

But things are not always so straightforward. A ban on fishing in a fishing community, even with the best intentions in mind (preservation of the marine flora and fauna in some areas) is likely to be met with hostility by the local community. After all, how many of us refuse to switch off our computers despite evidence that standby still consumes electricity that the rest of the world needs?

The space, be it symbolic, in time, or physical, between what is the best for an individual and for a collectivity can be filled in many ways. It is the starting point of human agency, most likely versus the collectivity or the state. In the beginning, when a sphere of life is not regulated, there is only the collectivity and the unregulated (by the state, the community might have its own unwritten rules). At some point, some institution decides that there is a need for a formal rule and adopts it. However, giving instructions that work out-of-the-box for a large territory is difficult - I would say impossible. The new instructions are likely to upset a part, or the majority, of the community. Some will abide, some will reject the new rules, some individuals or groups will be faster and some will be slower in accepting emit. Some others might remain in limbo acting "mostly" according to the rule but with some personal modifications. Some others will do the minimal needed not to get in trouble with the law or simply show compliance without really acting on the new instructions. Once the state receives its first feedback, it is up to the decision-makers to decide how much they can live with the current status quo – that is, a certain percentage abiding, a certain percentage not abiding and the ones in between. It is also up to the state, and its government, to make new attempts for change and decide whether it is worth it or not to invest resources into further behaviour or attitude change.

The reason why I see informality so important in a community, a society or a state, is that it is intimately related with policy making and the mechanisms of governance. Informality is like bacteria, some of them are harmful and many of them are dangerous. However, they also have good functions and in a world without them we would possibly have more health issues than in the current one. Informality is thus not an evil to eradicate but a mechanism to study, understand and control - at least partly since total control on informality is virtually impossible or too costly at best.

This book has been an attempt to shed light on some informal mechanisms of governance that, while they can be considered pieces of a global theory of informality, are certainly non-exhaustive and show that a wider understanding of the phenomenon is needed. It initially dealt with the perceived and "real" role of the state, showing the various meanings of welfare states and challenging the idea that the state is the sole source of welfare, by illustrating the existence of other, non-state controlled mechanisms of welfare production and consumption. The discourse on welfare was expanded to the production of labour, employment, and salaries. A few cases at the margin were provided of border towns, border crossings and the capacity to bridge the gap between supply and demand beyond the state, and what it allows, were called upon. Border crossings, it was shown, may be used to generate opportunities and take advantage of the earning potential through transaction costs. Although outlawed by the state, and fought by its institutions, the morality of cross-border trade is nuanced by a variety of local perceptions, expectations and the limited opportunities existing in some areas. These chapters were not used to justify illegal transactions in full but to show the discrepancies that can arise between individual and state moralities in a variety of situations.

The discourse then moved to the production of opportunities in the public sector or, better, in a specific case of the public sector, where public employment is only apparent or nominal, since de facto does not pay the bills. When this happens we fall, it was argued, into a different category of a semi-public worker where only a part of what is needed is provided by the state and the boundary between public and private, corruption and favour, legal and licit, become volatile and blurred. The main points of this discussion can be found in the chapter on private initiative where we show the complementarity, and to a certain extent competition, between not only the private and public sector but on how informality fills the spaces that are not claimed by neither of them.

The last three chapters gradually switched focus from economic to other aspects of informality. It becomes important, thus, to notice the degree to which informality is interrelated with traditions, culture and everyday life. Hospitality rituals were explored, together with their socio-economic significance, to integrate a cultural component in the use of informality and show that it is not all about money. There are a number of other (intangible) currencies, such as respectability, reputation, friendship and support that are also sought after and are important when deciding whether to engage in informal practices. The final chapter stretched this approach by taking a direction that I wanted to take many years ago but only quickly engaged with. The use of informality in mechanisms of governance has little, if anything, to do with economic governance plays a double role. On the one hand it may be regarded as closing the circle of informality, by showing its relevance in a variety of aspects; on the other one, however, it provided some suggestions for furthering the field of study of informality.

By way of conclusion, I would ask: can informality become mainstream research? Given the exponential increase in works on informality, explored from a variety of standpoints (economics, anthropology, sociology, management, geography), it is possible that informality will play a growing role in academic debates. After all, I could not imagine it would have gone this far when I started some years ago. However, given the fact research on informality has often started from a radical or critical perspective, with no one daring to come up with a theory of informality, I see the role of informality research with a limited potential at this stage. It is a word used increasingly to shed light on phenomena that were under perceived or understudied in the past but it is mostly used to state, "the current one is not the sole explanation we can find, we have to consider informality". For one thing, take the recent field of informal governance. It was not created to argue that things happen informally and are then formalised, but to show that some decisions are affected by informal mechanisms and processes that have been neglected so far. Finally, we should not become enthusiastic supporters of informality to the point of forgetting the role of formal mechanisms and formal governance that are used to give continuity to decisions beyond a single individual, which allows structures and countries to survive crisis in spite of regular change in their institutions and leading figures.

Perhaps this is the perverse pleasure of research on informality. To grant oneself the permission of criticising current approaches by maintaining that there is a side of the picture that has not been considered and that only an informality framework can help us to understand it. It is the joy and sorrow of critical research, to claim to be free from existing structures and mainstream ideas while rhetorically asking why the rest of the world does not consider us as important as we could claim to be.

SOVIET AND POST-SOVIET POLITICS AND SOCIETY

Edited by Dr. Andreas Umland

ISSN 1614-3515

1   Андреас Умланд (ред.)
    Воплощение Европейской
    конвенции по правам человека в
    России
    Философские, юридические и
    эмпирические исследования
    ISBN 3-89821-387-0

2   Christian Wipperfürth
    Russland – ein vertrauenswürdiger
    Partner?
    Grundlagen, Hintergründe und Praxis
    gegenwärtiger russischer Außenpolitik
    Mit einem Vorwort von Heinz Timmermann
    ISBN 3-89821-401-X

3   Manja Hussner
    Die Übernahme internationalen Rechts
    in die russische und deutsche
    Rechtsordnung
    Eine vergleichende Analyse zur
    Völkerrechtsfreundlichkeit der Verfassungen
    der Russländischen Föderation und der
    Bundesrepublik Deutschland
    Mit einem Vorwort von Rainer Arnold
    ISBN 3-89821-438-9

4   Matthew Tejada
    Bulgaria's Democratic Consolidation
    and the Kozloduy Nuclear Power Plant
    (KNPP)
    The Unattainability of Closure
    With a foreword by Richard J. Crampton
    ISBN 3-89821-439-7

5   Марк Григорьевич Меерович
    Квадратные метры, определяющие
    сознание
    Государственная жилищная политика в
    СССР. 1921 – 1941 гг
    ISBN 3-89821-474-5

6   Andrei P. Tsygankov, Pavel
    A.Tsygankov (Eds.)
    New Directions in Russian
    International Studies
    ISBN 3-89821-422-2

7   Марк Григорьевич Меерович
    Как власть народ к труду приучала
    Жилище в СССР – средство управления
    людьми. 1917 – 1941 гг.
    С предисловием Елены Осокиной
    ISBN 3-89821-495-8

8   David J. Galbreath
    Nation-Building and Minority Politics
    in Post-Socialist States
    Interests, Influence and Identities in Estonia
    and Latvia
    With a foreword by David J. Smith
    ISBN 3-89821-467-2

9   Алексей Юрьевич Безугольный
    Народы Кавказа в Вооруженных
    силах СССР в годы Великой
    Отечественной войны 1941-1945 гг.
    С предисловием Николая Бугая
    ISBN 3-89821-475-3

10 Вячеслав Лихачев и Владимир
    Прибыловский (ред.)
    Русское Национальное Единство,
    1990-2000. В 2-х томах
    ISBN 3-89821-523-7

11 Николай Бугай (ред.)
    Народы стран Балтии в условиях
    сталинизма (1940-е – 1950-е годы)
    Документированная история
    ISBN 3-89821-525-3

12 Ingmar Bredies (Hrsg.)
    Zur Anatomie der Orange Revolution
    in der Ukraine
    Wechsel des Elitenregimes oder Triumph des
    Parlamentarismus?
    ISBN 3-89821-524-5

13 Anastasia V. Mitrofanova
    The Politicization of Russian
    Orthodoxy
    Actors and Ideas
    With a foreword by William C. Gay
    ISBN 3-89821-481-8

14   Nathan D. Larson
     Alexander Solzhenitsyn and the
     Russo-Jewish Question
     ISBN 3-89821-483-4

15   Guido Houben
     Kulturpolitik und Ethnizität
     Staatliche Kunstförderung im Russland der
     neunziger Jahre
     Mit einem Vorwort von Gert Weisskirchen
     ISBN 3-89821-542-3

16   Leonid Luks
     Der russische „Sonderweg"?
     Aufsätze zur neuesten Geschichte Russlands
     im europäischen Kontext
     ISBN 3-89821-496-6

17   Евгений Мороз
     История «Мёртвой воды» – от
     страшной сказки к большой
     политике
     Политическое неоязычество в
     постсоветской России
     ISBN 3-89821-551-2

18   Александр Верховский и Галина
     Кожевникова (ред.)
     Этническая и религиозная
     интолерантность в российских СМИ
     Результаты мониторинга 2001-2004 гг.
     ISBN 3-89821-569-5

19   Christian Ganzer
     Sowjetisches Erbe und ukrainische
     Nation
     Das Museum der Geschichte des Zaporoger
     Kosakentums auf der Insel Chortycja
     Mit einem Vorwort von Frank Golczewski
     ISBN 3-89821-504-0

20   Эльза-Баир Гучинова
     Помнить нельзя забыть
     Антропология депортационной травмы
     калмыков
     С предисловием Кэролайн Хамфри
     ISBN 3-89821-506-7

21   Юлия Лидерман
     Мотивы «проверки» и «испытания»
     в постсоветской культуре
     Советское прошлое в российском
     кинематографе 1990-х годов
     С предисловием Евгения Марголита
     ISBN 3-89821-511-3

22   Tanya Lokshina, Ray Thomas, Mary
     Mayer (Eds.)
     The Imposition of a Fake Political
     Settlement in the Northern Caucasus
     The 2003 Chechen Presidential Election
     ISBN 3-89821-436-2

23   Timothy McCajor Hall, Rosie Read
     (Eds.)
     Changes in the Heart of Europe
     Recent Ethnographies of Czechs, Slovaks,
     Roma, and Sorbs
     With an afterword by Zdeněk Salzmann
     ISBN 3-89821-606-3

24   Christian Autengruber
     Die politischen Parteien in Bulgarien
     und Rumänien
     Eine vergleichende Analyse seit Beginn der
     90er Jahre
     Mit einem Vorwort von Dorothée de Nève
     ISBN 3-89821-476-1

25   Annette Freyberg-Inan with Radu
     Cristescu
     The Ghosts in Our Classrooms, or:
     John Dewey Meets Ceauşescu
     The Promise and the Failures of Civic
     Education in Romania
     ISBN 3-89821-416-8

26   John B. Dunlop
     The 2002 Dubrovka and 2004 Beslan
     Hostage Crises
     A Critique of Russian Counter-Terrorism
     With a foreword by Donald N. Jensen
     ISBN 3-89821-608-X

27   Peter Koller
     Das touristische Potenzial von
     Kam''janec'–Podil's'kyj
     Eine fremdenverkehrsgeographische
     Untersuchung der Zukunftsperspektiven und
     Maßnahmenplanung zur
     Destinationsentwicklung des „ukrainischen
     Rothenburg"
     Mit einem Vorwort von Kristiane Klemm
     ISBN 3-89821-640-3

28   Françoise Daucé, Elisabeth Sieca-
     Kozlowski (Eds.)
     Dedovshchina in the Post-Soviet
     Military
     Hazing of Russian Army Conscripts in a
     Comparative Perspective
     With a foreword by Dale Herspring
     ISBN 3-89821-616-0

29 Florian Strasser
    Zivilgesellschaftliche Einflüsse auf die
    Orange Revolution
    Die gewaltlose Massenbewegung und die
    ukrainische Wahlkrise 2004
    Mit einem Vorwort von Egbert Jahn
    ISBN 3-89821-648-9

30 Rebecca S. Katz
    The Georgian Regime Crisis of 2003-
    2004
    A Case Study in Post-Soviet Media
    Representation of Politics, Crime and
    Corruption
    ISBN 3-89821-413-3

31 Vladimir Kantor
    Willkür oder Freiheit
    Beiträge zur russischen Geschichtsphilosophie
    Ediert von Dagmar Herrmann sowie mit
    einem Vorwort versehen von Leonid Luks
    ISBN 3-89821-589-X

32 Laura A. Victoir
    The Russian Land Estate Today
    A Case Study of Cultural Politics in Post-
    Soviet Russia
    With a foreword by Priscilla Roosevelt
    ISBN 3-89821-426-5

33 Ivan Katchanovski
    Cleft Countries
    Regional Political Divisions and Cultures in
    Post-Soviet Ukraine and Moldova
    With a foreword by Francis Fukuyama
    ISBN 3-89821-558-X

34 Florian Mühlfried
    Postsowjetische Feiern
    Das Georgische Bankett im Wandel
    Mit einem Vorwort von Kevin Tuite
    ISBN 3-89821-601-2

35 Roger Griffin, Werner Loh, Andreas
    Umland (Eds.)
    Fascism Past and Present, West and
    East
    An International Debate on Concepts and
    Cases in the Comparative Study of the
    Extreme Right
    With an afterword by Walter Laqueur
    ISBN 3-89821-674-8

36 Sebastian Schlegel
    Der „Weiße Archipel"
    Sowjetische Atomstädte 1945-1991
    Mit einem Geleitwort von Thomas Bohn
    ISBN 3-89821-679-9

37 Vyacheslav Likhachev
    Political Anti-Semitism in Post-Soviet
    Russia
    Actors and Ideas in 1991-2003
    Edited and translated from Russian by Eugene
    Veklerov
    ISBN 3-89821-529-6

38 Josette Baer (Ed.)
    Preparing Liberty in Central Europe
    Political Texts from the Spring of Nations
    1848 to the Spring of Prague 1968
    With a foreword by Zdeněk V. David
    ISBN 3-89821-546-6

39 Михаил Лукьянов
    Российский консерватизм и
    реформа, 1907-1914
    С предисловием Марка Д. Стейнберга
    ISBN 3-89821-503-2

40 Nicola Melloni
    Market Without Economy
    The 1998 Russian Financial Crisis
    With a foreword by Eiji Furukawa
    ISBN 3-89821-407-9

41 Dmitrij Chmelnizki
    Die Architektur Stalins
    Bd. 1: Studien zu Ideologie und Stil
    Bd. 2: Bilddokumentation
    Mit einem Vorwort von Bruno Flierl
    ISBN 3-89821-515-6

42 Katja Yafimava
    Post-Soviet Russian-Belarussian
    Relationships
    The Role of Gas Transit Pipelines
    With a foreword by Jonathan P. Stern
    ISBN 3-89821-655-1

43 Boris Chavkin
    Verflechtungen der deutschen und
    russischen Zeitgeschichte
    Aufsätze und Archivfunde zu den
    Beziehungen Deutschlands und der
    Sowjetunion von 1917 bis 1991
    Ediert von Markus Edlinger sowie mit einem
    Vorwort versehen von Leonid Luks
    ISBN 3-89821-756-6

44 Anastasija Grynenko in
Zusammenarbeit mit Claudia Dathe
Die Terminologie des Gerichtswesens
der Ukraine und Deutschlands im
Vergleich
Eine übersetzungswissenschaftliche Analyse
juristischer Fachbegriffe im Deutschen,
Ukrainischen und Russischen
Mit einem Vorwort von Ulrich Hartmann
ISBN 3-89821-691-8

45 Anton Burkov
The Impact of the European
Convention on Human Rights on
Russian Law
Legislation and Application in 1996-2006
With a foreword by Françoise Hampson
ISBN 978-3-89821-639-5

46 Stina Torjesen, Indra Overland (Eds.)
International Election Observers in
Post-Soviet Azerbaijan
Geopolitical Pawns or Agents of Change?
ISBN 978-3-89821-743-9

47 Taras Kuzio
Ukraine – Crimea – Russia
Triangle of Conflict
ISBN 978-3-89821-761-3

48 Claudia Šabić
"Ich erinnere mich nicht, aber L'viv!"
Zur Funktion kultureller Faktoren für die
Institutionalisierung und Entwicklung einer
ukrainischen Region
Mit einem Vorwort von Melanie Tatur
ISBN 978-3-89821-752-1

49 Marlies Bilz
Tatarstan in der Transformation
Nationaler Diskurs und Politische Praxis
1988-1994
Mit einem Vorwort von Frank Golczewski
ISBN 978-3-89821-722-4

50 Марлен Ларюэль (ред.)
Современные интерпретации
русского национализма
ISBN 978-3-89821-795-8

51 Sonja Schüler
Die ethnische Dimension der Armut
Roma im postsozialistischen Rumänien
Mit einem Vorwort von Anton Sterbling
ISBN 978-3-89821-776-7

52 Галина Кожевникова
Радикальный национализм в России
и противодействие ему
Сборник докладов Центра «Сова» за 2004-
2007 гг.
С предисловием Александра Верховского
ISBN 978-3-89821-721-7

53 Галина Кожевникова и Владимир
Прибыловский
Российская власть в биографиях I
Высшие должностные лица РФ в 2004 г.
ISBN 978-3-89821-796-5

54 Галина Кожевникова и Владимир
Прибыловский
Российская власть в биографиях II
Члены Правительства РФ в 2004 г.
ISBN 978-3-89821-797-2

55 Галина Кожевникова и Владимир
Прибыловский
Российская власть в биографиях III
Руководители федеральных служб и
агентств РФ в 2004 г.
ISBN 978-3-89821-798-9

56 Ileana Petroniu
Privatisierung in
Transformationsökonomien
Determinanten der Restrukturierungs-
Bereitschaft am Beispiel Polens, Rumäniens
und der Ukraine
Mit einem Vorwort von Rainer W. Schäfer
ISBN 978-3-89821-790-3

57 Christian Wipperfürth
Russland und seine GUS-Nachbarn
Hintergründe, aktuelle Entwicklungen und
Konflikte in einer ressourcenreichen Region
ISBN 978-3-89821-801-6

58 Togzhan Kassenova
From Antagonism to Partnership
The Uneasy Path of the U.S.-Russian
Cooperative Threat Reduction
With a foreword by Christoph Bluth
ISBN 978-3-89821-707-1

59 Alexander Höllwerth
Das sakrale eurasische Imperium des
Aleksandr Dugin
Eine Diskursanalyse zum postsowjetischen
russischen Rechtsextremismus
Mit einem Vorwort von Dirk Uffelmann
ISBN 978-3-89821-813-9

60 Олег Рябов
«Россия-Матушка»
Национализм, гендер и война в России XX
века
С предисловием Елены Гощило
ISBN 978-3-89821-487-2

61 Ivan Maistrenko
Borot'bism
A Chapter in the History of the Ukrainian
Revolution
With a new introduction by Chris Ford
Translated by George S. N. Luckyj with the
assistance of Ivan L. Rudnytsky
ISBN 978-3-89821-697-5

62 Maryna Romanets
Anamorphosic Texts and
Reconfigured Visions
Improvised Traditions in Contemporary
Ukrainian and Irish Literature
ISBN 978-3-89821-576-3

63 Paul D'Anieri and Taras Kuzio (Eds.)
Aspects of the Orange Revolution I
Democratization and Elections in Post-
Communist Ukraine
ISBN 978-3-89821-698-2

64 Bohdan Harasymiw in collaboration
with Oleh S. Ilnytzkyj (Eds.)
Aspects of the Orange Revolution II
Information and Manipulation Strategies in
the 2004 Ukrainian Presidential Elections
ISBN 978-3-89821-699-9

65 Ingmar Bredies, Andreas Umland and
Valentin Yakushik (Eds.)
Aspects of the Orange Revolution III
The Context and Dynamics of the 2004
Ukrainian Presidential Elections
ISBN 978-3-89821-803-0

66 Ingmar Bredies, Andreas Umland and
Valentin Yakushik (Eds.)
Aspects of the Orange Revolution IV
Foreign Assistance and Civic Action in the
2004 Ukrainian Presidential Elections
ISBN 978-3-89821-808-5

67 Ingmar Bredies, Andreas Umland and
Valentin Yakushik (Eds.)
Aspects of the Orange Revolution V
Institutional Observation Reports on the 2004
Ukrainian Presidential Elections
ISBN 978-3-89821-809-2

68 Taras Kuzio (Ed.)
Aspects of the Orange Revolution VI
Post-Communist Democratic Revolutions in
Comparative Perspective
ISBN 978-3-89821-820-7

69 Tim Bohse
Autoritarismus statt Selbstverwaltung
Die Transformation der kommunalen Politik
in der Stadt Kaliningrad 1990-2005
Mit einem Geleitwort von Stefan Troebst
ISBN 978-3-89821-782-8

70 David Rupp
Die Rußländische Föderation und die
russischsprachige Minderheit in
Lettland
Eine Fallstudie zur Anwaltspolitik Moskaus
gegenüber den russophonen Minderheiten im
„Nahen Ausland" von 1991 bis 2002
Mit einem Vorwort von Helmut Wagner
ISBN 978-3-89821-778-1

71 Taras Kuzio
Theoretical and Comparative
Perspectives on Nationalism
New Directions in Cross-Cultural and Post-
Communist Studies
With a foreword by Paul Robert Magocsi
ISBN 978-3-89821-815-3

72 Christine Teichmann
Die Hochschultransformation im
heutigen Osteuropa
Kontinuität und Wandel bei der Entwicklung
des postkommunistischen Universitätswesens
Mit einem Vorwort von Oskar Anweiler
ISBN 978-3-89821-842-9

73 Julia Kusznir
Der politische Einfluss von
Wirtschaftseliten in russischen
Regionen
Eine Analyse am Beispiel der Erdöl- und
Erdgasindustrie, 1992-2005
Mit einem Vorwort von Wolfgang Eichwede
ISBN 978-3-89821-821-4

74 Alena Vysotskaya
Russland, Belarus und die EU-
Osterweiterung
Zur Minderheitenfrage und zum Problem der
Freizügigkeit des Personenverkehrs
Mit einem Vorwort von Katlijn Malfliet
ISBN 978-3-89821-822-1

75 Heiko Pleines (Hrsg.)
    Corporate Governance in post-
    sozialistischen Volkswirtschaften
    ISBN 978-3-89821-766-8

76 Stefan Ihrig
    Wer sind die Moldawier?
    Rumänismus versus Moldowanismus in
    Historiographie und Schulbüchern der
    Republik Moldova, 1991-2006
    Mit einem Vorwort von Holm Sundhaussen
    ISBN 978-3-89821-466-7

77 Galina Kozhevnikova in collaboration
    with Alexander Verkhovsky and
    Eugene Veklerov
    Ultra-Nationalism and Hate Crimes in
    Contemporary Russia
    The 2004-2006 Annual Reports of Moscow's
    SOVA Center
    With a foreword by Stephen D. Shenfield
    ISBN 978-3-89821-868-9

78 Florian Küchler
    The Role of the European Union in
    Moldova's Transnistria Conflict
    With a foreword by Christopher Hill
    ISBN 978-3-89821-850-4

79 Bernd Rechel
    The Long Way Back to Europe
    Minority Protection in Bulgaria
    With a foreword by Richard Crampton
    ISBN 978-3-89821-863-4

80 Peter W. Rodgers
    Nation, Region and History in Post-
    Communist Transitions
    Identity Politics in Ukraine, 1991-2006
    With a foreword by Vera Tolz
    ISBN 978-3-89821-903-7

81 Stephanie Solywoda
    The Life and Work of
    Semen L. Frank
    A Study of Russian Religious Philosophy
    With a foreword by Philip Walters
    ISBN 978-3-89821-457-5

82 Vera Sokolova
    Cultural Politics of Ethnicity
    Discourses on Roma in Communist
    Czechoslovakia
    ISBN 978-3-89821-864-1

83 Natalya Shevchik Ketenci
    Kazakhstani Enterprises in Transition
    The Role of Historical Regional Development
    in Kazakhstan's Post-Soviet Economic
    Transformation
    ISBN 978-3-89821-831-3

84 Martin Malek, Anna Schor-
    Tschudnowskaja (Hrsg.)
    Europa im Tschetschenienkrieg
    Zwischen politischer Ohnmacht und
    Gleichgültigkeit
    Mit einem Vorwort von Lipchan Basajewa
    ISBN 978-3-89821-676-0

85 Stefan Meister
    Das postsowjetische Universitätswesen
    zwischen nationalem und
    internationalem Wandel
    Die Entwicklung der regionalen Hochschule
    in Russland als Gradmesser der
    Systemtransformation
    Mit einem Vorwort von Joan DeBardeleben
    ISBN 978-3-89821-891-7

86 Konstantin Sheiko in collaboration
    with Stephen Brown
    Nationalist Imaginings of the
    Russian Past
    Anatolii Fomenko and the Rise of Alternative
    History in Post-Communist Russia
    With a foreword by Donald Ostrowski
    ISBN 978-3-89821-915-0

87 Sabine Jenni
    Wie stark ist das „Einige Russland"?
    Zur Parteibindung der Eliten und zum
    Wahlerfolg der Machtpartei
    im Dezember 2007
    Mit einem Vorwort von Klaus Armingeon
    ISBN 978-3-89821-961-7

88 Thomas Borén
    Meeting-Places of Transformation
    Urban Identity, Spatial Representations and
    Local Politics in Post-Soviet St Petersburg
    ISBN 978-3-89821-739-2

89 Aygul Ashirova
    Stalinismus und Stalin-Kult in
    Zentralasien
    Turkmenistan 1924-1953
    Mit einem Vorwort von Leonid Luks
    ISBN 978-3-89821-987-7

90 Leonid Luks
Freiheit oder imperiale Größe?
Essays zu einem russischen Dilemma
ISBN 978-3-8382-0011-8

91 Christopher Gilley
The 'Change of Signposts' in the Ukrainian Emigration
A Contribution to the History of Sovietophilism in the 1920s
With a foreword by Frank Golczewski
ISBN 978-3-89821-965-5

92 Philipp Casula, Jeronim Perovic (Eds.)
Identities and Politics During the Putin Presidency
The Discursive Foundations of Russia's Stability
With a foreword by Heiko Haumann
ISBN 978-3-8382-0015-6

93 Marcel Viëtor
Europa und die Frage nach seinen Grenzen im Osten
Zur Konstruktion ‚europäischer Identität' in Geschichte und Gegenwart
Mit einem Vorwort von Albrecht Lehmann
ISBN 978-3-8382-0045-3

94 Ben Hellman, Andrei Rogachevskii
Filming the Unfilmable
Casper Wrede's 'One Day in the Life of Ivan Denisovich'
Second, Revised and Expanded Edition
ISBN 978-3-8382-0044-6

95 Eva Fuchslocher
Vaterland, Sprache, Glaube
Orthodoxie und Nationenbildung am Beispiel Georgiens
Mit einem Vorwort von Christina von Braun
ISBN 978-3-89821-884-9

96 Vladimir Kantor
Das Westlertum und der Weg Russlands
Zur Entwicklung der russischen Literatur und Philosophie
Ediert von Dagmar Herrmann
Mit einem Beitrag von Nikolaus Lobkowicz
ISBN 978-3-8382-0102-3

97 Kamran Musayev
Die postsowjetische Transformation im Baltikum und Südkaukasus
Eine vergleichende Untersuchung der politischen Entwicklung Lettlands und Aserbaidschans 1985-2009
Mit einem Vorwort von Leonid Luks
Ediert von Sandro Henschel
ISBN 978-3-8382-0103-0

98 Tatiana Zhurzhenko
Borderlands into Bordered Lands
Geopolitics of Identity in Post-Soviet Ukraine
With a foreword by Dieter Segert
ISBN 978-3-8382-0042-2

99 Кирилл Галушко, Лидия Смола (ред.)
Пределы падения – варианты украинского будущего
Аналитико-прогностические исследования
ISBN 978-3-8382-0148-1

100 Michael Minkenberg (ed.)
Historical Legacies and the Radical Right in Post-Cold War Central and Eastern Europe
With an afterword by Sabrina P. Ramet
ISBN 978-3-8382-0124-5

101 David-Emil Wickström
Rocking St. Petersburg
Transcultural Flows and Identity Politics in the St. Petersburg Popular Music Scene
With a foreword by Yngvar B. Steinholt
Second, Revised and Expanded Edition
ISBN 978-3-8382-0100-9

102 Eva Zabka
Eine neue „Zeit der Wirren"?
Der spät- und postsowjetische Systemwandel 1985-2000 im Spiegel russischer gesellschaftspolitischer Diskurse
Mit einem Vorwort von Margareta Mommsen
ISBN 978-3-8382-0161-0

103 Ulrike Ziemer
Ethnic Belonging, Gender and Cultural Practices
Youth Identitites in Contemporary Russia
With a foreword by Anoop Nayak
ISBN 978-3-8382-0152-8

104 Ksenia Chepikova
     ‚Einiges Russland' - eine zweite
     KPdSU?
     Aspekte der Identitätskonstruktion einer
     postsowjetischen „Partei der Macht"
     Mit einem Vorwort von Torsten Oppelland
     ISBN 978-3-8382-0311-9

105 Леонид Люкс
     Западничество или евразийство?
     Демократия или идеократия?
     Сборник статей об исторических дилеммах
     России
     С предисловием Владимира Кантора
     ISBN 978-3-8382-0211-2

106 Anna Dost
     Das russische Verfassungsrecht auf dem
     Weg zum Föderalismus und zurück
     Zum Konflikt von Rechtsnormen und
     -wirklichkeit in der Russländischen
     Föderation von 1991 bis 2009
     Mit einem Vorwort von Alexander Blankenagel
     ISBN 978-3-8382-0292-1

107 Philipp Herzog
     Sozialistische Völkerfreundschaft,
     nationaler Widerstand oder harmloser
     Zeitvertreib?
     Zur politischen Funktion der Volkskunst
     im sowjetischen Estland
     Mit einem Vorwort von Andreas Kappeler
     ISBN 978-3-8382-0216-7

108 Marlène Laruelle (ed.)
     Russian Nationalism, Foreign Policy,
     and Identity Debates in Putin's Russia
     New Ideological Patterns after the Orange
     Revolution
     ISBN 978-3-8382-0325-6

109 Michail Logvinov
     Russlands Kampf gegen den
     internationalen Terrorismus
     Eine kritische Bestandsaufnahme des
     Bekämpfungsansatzes
     Mit einem Geleitwort von
     Hans-Henning Schröder
     und einem Vorwort von Eckhard Jesse
     ISBN 978-3-8382-0329-4

110 John B. Dunlop
     The Moscow Bombings
     of September 1999
     Examinations of Russian Terrorist Attacks
     at the Onset of Vladimir Putin's Rule
     Second, Revised and Expanded Edition
     ISBN 978-3-8382-0388-1

111 Андрей А. Ковалёв
     Свидетельство из-за кулис
     российской политики I
     Можно ли делать добро из зла?
     (Воспоминания и размышления о
     последних советских и первых
     послесоветских годах)
     With a foreword by Peter Reddaway
     ISBN 978-3-8382-0302-7

112 Андрей А. Ковалёв
     Свидетельство из-за кулис
     российской политики II
     Угроза для себя и окружающих
     (Наблюдения и предостережения
     относительно происходящего после 2000 г.)
     ISBN 978-3-8382-0303-4

113 Bernd Kappenberg
     Zeichen setzen für Europa
     Der Gebrauch europäischer lateinischer
     Sonderzeichen in der deutschen Öffentlichkeit
     Mit einem Vorwort von Peter Schlobinski
     ISBN 978-3-89821-749-1

114 Ivo Mijnssen
     The Quest for an Ideal Youth in
     Putin's Russia I
     Back to Our Future! History, Modernity, and
     Patriotism according to Nashi, 2005-2013
     With a foreword by Jeronim Perović
     Second, Revised and Expanded Edition
     ISBN 978-3-8382-0368-3

115 Jussi Lassila
     The Quest for an Ideal Youth in
     Putin's Russia II
     The Search for Distinctive Conformism in the
     Political Communication of Nashi, 2005-2009
     With a foreword by Kirill Postoutenko
     Second, Revised and Expanded Edition
     ISBN 978-3-8382-0415-4

116 Valerio Trabandt
     Neue Nachbarn, gute Nachbarschaft?
     Die EU als internationaler Akteur am Beispiel
     ihrer Demokratieförderung in Belarus und der
     Ukraine 2004-2009
     Mit einem Vorwort von Jutta Joachim
     ISBN 978-3-8382-0437-6

117 Fabian Pfeiffer
     Estlands Außen- und Sicherheitspolitik I
     Der estnische Atlantizismus nach der
     wiedererlangten Unabhängigkeit 1991-2004
     Mit einem Vorwort von Helmut Hubel
     ISBN 978-3-8382-0127-6

118 Jana Podßuweit
     Estlands Außen- und Sicherheitspolitik II
     Handlungsoptionen eines Kleinstaates im
     Rahmen seiner EU-Mitgliedschaft (2004-2008)
     Mit einem Vorwort von Helmut Hubel
     ISBN 978-3-8382-0440-6

119 Karin Pointner
     Estlands Außen- und Sicherheitspolitik III
     Eine gedächtnispolitische Analyse estnischer
     Entwicklungskooperation 2006-2010
     Mit einem Vorwort von Karin Liebhart
     ISBN 978-3-8382-0435-2

120 Ruslana Vovk
     Die Offenheit der ukrainischen
     Verfassung für das Völkerrecht und
     die europäische Integration
     Mit einem Vorwort von Alexander
     Blankenagel
     ISBN 978-3-8382-0481-9

121 Mykhaylo Banakh
     Die Relevanz der Zivilgesellschaft
     bei den postkommunistischen
     Transformationsprozessen in mittel-
     und osteuropäischen Ländern
     Das Beispiel der spät- und postsowjetischen
     Ukraine 1986-2009
     Mit einem Vorwort von Gerhard Simon
     ISBN 978-3-8382-0499-4

122 Michael Moser
     Language Policy and the Discourse on
     Languages in Ukraine under President
     Viktor Yanukovych (25 February
     2010–28 October 2012)
     ISBN 978-3-8382-0497-0 (Paperback edition)
     ISBN 978-3-8382-0507-6 (Hardcover edition)

123 Nicole Krome
     Russischer Netzwerkkapitalismus
     Restrukturierungsprozesse in der
     Russischen Föderation am Beispiel des
     Luftfahrtunternehmens "Aviastar"
     Mit einem Vorwort von Petra Stykow
     ISBN 978-3-8382-0534-2

124 David R. Marples
     'Our Glorious Past'
     Lukashenka's Belarus and
     the Great Patriotic War
     ISBN 978-3-8382-0574-8 (Paperback edition)
     ISBN 978-3-8382-0675-2 (Hardcover edition)

125 Ulf Walther
     Russlands "neuer Adel"
     Die Macht des Geheimdienstes von
     Gorbatschow bis Putin
     Mit einem Vorwort von Hans-Georg Wieck
     ISBN 978-3-8382-0584-7

126 Simon Geissbühler (Hrsg.)
     Kiew – Revolution 3.0
     Der Euromaidan 2013/14 und die
     Zukunftsperspektiven der Ukraine
     ISBN 978-3-8382-0581-6 (Paperback edition)
     ISBN 978-3-8382-0681-3 (Hardcover edition)

127 Andrey Makarychev
     Russia and the EU
     in a Multipolar World
     Discourses, Identities, Norms
     With a foreword by Klaus Segbers
     ISBN 978-3-8382-0629-5

128 Roland Scharff
     Kasachstan als postsowjetischer
     Wohlfahrtsstaat
     Die Transformation des sozialen
     Schutzsystems
     Mit einem Vorwort von Joachim Ahrens
     ISBN 978-3-8382-0622-6

129 Katja Grupp
     Bild Lücke Deutschland
     Kaliningrader Studierende sprechen über
     Deutschland
     Mit einem Vorwort von Martin Schulz
     ISBN 978-3-8382-0552-6

130 Konstantin Sheiko, Stephen Brown
     History as Therapy
     Alternative History and Nationalist
     Imaginings in Russia, 1991-2014
     ISBN 978-3-8382-0665-3

131 *Elisa Kriza*
Alexander Solzhenitsyn: Cold War
Icon, Gulag Author, Russian
Nationalist?
A Study of the Western Reception of his
Literary Writings, Historical Interpretations,
and Political Ideas
With a foreword by Andrei Rogatchevski
ISBN 978-3-8382-0589-2 (Paperback edition)
ISBN 978-3-8382-0690-5 (Hardcover edition)

132 *Serghei Golunov*
The Elephant in the Room
Corruption and Cheating in Russian
Universities
ISBN 978-3-8382-0570-0

133 *Manja Hussner, Rainer Arnold (Hgg.)*
Verfassungsgerichtsbarkeit in
Zentralasien I
Sammlung von Verfassungstexten
ISBN 978-3-8382-0595-3

134 *Nikolay Mitrokhin*
Die "Russische Partei"
Die Bewegung der russischen Nationalisten in
der UdSSR 1953-1985
Aus dem Russischen übertragen von einem
Übersetzerteam unter der Leitung von Larisa Schippel
ISBN 978-3-8382-0024-8

135 *Manja Hussner, Rainer Arnold (Hgg.)*
Verfassungsgerichtsbarkeit in
Zentralasien II
Sammlung von Verfassungstexten
ISBN 978-3-8382-0597-7

136 *Manfred Zeller*
Das sowjetische Fieber
Fußballfans im poststalinistischen
Vielvölkerreich
Mit einem Vorwort von Nikolaus Katzer
ISBN 978-3-8382-0757-5

137 *Kristin Schreiter*
Stellung und Entwicklungspotential
zivilgesellschaftlicher Gruppen in
Russland
Menschenrechtsorganisationen im Vergleich
ISBN 978-3-8382-0673-8

138 *David R. Marples, Frederick V. Mills (eds.)*
Ukraine's Euromaidan
Analyses of a Civil Revolution
ISBN 978-3-8382-0660-8

139 *Bernd Kappenberg*
Setting Signs for Europe
Why Diacritics Matter for
European Integration
With a foreword by Peter Schlobinski
ISBN 978-3-8382-0663-9

140 *René Lenz*
Internationalisierung, Kooperation
und Transfer
Externe bildungspolitische Akteure in der
Russischen Föderation
Mit einem Vorwort von Frank Ettrich
ISBN 978-3-8382-0751-3

141 *Juri Plusnin, Yana Zausaeva, Natalia Zhidkevich, Artemy Pozanenko*
Wandering Workers
Mores, Behavior, Way of Life, and Political
Status of Domestic Russian Labor Migrants
Translated by Julia Kazantseva
ISBN 978-3-8382-0653-0

142 *Matthew Kott, David J. Smith (eds.)*
Latvia – A Work in Progress?
100 Years of State- and Nation-building
ISBN 978-3-8382-0648-6

143 Инна Чувычкина (ред.)
Экспортные нефте- и газопроводы
на постсоветском пространстве
Анализ трубопроводной политики в свете
теории международных отношений
ISBN 978-3-8382-0822-0

144 *Johann Zajaczkowski*
Russland – eine pragmatische
Großmacht?
Eine rollentheoretische Untersuchung
russischer Außenpolitik am Beispiel der
Zusammenarbeit mit den USA nach 9/11 und
des Georgienkrieges von 2008
Mit einem Vorwort von Siegfried Schieder
ISBN 978-3-8382-0837-4

145 *Boris Popivanov*
Changing Images of the Left in
Bulgaria
The Challenge of Post-Communism in the
Early 21st Century
ISBN 978-3-8382-0667-7